D1250791

McKillop
Library
Salve Regina UNIVERSITY

THE CONNOISSEUR PERIOD GUIDES

# *The Regency Period*

*The Connoisseur Period Guides*

to the Houses, Decoration, Furnishing and Chattels of the Classic Periods

Edited by Ralph Edwards & L. G. G. Ramsey

❦

The Tudor Period
1500—1603

The Stuart Period
1603—1714

The Early Georgian Period
1714—1760

The Late Georgian Period
1760—1810

The Regency Period
1810—1830

The Early Victorian Period
1830—1860

❦

The Banqueting Room of Brighton Royal Pavilion. The table is set with silver loaned by the Trustees of the Marquess of Londonderry and reproduces the Royal banquet of King George IV.

# THE REGENCY PERIOD

## 1810-1830

**Reynal & Company**

New York

*Designed and produced by Rainbird, McLean Ltd*
*11 Charlotte Street, London W 1*
*The text printed by Richard Clay and Company Ltd*
*Bungay, Suffolk*
*The monochrome plates printed by Robert MacLehose*
*Glasgow*
*The colour plates printed by Henry Stone and Son (Printers) Ltd*
*Banbury*



PRINTED IN GREAT BRITAIN

# Contents

## Colour Plates

Engraved Advertisement from Robert Brindley's
*Plymouth, Devonport and Stonehouse Directory*, 1830

# Acknowledgments

The colour photograph used for the jacket is of the Banqueting Room of Brighton Royal Pavilion. The table is set with silver loaned by the Trustees of the Marquess of Londonderry and reproduces the Royal banquet of King George IV. The photograph was taken by A. F. Kersting.

The typographical border on the title page is adapted from that used on the wrapper of *The Beauties of Brighton*, printed by and for R. Sickelmore Jun., Brighton, *c.* 1830, and reproduced on page 49 of J. R. Abbey's *Scenery of Great Britain and Ireland*, 1952.

For the illustrations on pages 36, 92, 171, 172, 173 and 174 acknowledgment is made to St Bride Printing Library, for the loan of Vincent Figgins' Specimen books of 1821 and 1835.

For the loan of various books, including the one illustrated in plate 94, grateful acknowledgment is made to Berthold Wolpe, Esq.

The photograph used for plate 95 was taken by Jarrold & Sons Ltd, Norwich, for plates 8A, 13, 17B, 19A and 20 by A. F. Kersting, for plates 5A, B, 6A, B, 7, 8B, 9A, B, 10A, B, 11B, 12B, 14B, 15A, B, 16A, B and 17A by Clifford Musgrave, and for plate 12A by J. F. Smith.

For the following plates acknowledgment is made to the Victoria and Albert Museum, who hold the copyright of the photographs: 69B, 71B, 72B and 73B.

Acknowledgment is made to Temple Williams for plates 21A, D, 28A, 29B and 31, Pratt and Sons for plates 21C, 22B, 23A, B, 24A, B and 25B, Hotspur for plates 25A and 28B, Christie, Manson and Woods for plates 57D, 58A, and 61A, and Delomosne & Son Ltd for plates 62A and C.

For the following illustrations acknowledgment is made to Hulton Picture Library: plates 3A, 4, 89A, 90A, D, 91A, B, and the line illustration on page 163.

The line drawings are by Betty Bradford, Audrey Frew, Diana Holmes and Carol Oblath.

The Index was made by the Reverend Guy Daniel, M.A.

# Foreword

L. G. G. RAMSEY

As some of the specialist contributors to its pages have experienced (to their chagrin), the decades covered by this volume bear no precise historical relationship to the years of the Regency in England (1811–20). The English Regency period has also even been dated from 1795, the date of the marriage of the Prince of Wales to Caroline of Brunswick. The years, in fact, here selected are more as a designation of a convenient and effective follow-on to the preceding volume and as a suitable precursor to the next, and final, one.

The years now surveyed have been described as 'The Age of Elegance'. The long, costly wars against Napoleon had left England as a great oceanic Power: and ruling princes, statesmen and generals from most of Europe (and how Czar Alexander marvelled at the Surrey countryside through which his carriage took him) were arriving to pay homage to a nation which, for twenty years, had 'put a soul into the resistance to Napoleon' and which had finally beaten him and his Grande Armée down. Yet what economic distress – something, as it were, of a shadow stalking across England – was soon to emerge, following the victorious, peace-making years: and what an extreme instability of temperament, seasoned with a certain exuberant vitality, was presented by George Augustus himself; probably the most extraordinary aspect of this Prince being his patronage of the arts, in which he displayed a reckless extravagancy, especially with the taxpayers' money.

It was symptomatic, too, of the changing social ideas of the period that much of the formal grace which had distinguished the great English country-house interiors in the eighteenth century was disappearing. George Smith, 'Upholsterer and Furniture Draughtsman to His Majesty', in casting about for novelties, and as if sensing the growing poverty of ideas, was stressing the perfection not only of Greek ornament, but also of Egyptian, Etruscan, Roman, Gothic and French motifs. Every room was a masquerade in itself. From Egypt, also, came a constant flow of antiquities, including the sarcophagus of Seti I acquired by Sir John Soane from Giovanni Battista Belzoni in 1824 for £2,000. An adventurous generation of art dealers was also scouring the Continent for antiquities, whilst auctioneer James Christie ensured that important collections, such as that, for example, belonging to the Duc d'Orléans, were offered for sale in London. It was the period of 'Regency plate', an absorbing subject in which it is necessary to consider to what extent the Regent himself was responsible for the style implied by that term, to what degree the royal collections benefited during the period concerned, and the debt, if any, that English art as a whole owes to the Regent's personal taste and patronage.

One of the most academically interesting chapters in this book, as in other volumes in this series of *Connoisseur Period Guides*, is that devoted to Architecture and Interior Decoration. Here the Regent is engaged in all manner of costly projects, in collaboration with his favourite John Nash, finding particular expression in the gigantic programme of public works carried out in London (the Metropolitan Improvements) between 1812 and 1828. And if the culmination of splendour in the classical style of the period may be studied in such great palatial establishments as Belvoir Castle, Windsor Castle, Apsley House and Londonderry House, the height of magnificence in Regency exoticism was reached in the Royal Pavilion at Brighton, the Banqueting Room of which is the subject of the dust jacket to this book.

The Arms of George III (from 1801), George IV and William IV. From Vincent Figgins' Specimen Book of 1835

*The Age of the Prince Regent*

The Duke of Wellington in 1817, from an engraving by Mécou after a miniature by Isabey (enlarged).

# The Age of the Prince Regent

IAN R. CHRISTIE

## *The Rulers*

When, at the end of 1810, the mind of George III lapsed finally into the twilight of insanity, the kingly role passed to the member of the Hanoverian house least fitted to bear it – George Augustus, Prince of Wales, who in 1820 succeeded his father as George IV. At no period in modern times has the British throne been so dragged into disrepute as by the Regent and his six brothers, 'the dull dregs of their race, who flow through public scorn'; men seeming, in the view of one worthy county member of parliament, 'to be the only persons in the country who were wholly regardless of their own welfare and respectability'. They were, according to Wellington, 'the damnest millstones about the neck of any government'; and the Whig, Brougham, when asked why he prayed so hard for the Regent's health, declared that if he died the Tory Ministry would then be released from all its embarrassments.

The Prince Regent inherited the exuberant vitality but not the steadiness of character of his father. Married, in the eyes of Rome, but not by the law of England, to Maria Fitzherbert, and separated both from her and from his legal wife, Caroline of Brunswick, his swerving devotion to one elderly mistress after another outraged the increasingly stern moral outlook of a great part of the nation. His patronage of the arts revealed a reckless generosity – with the taxpayers' money – which his ministers had constantly to resist. Cultured and affable, he had to the full the royal gift of personal attraction: 'You lose', wrote Sir Walter Scott, 'the thoughts of the Prince, in admiring the well-bred accomplished gentleman.' For a short time after his accession his efforts to cultivate popularity were not unsuccessful, and he scored a triumph with his visit to Dublin – the only one ever made by a Hanoverian monarch. He was not without shrewdness, and he displayed a genuine affection for his family, especially for his only child, the ill-fated Charlotte, whose death in childbed, less than a year after her supremely happy marriage to Leopold of Saxe-Coburg, deeply affected him. But these good qualities were betrayed by his instability of temperament. Those who were in constant contact with him saw another side. Obese, self-indulgent, vain, wayward, deceitful, supremely egotistic – to Greville, 'a spoiled, selfish, odious beast' – pursuing with undignified rancour the wife whom he had married unwillingly and under pressure, and whose conduct, if equivocal, was not a tithe so disreputable as his own, no figure could be more calculated to bring monarchy into the gravest discredit: it was as well, perhaps, that a generation of conflict with revolution had so sharpened British attachment to the monarchy as to other existing institutions, that for the time being much might be forgiven its representative.

Government in this age rested in the hands of the pupils and associates of William Pitt. If none of them, save perhaps Canning, showed a spark of Pitt's genius, nevertheless their leaders had gifts of a high order, a capacity for sound administration, and a determination to do what they thought right regardless of the Regent's whims. For most of these years the highest place was held by one man,

Lord Liverpool, Prime Minister from 1812 to 1827, frank, amiable, sensitive, 'the honestest man that could be dealt with', an able manager of men, dexterous at reconciling the conflicting views of his colleagues, soothing and pliable, but capable of a firm stand at times of crisis. The tremendous respect accorded to his high moral character was one of the greatest assets of his ministry; and in parliament his sound but sober, even pedestrian, explanations of policy carried more weight than the glancing brilliance of a Canning. For the first ten years of his ministry his chief lieutenant was the Foreign Secretary, Castlereagh, stubborn, reserved, cautious, laborious, but withal a man of vision and resource; and after him, Canning, in so many ways the opposite of both, brilliant, epigrammatic, volatile, flamboyant, and impetuous. Alongside these statesmen brooded the aloof personality of Wellington, lonely, sensitive, punctilious, realistic, a master of the strategic retreat in politics as in his own profession of war, and after his victory at Waterloo a figure of European fame. In their train were the professional administrators of humbler rank but no less ability, Herries and Huskisson, the exponents of the new economic teaching to which Liverpool himself also subscribed.

These men and their colleagues in government have gone down in the history books as 'Tories'; but they thought of themselves more as 'the friends of Mr Pitt', from whom they inherited a medley of liberal and conservative traditions; and the 'Toryism' which embraced Huskisson's political economy, the pro-Catholic sentiment and Liberal trends in foreign policy of Canning, and the enlightened administration at the Home Office of Robert Peel, was an elastic concept, if indeed it had much meaning at all. In the first years after the war an understandable fear of revolution led them into policies of repression, and the same fear made them obstinately opposed to constitutional change; but they were by no means entirely reactionaries, and, especially in the 'twenties, after these fears had subsided, they made many creative contributions to British advancement. The men who came to dominate the administration in these later years were well aware of the dangers of blind reaction: 'those', said Canning, 'who resist indiscriminately all improvements as innovations may find themselves compelled at last to submit to innovations although they are not improvements'. Law, fiscal administration, and economic life all benefited greatly at their hands.

Opposition, conducted by the heirs of Fox and Shelburne, initially with the support of Pitt's old associate, Lord Grenville, was spasmodic, and its inspiration was at times more personal than political. Bitterly disappointed at the Regent's refusal to give them power when the right to do so passed into his hands, they laboured to embarrass him and his ministers, digging still deeper the pit which separated them from office. They despaired of victory against Napoleon, would have withdrawn Wellington's army from Portugal and acquiesced in a stalemate – one at least of the reasons which, initially, kept the Prince from turning to them. Later they exploited the undignified wrangles between the Regent and his wife, and raised against the administration traditional eighteenth-century cries of extravagance, corruption and threats to liberty. But they shaped policies out of immediate circumstances which might embarrass the ministers, not on sound principles; and they had no solution for the social and economic dislocation that were the real problems of the age. They made Catholic Emancipation one of their causes, but on this they were divided from a part only of the Tories. On parliamentary reform their aristocratic wing was for long lukewarm. The more strident demands of such radicals as Whitbread, Romilly, Burdett, or Brougham grated on the ears of a Lansdowne or a Grey; and in the 'twenties, divided on this ground, and also by personal antipathies, they ceased for a time to act as a party at all. More and more, contemporaries were aware of the artificiality of faction fights between two ghosts: 'Whig and Tory, Foxite and Pittite, Minister and Opposition have ceased to be distinctions, but the divisions of classes and great interests are arrayed against each other,' Fox's nephew, Holland, wrote in 1826. The last years of the Regency saw a growing tendency towards coalitions and a shifting of loyalties.

There had been little change since the eighteenth century in the working of the constitution or in the distribution of political power. Power remained in the hands of the wealthy landed class, who controlled local government in the shires and dominated the Houses of Parliament. The oligarchs had even risen in wealth and influence. Agriculture had so prospered through war demands and the increase of population, that rents in many parts were five times what they had been a generation before. In Cheshire alone, about 1814, there were fifty landed estates of from £3,000 to £10,000 a year, an income worth six or seven times as much in modern currency. Rents fell heavily after 1814, but still remained substantially higher than before the French Revolution; and there were many peers and gentlemen who found their estates appreciate to fantastic levels, through the exploitation of mineral deposits previously unknown, or for which there had been no market until the coming of steam power and the canal. From these classes came five-sixths of the House of Commons, and nearly two-thirds of the seats, in pocket boroughs like Calne or depopulated Old Sarum, were at the disposal of some two hundred peers and commoners. Political parties were still loose and indeterminate; they could provide an element of the support for the King's Government, but never the whole. As in the previous reign, the ministry depended on parlimentary support from independent members and from those who belonged to the Court and administration group. This last was a dwindling force. Suppressions of sinecures in response to parliamentary demands for economy, and deliberate attempts to improve the professional character of the revenue services – Liverpool sacrificed political advantage by removing from the sphere of political patronage the appointments to the higher offices of the customs department – were reducing the traditional methods which drew a parliamentary phalanx in the train of the Government. In another respect, too, administration was more weak in the face of Parliament and more responsive to opinion within and outside it than had been the case a generation before. Public opinion, roused and directed by an expanding Press, was increasing in political importance. It played a decisive part in securing the abolition of income tax in 1816 and the return to a Gold Standard after 1819. In the 'twenties the ministers consciously sought the support of the commercial interests for their economic policy and Canning broke all precedents by his publication of despatches intended to secure public approbation of his diplomacy.

### *Britain and the world*

In the opening years of the Regency the minds and energies of the nation's leaders were absorbed by the great war against Napoleon – a struggle in which as yet only the eye of faith could descry a path to victory. Britain at sea, Napoleon on land, each seemed supreme, and impervious to attack; and, in default of other means, each sought the other's ruin by economic war – Britain by the blockade, Napoleon by his 'Continental System' designed in vain to strangle British trade with Europe. The year 1812 brought further embarrassment. The blockade provoked a declaration of hostilities by the United States – the beginning of the two-years war ended in 1814 by the Treaty of Ghent – and, although the American naval and military threat was not very formidable, the consequent interruption of trade had severe effects upon British industry. Among the Government's critics there were not lacking counsellors of despair, to whom a continuation of the war seemed futile: better to make trial once more if one might trust the Corsican. But this was not the view of the King's ministers. They knew the deadly dangers of appeasement. So long as the slightest weak spot appeared in Napoleon's Fortress of Europe they were prepared to sap and mine, in hopes of an internal explosion which might shatter the dictator of the Continent and all his works. Spanish guerilla resistance to French domination proved their opportunity, and they had faith in Wellington's appraisal: 'If we can maintain ourselves in Portugal, the war will not cease in the Peninsula, and, if the war lasts in the Peninsula, Europe will be saved.' 'If', indeed: but this general of sepoys was proving himself a genius in war. The brilliant military prologue to the Regency was the scorched earth of northern Portugal and the lines of Torres Vedras; and a month after power passed into the Prince's hands, the last French attempt to drive the British out of Portugal ended with the withdrawal of Massena's armies, reduced nearly to half by starvation and disease.

British tenacity in the Peninsula soon reaped its reward. Others observed that France was not invincible. Russia grew recalcitrant in her role of satellite, and Napoleon, gambling with failing judgement for ever higher stakes, flung the flower of his army against Moscow, only to lose both army and reputation in the Russian snows. While Wellington bestrode Spain to the Pyrenees, central Europe rose once more against the French, and Britain became again pay-mistress of a European coalition, strong enough this time to beat Napoleon down.

Rarely have British statesmen shown more awareness of the interdependence of Britain and the Continent than did Castlereagh and his colleagues in the years of peace-making from 1813 to 1815. The war had left Britain the great oceanic Power: the opportunities for imperial development were incalculable and the temptation to isolation strong; but at the same time it had emphasized her dependence on events in Europe. British policy in Europe had two essential aims, defined by Castlereagh as the reduction of the French state to its former limits and the guarantee of this limitation by the other Powers: 'it is the fear of our union that will keep France down'. To these ends there must be territorial adjustments to establish a cordon on France's frontiers, conflicting ambitions in Central Europe must be checked to prevent a fatal breach between the Great Powers, and the war-time alliance must be extended to guarantee the peace. All these things Castlereagh successfully accomplished by 1815. He hoped for more. Two years of constant personal contact with the rulers of Europe had convinced him that nothing could so greatly conduce to the peace and prosperity of the Continent. It seemed to him 'a new discovery in the European government, at once extinguishing the cobwebs with which diplomacy obscures the horizon, bringing the whole bearing of the system into its true light, and giving to the councils of the Great Powers the efficiency, and almost the simplicity of a single state'. Here was a noble vision, that Europe might be kept at peace by congresses. But the dream soon faded. When the Tsar sought to turn the Concert of Europe into an instrument for the suppression of revolution, with a right to interfere in the internal affairs of any state, British participation became impossible. As Castlereagh pointed out, Britain's form of government was itself founded on a revolution. She could not, her people would not, subscribe to a doctrine which sanctified absolutism and proscribed the right of revolt: 'The House of Hanover could not well maintain the principles upon which the House of Stuart forfeited the throne.'

By Castlereagh's death in 1822, Britain's association with the Congress system was plainly foundering. Reluctantly he had been driven towards a breach. But his successor was an isolationist by conviction. Canning, defending purely national interests, broke with the Congress completely over Latin America and with pleasure saw it drive to destruction on the Eastern Question. Spanish America, asserting its freedom during the upheaval of the Napoleonic Wars, had become a vast free-trade area open to British commerce. Spain sought the re-establishment of her imperial authority. But to permit the restoration of a protectionist Spanish imperial system was unthinkable; and when Spain turned for aid to France, to let France gain exclusive commercial advantages was also unthinkable; and so, forestalling both France and the United States, came Canning's recognition of the Latin American republics, swinging them decisively into the commercial and diplomatic orbit of Great Britain, offsetting French influence in the Peninsula, calling, as he put it, 'the New World into existence to redress the balance of the Old'. The Congress Powers were rudely informed they had no ground for interference: 'it was a maritime and commercial question of concern to England ... the influence of the Continental Powers ceased with the bounds of Europe'. Faced in the Near East with the Greek struggle for independence, Canning stirred not a finger to keep united the Russian and Austrian keys of the Congress arch: over the ruins of the Congress system rose his alliance with Russia and France, to impose a settlement in Greece which would spare Britain any danger from an advance of Russian power.

*A land of promise and a land of grief*

So great was the increase of Britain's wealth that her economy rode buoyantly through the long war against France. Despite vicissitudes, its expansion was sustained after the peace. This prosperity owed much to the oceanic supremacy and the expansion of Empire assured at Trafalgar. Many conquests were, it is true, returned at the peace. Britain was comparatively moderate in her territorial demands, and retentions of conquests – notably the Cape Colony and Ceylon – were determined mainly by strategic considerations. More important, older parts of the Empire could be held and extended. In India needs of defence advanced British territories and protectorates over the greater part of the Maratha states and led to annexations from Nepal; and a little later Burmese advances into the Brahmaputra valley provoked the British annexation of Aracan and Tenasserim and the establishment of a protectorate over Assam. British colonization within the Empire was as yet mainly confined to the Canadas and the colonies of the St Lawrence estuary, where the population nearly doubled in the fifteen years after the peace of 1815, and this area was of growing though still relatively minor commercial importance. Other lands suitable for settlement were relatively remote or offered little opportunity. A trickle of British settlers was added to the Dutch population at the Cape. New South Wales and Tasmania were in 1811 still convict settlements with very few free settlers. By 1830 the population of New South Wales was still only about 50,000, more or less equally divided between free settlers and those who had come as convicts; that of Tasmania was about half this figure. The potential wealth of the southern continent was becoming evident, and a small flourishing export trade in wool to Great Britain had been established. But only in 1829, when the French threatened to forestall us, was Western Australia annexed and the whole land thus opened to British exploitation.

At the heart of Britain's mounting prosperity were the increase in her population and the native vigour and ingenuity of her people. In 1811 the population of England and Wales was just over ten million. In twenty years it increased to nearly fourteen million. In the same period Scotland's population of one and three-quarter million increased by half a million and Ireland's of some six million by over a million and a half. In 1811 already rather more than half the people of England and Wales were employed in commerce, navigation, and manufacture, less than half in agriculture and mining. In the next twenty years, although agricultural production practically kept pace with demand, the numbers employed in it rose very little: practically all the increase in population was absorbed in industry and allied pursuits. Urbanization was proceeding apace, especially in Lancashire, Durham, the Midlands and South Wales, while greater London grew at an unprecedented rate, adding in twenty years half a million souls to the million within its confines in 1811.

Great as was the increase of the population, Britain's mounting industrial power more than kept pace. The key to the future lay in the sources of energy locked away in her coal-seams, and the exploitation of these was assured by various new techniques, particularly improved winding gear and the use of pit-props. The statue to Sir Humphry Davy in Helston churchyard pays tribute to the protection to life brought by the invention of his safety lamp; but the nation also owed to him a greatly increased command of its most valuable natural resources, for the safety lamp removed one of the most serious obstacles to deeper working: about 1830 it was described as operating 'as a complete renovation to many of the collieries which were then in a state of exhaustion'. Iron production, which might otherwise have been curtailed for lack of fuel, was also advancing, finding, as war requirements came to an end, new uses in the manufacture of machines, bridges, gas and water piping and countless other requirements. The Scottish iron industry benefited greatly from Neilson's discovery in 1829 of the use of the hot air blast in smelting, which brought substantial economies in the consumption of coal of the types mainly produced by the Scottish pits. The most spectacular advance was made by the cotton industry, which by 1831 was consuming three times as much raw cotton as in 1811 and had secured a lucrative and unlimited market in India, where it undercut native domestic manufacture. About 1811 water was still the main source of motive power for the factories, but by 1830 steam power was well on the way to supplanting it. Power-loom weaving in factories was steadily ousting the handloom weaver. The number of power-looms in the country doubled and redoubled in the ten years before 1830; about 1826 it was calculated that a youth in charge of steam-driven machinery could produce six times the output of a skilled handloom weaver in the prime of life, and costs of production were so reduced that by 1830 the prices of cottons had fallen to a fifth of their level about 1815. The cotton handloom weavers became an impoverished and declining class. They could no longer command high wages, and, except in the fancy lines, were sure of employment only in boom periods, when demand exceeded factory capacity. But there were estimated to be still over 200,000 of them about 1830, the worst-hit victims of industrialization, constituting a grave social problem to which no government of the day could see any ready solution. The railway age was yet to come. These last decades before the railway began to revolutionize transport were the heyday of highways and canals, with no important centre of population more than fifteen miles from a waterway and coach services at ten miles an hour on McAdam's roads. But the essential pioneer work on the railways had been done by 1830. By the 'twenties, Trevithick, George Stephenson and others had proved the practical possibilities of steam traction. The business partnership of Stephenson and Edward Pease led to the opening of the Stockton–Darlington line in 1825, with results which, if not regarded as decisive, at least commanded attention. The rate of carriage per ton of merchandise to Darlington was cut from fivepence to a fifth of a penny per mile, carriage of minerals from sevenpence to three halfpence, and the cost of coal at Darlington was more than halved. In 1830 followed the Liverpool–Manchester line, for which Stephenson was the construction engineer, and its success overcame all doubts of the usefulness of extensive railway networks throughout the country: in 1829, at the trials at Rainhill near Liverpool, Stephenson's *Rocket*, which secured him the contract for locomotives, attained the then phenomenal speed of thirty miles an hour. There were other portents. A few small steam-driven vessels were coming into use on inland waterways before 1820; and a little later services across the Channel and the Irish Sea began. Oceanic steamships still lay in the future, and the iron-built ship was as yet a curiosity. But at sea, as on land, the way had been prepared for the tremendous advances in transport of the early Victorian age.

Changes of such magnitude in trade and industry, though they added greatly to the nation's general wealth and prosperity, were not achieved without much hardship and social dislocation. In the early years, dislocation due to war – especially interruption of trade with the United States – and later alternate boom and depression, created grave problems of unemployment, aggravated particularly after 1815 by the ending of war contracts and the demobilization of nearly a quarter of a million men. Slump and boom alike gave rise to industrial unrest, as workmen resisted attempts to lower wages and turned to the destruction of the machines to which they attributed their loss of work, or else sought their share of rising profits in higher pay. Certain skills, like that of the handloom weavers, were becoming redundant, and those who practised them had the hardest time of all, as the market for their labour narrowed inexorably, squeezing them gradually out of economic existence. Distress also stalked the agricultural south. Much of the rural area of southern England was suffering from over-population. If the widespread Speenhamland system of subsidizing agricultural wages out of rates had not encouraged the birth-rate, it was nevertheless a major cause of this state of affairs by keeping in their villages on a pittance men who might otherwise have migrated to the towns in search of work. With labour plentiful no part of the profits made by landlords and farmers was passed on to the labourer. Enclosures, which rose sharply during the war, made matters worse by depriving the peasant of the chance to eke out his living from the common, and those who turned in desperation to poaching their landlord's hares or pheasants ran the risk of transportation under the ferocious laws for the preservation of game. If bread prices rose from a sudden scarcity, the men who grew the wheat found themselves facing actual starvation: the labourers who rioted in Suffolk in 1816 followed a flag inscribed with the words 'Bread or Blood'. A Bedfordshire labourer declared before a committee on wages in 1824 that he and his family lived mainly on bread and cheese and water, and that sometimes for a month together he never tasted meat: in the 'twenties wages and poor relief together did not provide subsistence.

### *Government and the people*

Those who controlled the country's destinies were only too aware of the stresses imposed by economic development, and were not without a will to solve them. But they were hampered by at least two major circumstances – their conviction of the correctness of the doctrines of *laissez-faire* preached by the leading thinkers on political economy, and the oligarchical character of the State, which gave predominance to certain group interests and caused any stirring of the masses to be regarded as dangerous. Also the situations which faced them were unprecedented. No society in human experience had undergone such radical transformations, and it was small wonder that the policies adopted by governments were sometimes sectional and appeared to be unfeeling and harsh. Not least, politicians were dogged by memories of the disasters which had befallen France and Europe after the revolutionary outbreak of 1789.

In a parliament composed mainly of landowners a protectionist policy for agriculture seemed essential, and the slump of 1815 was hastily met by a Corn Law excluding foreign wheat till the home price touched 80 shillings per quarter. Rightly or wrongly, this was regarded as inflicting dear bread upon the people, and aroused much popular discontent; and in 1825 the farmers had to see the Government take power to admit warehoused corn for consumption in time of dearth at a reduced duty and to admit more foreign corn at a low duty at discretion, while three years later the level of protection was reduced. More dangerous to the landowning interests than the agitation of the common people was the challenge from the rising class of merchants and manufacturers. During the last twenty years of the unreformed Parliament there were usually well over a hundred representatives of these groups in the Commons, and government was becoming increasingly responsive to their pressure. More plausibly than the land-owners, they could plead that their panacea – free trade – would benefit not just themselves but the country as a whole. Free interchange of commodities between nations would benefit all and reduce the tensions between them; while for Britain in particular it was necessary to secure cheap food and enable foreign countries to pay for British goods in return. In the 'twenties the increasing attention paid to commerce by the ministers aroused the jealousy of representatives of the landed interest, convincing them that in face of this rivalry old party animosities were of no account. Coke of Holkham told the Commons in 1822 that 'unless there should be a union of both Whigs and Tories, unless the country gentlemen on both sides of the House should combine their efforts the total destruction of the agricultural interest must ensue'. The battle was joined that would lead more than twenty years later to the repeal of the Corn Laws and the end of Protection.

Up till the 'thirties the industrialists' demands for cheaper corn for the workmen were not loud enough to flutter the nerves of the landed interest; but their pressure was subverting the old foundations of commercial policy and opening the way to the age of *laissez-faire*. In Huskisson, Liverpool and Herries they found after 1820 a trio of ministers whose views on commercial matters were sufficiently forward-looking to meet some at least of their demands, and who struck decisive blows at the restrictive commercial and navigational system of the eighteenth-century Empire. Up till 1822 the old system, mercantilist in character, still predominated. With some exceptions, overseas dependencies could trade only with the mother country or between each other. Traffic with foreign territories was restricted. The Empire formed a system of closed monopolies, and tariff barriers protected from foreign competition the industries of the homeland. Tariffs were attacked by the industrialists, who held the now quite justified belief that they could outsell the rest of the world if only they were given a free hand by access to markets without the penalties of duties charged either by their own or foreign governments. They hoped that a lowering of duties at home would be answered by similar action on the part of the foreigner. And from 1822 they got their way with the throwing open of the colonies to direct trade with Europe, the passage of a Reciprocity of Duties Act, and a series of further measures reducing British tariffs.

Also they attacked the shipping restrictions maintained under the Navigation Acts, by which the carrying trade between Great Britain and the dependencies was reserved to the ships of the mother country or of the dependencies themselves. The main defence for this monopoly of the Empire's carrying trade was still, as it had been in the eighteenth century, the provision of seamen for the Navy in time of war. On purely economic grounds it was much less defensible. The commercial interests blamed it for keeping artificially high the cost of freight. And though the ship-owners defended themselves hotly against this charge, they had no answer to the attack from a different quarter, when foreign governments insisted that their ships must be admitted to a share of the trade with the British colonies, otherwise British ships bringing colonial produce would be excluded from their ports. In the eighteen-twenties radical changes in the Navigation Laws were enacted in response to this combination of foreign and domestic pressure.

This enlightened policy had already gone far by 1828, and Huskisson and Herries were ready to take it further, by means not at all to the taste of the landed interest. At the moment when office was snatched from them in 1828 they were prepared to introduce some form of income tax or property tax which would have financed still more sweeping reductions of the revenue duties, which they regarded as 'most obstructive' to the industry of the country, 'most detrimental to it in its growing rivalry with the manufacturers of the Continent, and ... obnoxious to the public feeling'. Had they remained in office the work of Peel in the 'forties might have been anticipated by over a decade.

Material benefits were a major object of these commercial reforms. But to Huskisson at the Board of Trade, the minister chiefly concerned, the new policy had also another and more important object. He thought also in terms of political advantage. He argued that the American Revolution had been due more to British regulation of colonial trade than to any other single cause, and he wished to prevent repetitions of this disaster. *Laissez-faire* meant the abrogation of commercial control. By steering clear of action damaging to the interests of the colonies, their loyalty, he thought, might be kept at least for a time; and even afterwards, if they insisted upon their ultimate independence, the ties of friendly intercourse might be maintained. In 1825 he appealed to the House of Commons: 'Let us, as the parent state, fulfil our duties with all proper kindness and liberality. This is true wisdom: affording us on the one hand, the best chance of perpetuating a solid and useful connection, and on the other the best hope if ... that connection is ever to be dissolved, that separation may not be embittered by acrimony and bloodshed; and the certain consolation that, however brought about, it will not have been hastened or provoked by vexatious interference or oppressive pretensions on our part.'

Government response to the half-articulate mutterings of the masses was varied and by no means entirely negative. At first, indeed, it saw the problem of internal policy as one of order and little else, grappling with it by suspensions of Habeas Corpus, by strong backing for magistrates who called in the military, and by suppression and restriction of public meetings and the radical press. Such a policy was not entirely without justification. There was a lunatic fringe among the discontented inclined to appeal to force: in 1820 the Thistlewood group conspired to murder the Cabinet and proclaim a revolutionary régime. But repression for its own sake was no part of the Government's intentions, and with the more prosperous 'twenties these measures were soon relaxed. Prevention of crime was pursued both by the introduction of a more humane and therefore more effective criminal code and by the institution, in 1829, of the Metropolitan Police. On a different level were the Government's grants of money for the building of churches – a million pounds in 1817 – designed partly to counter the spread of Methodism, but of importance in bringing to the rootless immigrant populations of the unparished industrial towns an element of social cohesion and moral guidance. Yet another step in 1824 and 1825 was the legalization of limited trade-union activity, through which, it was hoped, labour might find and understand – and so accept – the role allotted to it by the political economists.

With radicalism Government would have nothing to do. It dismissed as chimerical the pleas of Cartwright, Orator Hunt, or William Cobbett, that Britain's welfare depended on a reform of Parliament, to make it truly representative of the people's views. But the pressure of middle-class radicalism for economy and improvements in administration could not be wholly withstood. It led to the abolition of sinecures and patronage and a growing professionalization of the revenue services. Under Peel's ægis the legal system was overhauled, stripped of medieval anomalies and obstructive technical processes, made less expensive and more accessible for the public. The Court of Chancery had become a by-word for inefficiency and was years in arrears: one critic observed that its work was divided into two parts – one, under the Chancellor, was *oyer sans terminer*, the other, under the Vice-Chancellor, *terminer sans oyer*. Peel's committee of inquiry into its operations was an indispensible preliminary to essential reforms.

Towards the close of the period, reforms of a different order began, when the political monopoly of the Church of England, a corner-stone of English polity since the Restoration, was destroyed by the two Emancipation Acts of 1828 and 1829.

The Protestant Dissenters were at law still excluded from public life. In practice they had for long been virtually admitted within the pale of the Constitution, and were sheltered from most of the consequences of their anomalous legal position by the operation of the annual indemnity acts. Practically the only sphere of public life barred to them was the borough corporation, and this was more because of the oligarchical structure which there obtained than because of the law. The legal situation of the Dissenters was illogical and quite indefensible, and when their demand for justice was raised in Parliament in 1828, hardly anyone was prepared seriously to resist it.

A year later the partisans of the Established Church had to swallow the admission of Roman Catholics also to full political rights. Catholic Emancipation in 1829 was the sequel to over thirty years of agitation. Throughout this period the Catholic question was, in effect, the Irish question. The English Roman Catholics were few and unimportant, and in the main reconciled to exclusion from public life. But the Roman Catholics in Ireland were an overwhelming majority of the population. They were, however, still victims of political discrimination, for Pitt had found it impossible to carry emancipation as he had wished to do in 1800, when the Union between Great Britain and Ireland was enacted. Catholics in Ireland could vote in elections, but they could not enter Parliament, and they were debarred from the higher civil and military offices. They were taxed to maintain an alien Church, of which only about a tenth of the inhabitants of Ireland were communicants. The success of the campaign for their emancipation was due to two circumstances: the emergence of a born leader and an effective organization. The leader was Daniel O'Connell, the organization was the Catholic Association. Many outstanding qualities brought O'Connell to the forefront of the Catholic movement: his integrity in the pursuit of Irish interests, his enthusiasm and zeal, his power of oratory, and his exceptional legal skill and knowledge. His ability as a lawyer was of particular importance to a cause always facing the necessity of evading legislation intended to crush it altogether, and to followers who were inevitably in conflict with those who administered the law. These gifts, employed with all the exuberant energy of which he was capable, soon made O'Connell a national hero.

In 1823 O'Connell re-created the Catholic Association, as an instrument to awaken political consciousness among the Irish Catholic peasantry – not the first or last time that a Church has contributed to the development of a national consciousness – and as a means of putting pressure on the British Government. Held together by the Catholic priesthood and hierarchy, the Association soon became a state within a state, administering its own equitable jurisdiction without reference to, and in defiance of, the central authority at Dublin which represented British rule. From 1826 it began to intervene effectively in parliamentary elections, protecting the humble voters from the consequences of defying the instructions of their Protestant landlords, and securing the return of champions of Emancipation. The climax of these demonstrations of power was the return of O'Connell himself for County Clare in 1829, although he was a Catholic and not legally eligible. This gesture of strength made it clear that the power of Protestant ascendancy over Irish elections was completely broken, and that the events in Clare would be repeated at the next general election in nearly every county in Ireland. The British Government had no choice but to give way or to take police action, which Peel thought would lead straight to civil war. Catholic emancipation was conceded to a nationalist demand which few in their consciences were prepared to resist by the only means possible – by force.

*Mental horizons*

The virility displayed by the British people of this age in their international relationships and their development of commerce and industrial resources was paralleled by the vigour of their intellectual life; and while much of the cultural efflorescence of the Regency is a subject for other writers in this volume, its literature, science, and spiritual life require mention here.

The literature of the Regency afforded a wonderful diversity of riches. In these years the younger Romantic poets flowered and died – Byron, the 'Titan', lonely and passionate rebel, the lyric and prophetic Shelley, and Keats, with his sensual love of natural beauty. Scott's romantic novels had captured the public and were bringing him a European reputation. On a different scale, Jane Austen was writing her exquisite miniatures of country-house life, and a little later Miss Mitford's sketches of 'Our Village' illustrated the less sophisticated delights and wonders of rural society. Among the essayists, Charles Lamb was launching into his best work after 1808 – the *Essays of Elia* were written during the 'twenties. New opportunities for this *genre* were opened by the expansion of the periodical press – the *Quarterly Review* was founded in 1809, followed within the next few years by *Blackwood's* and the *Westminster Review* – and were exploited by (among others) Hazlitt, de Quincey, Jeffrey, John Gibson Lockhart, and the Mills, father and son. Travel literature was increasing in popularity: Cobbett's *Rural Rides* appeared during the 'twenties. In the reviews literature touched – often more than touched – on the fringe of politics. Otherwise literary art in this period was on the whole devoid of conscious social purpose, although Shelley and one or two others foreshadowed the trend of the following generation, in which it became more nearly associated with great public questions. Philosophic thought provoked both a revolutionary and a reactionary current. On the one hand stood the gospel of universal love preached by Shelley, evolved from rationalist assumptions of human perfectibility. On the other might be traced a movement, earlier visible in the last writings of Burke, and given expression in the work of the Lake Poets, of recoil from the bare reason back to the emotions as a truer guide to the inner meaning of things, basing upon them an innately conservative attitude to problems of political obligation and social structure.

Meanwhile the scientific mind enlarged its horizons. In pure science there was no great name at this period. The best work of Dalton and of Davy had already been done, and though Faraday was serving his apprenticeship to scientific inquiry, his greatness was revealed only in the next generation. It was in practical applications of scientific knowledge that advances were made in many and varied fields. Civil and mechanical engineering were emerging as professions. By 1830 George Stephenson had established himself as a railway engineer. McAdam, whose name gave a new word to the language, reached the height of his reputation as a constructor of highways. In 1819 he published his *Practical Essay on the Scientific Repair and Preservation of Roads*; and though his techniques were at first derided by scoffers who quipped about 'quack-adamizing', they were soon accorded general recognition: in 1827 he was appointed Surveyor-General of Roads. Other great achievements in the construction of roads, bridges and canals were due to Telford, under whose supervision the work on the Caledonian Canal was completed in 1822. In 1818 Telford was one of the founders of the society which a few years later became the Institution of Civil Engineers. A marked advance was made by the medical profession when, in 1815, the Society of Apothecaries secured an Act giving it power to examine all entrants into the profession. A regular training for apprentice doctors was thus assured. Also, the Regency coincided with the most fruitful period in the career of Charles Bell, whose discoveries concerning human and animal physiology rank in importance in medical science with Harvey's demonstration of the circulation of the blood nearly two centuries before. Bell published in 1811 his *Idea of a New Anatomy of the Brain*, and in 1830 gathered together the fruits of twenty years of research in his volume *The Nervous System of the Human Body*. In the same period Marshall Hall had begun his distinguished career as a medical researcher, teacher, and physician, though his most important contributions to medical knowledge were not made till after 1830.

The structure and the problems of society were also made the subject of scientific inquiry. John Rickman applied statistical methods to the analysis of the census returns, and the habit of gathering statistics about various aspects of economic life made rapid headway. Economic dislocation, and the currency problems produced by war-time inflation, stimulated economic thinking – David Ricardo began his career as a pamphleteer on the bullion question in 1809 – but the political economists also turned their attention to more general problems, such as distribution and the theory of value. James Mill, Malthus, and others were also writing on economic questions, but Ricardo, who in 1817 published his main work, *Principles of Political Economy and Taxation*, was the principal founder of what has been called the classical school of political economy. Mill, one of his close associates and a fellow founder in 1820 of the Political Economy Club, was better known for his exposition of Bentham's philosophy of Utilitarianism, and in his *Essay on Government*, published in 1820, setting forth the logical necessity for an adult male franchise if government and people were to be kept in step, he preached the beliefs and objects of political radicalism based upon Benthamite principles.

If Mill, Bentham, and some of their associates were sceptics, nevertheless the great clash between religion and science still lay in the future. Not till later was the controversy over *The Origin of Species* to set priest and scientist at odds. Men of culture still combined their knowledge of material things with a faith resting on literal acceptance of the Scriptures. But there were already vague rumblings of the impending battle in clerical dislike of the 'march of mind'. Purely secular pursuit of knowledge was condemned by some, as in the words of Dr Howley: 'The diffusion of knowledge, disjoined from religious instruction, stands in the same relation to ignorance as positive evil to the absence of good'. Churchmen looked askance at the Mechanics' Institutes popularized by Brougham, and at his society for the Diffusion of Useful Knowledge, which published informative literature at cheap rates. Towards the close of the period, their reaction was immediate to the foundation of the University of London, shortly to become University College, as a University for non-sectarian education: King's College, London, followed quickly as a Church foundation. But the Church's monopoly through the two older universities was now for the first time broken.

The end of the eighteenth century had seen a religious revival in full tide, and the impetus of this was not yet spent. Methodism was still spreading, especially in the industrial districts, and within the Church of England itself Evangelicalism now began to take a firmer hold. In some ways the Church was becoming more alive to its responsibilities. Much was done after 1809 to augment and endow benefices in the new growing towns, and up to 1824 Parliament voted two and a half million towards this work. But sectarian squabbles hampered the effort to provide elementary education, and for many reasons the Church of England laboured under difficulties during the later years of George IV's reign. As magistrates its clergy came into conflict with the labouring poor. As collectors of tithe they alienated the farmer and discouraged agricultural enterprise. And the Church remained a haunt of privilege and abuses. Plurality and non-residence were still widespread: for instance, Bishop Sharpe of Ely, his son, and his son-in-law, drew more than £30,000 yearly from church endowments, whilst at the other end of the scale, too many parishes were still left to the ministrations of penniless curates. Evangelicalism did little to break down these abuses, and its hostility towards secular learning contributed in these years to that intellectual isolation of the Church which in the next generation was to prove disastrous.

George Stephenson's *Rocket*.

(A) The Duke of Wellington, by T. PHILLIPS. *Courtesy the Earl of Shrewsbury.* (B) Robert Banks Jenkinson 2nd Earl of Liverpool, by SIR THOMAS LAWRENCE. *National Portrait Gallery.* (C) George IV, Regent 1811–20, reigned 1820–30, by SIR THOMAS LAWRENCE. *National Portrait Gallery.* (D) Robert Stewart, 2nd Marquess of Londonderry (Lord Castlereagh), by SIR THOMAS LAWRENCE. *National Portrait Gallery.* (E) George Canning, by SIR THOMAS LAWRENCE. *National Portrait Gallery.*

PLATE 1

*facing page 12*

(A) Politics for popular consumption: the radical, Samuel Whitbread, is worsted by Castlereagh. A print published by S. Knight of Sweeting Alley, 1815. *British Museum.*

(B) The 'lunatic fringe' among the discontented. Members of the Thistlewood group resisted arrest with fatal results for one of the police officers concerned. Coloured etching by George Cruikshank, 1820. *St Marylebone Public Library.*

PLATE 2

(A) The Royal Cockpit, Birdcage Walk, 1808. An aquatint by Rowlandson and Pugin from *The Microcosm of London*, 1808.

(B) A Cricket Match in the 1820's. North-east view of the cricket-fields at Darnall, near Sheffield. Coloured aquatint by Robert Cruikshank, 1827. *Marylebone Cricket Club.*

PLATE 3

In the heart of London's commercial world: the Customs House from the River Thames. From *The Microcosm of London*, 1808.

PLATE 4

*Architecture and Interior Design*

# Architecture and Interior Design

CLIFFORD MUSGRAVE

By the opening of the Regency in 1811 architecture in Britain had been given its main directions for the next twenty to thirty years. The classical inspiration had gained new impetus from two influences. One was the vitalizing force of Greek architecture, sensationally revealed in the series of folios *The Antiquities of Athens*, published by James Stuart and Nicholas Revett, in the years from 1762 onwards. Another invigorating impulse was the impact of the cult of the Picturesque, which during the eighteenth century had confined itself mostly to landscape gardening and rural buildings, upon the planning of town architecture, imparting to it new variety and individuality.

The play of these forces, both independently and upon each other, brought into being the fascinating and at times bewildering range of Regency styles. Running through this rich diversity, two main trends of taste are discernible. One phase is that of the restrained, elegant classical tradition evolved after Adam by Dance, Soane, Holland and Wyatt, of simplicity and good proportion in form and decoration. This mood, though most prevalent in the earlier part of the Regency, up to 1815, nevertheless persisted to the end of the period.

After Waterloo the second phase becomes more strongly apparent. It is the time of a more sumptuous, florid and amply proportioned richness in classical decoration, especially of palatial interiors. It is an age of the growing Picturesque transformation of houses, of the full tide of the Grecian Revival, and the rich flood of Regency medieval romanticism.

### *The picturesque*

Ideas of the Picturesque had been developing ever since, early in the eighteenth century, William Kent revolted against the symmetrical formal gardening favoured until then, and in the words of Horace Walpole 'leap'd the fence and found that all Nature was a garden'.

Controversy over the picturesque methods of Lancelot ('Capability') Brown caused several important works to be published during the years 1794–5, which established the 'Principles of the Picturesque'. The most important of these was *The Landscape, a Didactic Poem* by Richard Payne Knight, a wealthy and eccentric but highly capable scholar and connoisseur. Another work, *Sketches and Hints on Landscape*, 1785, was that of the professional landscape gardener, Humphrey Repton. He claimed in fact to be the first to use the title.

Knight also made a sound practical contribution to the newly rationalized science of the Picturesque. This was Downton Castle, the house he built for himself near Ludlow in 1774, the precursor of all the castellated mansions, both large and small, which became such distinguishing landmarks of the Regency scene, the movement culminating eventually in the rebuilding of Windsor Castle for King George IV from 1824 to 1836.

About 1796 Repton took into partnership John Nash (1752–1835). He had been an assistant in the office of Sir Robert Taylor, and after an early bankruptcy, had moved to Wales, where, during some twelve years, he built up a good practice as an architect of country houses. While with Repton

Fig. 1. Luscombe Castle, Devon, by John Nash, 1804. From *Jones' Views of the Seats of Noblemen and Gentlemen in England, etc.*, 1829

One of Nash's most charming small domestic castles.

Nash undertook all the architectural work involved in the improvement of country estates.

A natural flair for the element of drama in architecture combined with the experience of six years' partnership with Repton caused Nash virtually to inherit the leadership of the Picturesque movement, and he was soon well advanced on the path that was to lead him to fame as the designer who more than any other sums up in his work the architectural achievement of the Regency age.

Nash's early work included many designs for castellated mansions, but none survive of his larger examples, like his own at East Cowes, Caerhayes in Cornwall, and Ravensworth in Co. Durham; but his castellated style still exists on a delightful small scale at Luscombe, near Dawlish, in South Devon, where the house he finished in 1804 lies at the head of a long valley, flanked by cedars that Repton planted (Fig. 1). The delightful Kentchurch Court, Hereford,* is one of Nash's earliest domestic castles (*c.* 1795). Two of his smaller castles were built near each other in Sussex for the sons of Walter Burrell the historian. One, Knepp Castle (1806), is happily still preserved as a home by the same family (Pl. 5A). West Grinstead Park is derelict and almost certain to be demolished. All of them, with their large drum towers, tall narrow watch-towers, and square entrance towers, and their battlements and machicolations, derive from Downton.

The architect P. F. Robinson observed 'a passion for dwelling in cottages has been apparent',

* Indicates that the house is open to the public.

and in books of designs that appeared year by year he and other architects, like J. B. Papworth, excelled themselves and each other in producing notions for cottages, summer-houses, dairies, cowsheds, and conservatories that became more and more romantically extravagant as the years of classical restraint receded. Nash's interpretation of the *cottage orné* (Pl. 5B) is seen in perfection at the model village of Blaise Hamlet,* near Bristol, built in 1812, where he gathered together a collected edition of cottage designs he had executed in various places. Here his rustic fantasy may be seen in a delightful combination of dove-cot gables, clustered chimneys of brickwork moulded in lozenge, spiral and chequered designs, broad-eaved thatched roofs, arbours and porches and leaded windows.

Two of Nash's most notable early designs for private houses embody features that were to become distinctive contributions to the Regency commonwealth of styles. Southgate Grove, now Grovelands Hospital (1797), set the type of his later classical villas, and has a quality of gaiety and robustness that was welcome after the excessive delicacy of the Adam school. More refreshingly unfamiliar to the English scene were his houses like Cronkhill, Shropshire (1802), and Sandridge, Devon (1805), which established the type of the Italian villa, having the round towers with flattish conical roofs, the arched loggias and round-headed windows of the houses seen in such paintings of the Roman countryside as Claude Lorrain's *Landscape with a View of the Ponte Molle* at Birmingham Art Gallery.

One of the strongest influences pervading the architecture of the Regency, and one of the most subtle in bringing about the fusion of classical and Picturesque, was the intensely individual style of Sir John Soane (1753–1837), whose early career has been discussed in a previous volume. In his domestic interiors Soane brought to a new pitch the severity favoured by Dance, Holland and Wyatt, giving his rooms their characteristic dignity and simple beauty by means of semi-circular or semi-elliptical arched recesses with curved apses, and ceilings of shallow, flattened vaults as at Aynhoe, Northants (1800–2).* His ornament was confined to narrow ribbed mouldings, Greek key pattern decoration, and incised groovings, with occasionally recessed ceiling panels with rosettes, or small sculptured plaques with figures in relief, as at Pitzhanger Manor (1800–3),* at one time his own house, and now Ealing Public Library.

Soane's genius was for the handling of masses in a broad yet dramatic fashion with severe subordination of decorative detail. The Mausoleum and Picture Gallery* that he built for Sir Francis Bourgeois at Dulwich, now restored after damage during the war, is among the supreme examples of this quality in his work.

Soane gave similar treatment to his own house at No. 13 Lincoln's Inn Fields, which with No. 14 he added in 1812 to No. 12, where he had lived since 1792. Against the reticent brick façade of the three houses, Soane built a projecting frontispiece of stucco which he gave his characteristic pilaster-like treatment with recessed lines and key-pattern ornament. It was intended to form one of the side wings of an extended design across Nos. 13, 14 and 15, with a colonnade of coupled Ionic columns forming the centre, but the whole magnificent project was never completed. No. 13, now Sir John Soane's Museum,* was created to serve as dwelling-house, office, museum and gallery, to illustrate 'the union of architecture, sculpture and painting', and in the immense collection of casts, models, drawings, paintings, pottery, sculpture and antiques, the house embraces all the motifs of ancient architecture which were the inspiration of his time.

The rooms of the house have a multiplicity of shallow domes and vaults, lantern lights and clearstorys, arched openings and mirror-friezes, all creating those endless indeterminate vistas and recessions with which even in this circumscribed space, as in his earlier arched, domed and vaulted halls at the Bank of England, Soane strove to create the sense of infinity.

### *The Regency house*

The Regency age was not, like the eighteenth century, one to favour the building of great country houses. The number of immense aristocratic fortunes was smaller, and the Napoleonic

Wars caused restrictions of material. The Regency was pre-eminently the age of the smaller house, and in it Picturesque ideas inspired the individuality and charm which are so characteristic of the time.

The diversity of styles consisted in a wide range of variations upon a few basic themes. The underlying tradition was classical, flowing smoothly on from the restrained neo-classical phase of the late eighteenth century. The curved window bays and low roof parapets favoured by Wyatt became some of the most distinctive features of Regency building. These bays, of semi-circular or sometimes shallower segmental form, with sash windows shaped to the curve, rose to differing levels, sometimes through one or two storeys only, at times to roof level. In the early Regency this point was marked by a slender cornice with brick dentils; later a more heavily modelled and deeper cornice gave emphasis to the upper walls, and became characteristic. Frequently instead of the shallow roof, almost concealed behind the parapet, the Italian type of roof with overhanging eaves came to be favoured. Angular bays usually belong to the later Regency years, although of mid-eighteenth century and earlier origin.

Early in the period the brown brick of former years gave place increasingly to yellow stock bricks, which add gaiety to so many of the Regency houses of London and the seaside, but bricks of deep red continued to be used. The plain square or rectangular brick house of the eighteenth-century tradition, with its simple classical porch as the only adornment, persisted to defy the fevers of the Picturesque right through the Regency period up to the 'thirties and 'forties till its evolution into the square Victorian villa.

An excellent example of the Regency brick villa is Clissold House, Stoke Newington,* built by J. Woods about 1820–30, and now a tea-house. The central block has a projecting Doric portico of six columns, with balcony above a stone parapet and flat roof, and is flanked by single-storey wings with bowed ends.

In flat-fronted houses the severity of the plain façade was sometimes modified by recessed relieving arches of semi-circular or flattened curves above the window, as at Keats' House, Hampstead.*

The adornment of even the severest type of house by window-balconies (Pl. 6A) with delicate cast or wrought-iron railings was customary, and as Picturesque influence became more pervasive the window-canopy which now seems inseparable from the idea of the Regency house, especially at the seaside, became generally adopted. These delightful appendages of sheet metal of tented or Chinese pagoda form, sometimes fluted, did not come widely into use until after their introduction, together with verandas and trellis (Pl. 6B), by P. F. Robinson at Brighton Pavilion* in 1802, as part of the transformation of Henry Holland's building from its original prim severity to the gaiety and friendliness of a rural *cottage orné*. Many Brighton houses had balconies at an early date, but were not given canopies or verandas until about 1815 or later. The later canopies, of about 1820 onwards, were like ladies' bonnets, having a bulbous upper part and a skirt-like rim, separated by a broad ribbon (Pl. 7).

The covering of the ground-floor walls by stucco, which had been popularized by Adam, continued generally into the early Regency, the surface frequently being rusticated with deep horizontal joints emphasizing the long, reposeful proportions of a façade, especially that of a street terrace. The use of painted stucco for covering entire house fronts became more common from 1810 onwards, and was to form another of the celebrated characteristics of Regency building, culminating in its use for John Nash's great palatial terraces of Regent's Park. The hackneyed jibe against Nash from the *Quarterly Review* of 1826 is quoted again, if only that the use of the material may to some extent be vindicated.

> Augustus of Rome was for building renown'd,
> And of marble he left what of brick he had found;
> But is not our Nash, too, a very great master?
> He finds us all brick and he leaves us all plaster.

Aesthetically, at least, Nash was justified in using painted stucco, for with it he was able to give the terraces the gaiety and brilliance which are among their chief beauties, when seen flashing

Fig. 2. Grange Park, Hampshire, by William Wilkins, 1810. From *Jones' Views of the Seats of Noblemen and Gentlemen in England, etc.*, 1829.

A country house in the severest manner of the Greek revival.

in the sunshine across the green of Regent's Park on a summer's day, or in the clear evening light of spring or autumn. The Regency terraces of seaside towns like Brighton and Hastings would lose much of their quality of shining elegance without stucco. It was at the seaside, as Humphrey Repton explained, that the two virtues of the material first appeared. One, to obtain the utmost play of light and shadow upon buildings; the other, to seal brickwork against driving rain and winds heavily laden with salt spray.

Kent Grange, Hampstead (*c.* 1810), is a stucco house of unusually charming character, with its interplay of curves in double window bays, ironwork balconies and upper windows set within arched wall-recesses. For the moderate-sized country house of stucco may be cited Bignor Park, Sussex, built in restrained neo-classical style between 1826 and 1831, by Henry Harrison, an architect of whom little work is recorded.

Characteristic of the more informal and intimate tendencies of the Regency was the change in the conception of the villa, a term which no longer signified the imposing Palladian villa of Burlingtonian days, but now indicated almost every type of separate house of individual design between the cottage and the mansion.

The standard for those of medium or larger size was set by the villas of Regent's Park, which ranged from the severest manner of the Greek Revival (Fig. 2), as in the Doric Villa by York Terrace, to freer exercises in the Grecian taste, like The Holme, which Decimus Burton built for his father, and villas embodying strong Italian influence in round-headed windows and deeply overhanging eaves. No. 1 Gloucester Gate, by J. J.

Scoles, and many other villas of the Park, displayed the imaginative handling of the Classical tradition inspired by Picturesque ideas, in the way the masses of a building, while embodying Grecian detail, were broken up or detached to form a varied composition of dramatic and interesting outlines.

One of the most original domestic designs of the early Greek Revival is the Doric House, Sion Hill, Bath, built about 1810 with a Doric colonnade of two storeys, as a house and picture-gallery for the painter Thomas Barker by J. M. Gandy, A.R.A. (1771–1843), the friend and disciple of Soane.

For the expression of romantic moods in villa and cottage, however, the Gothic style was supreme, but less in the elaborate rococo manner of Strawberry Hill than in the playful style of Stephen Wright's Milton Manor, Abingdon.* Shelley's House at Great Marlow displays this gay spirit in its charming flattened ogival pointed windows. Extremes of Picturesque medieval fantasy are reached at Belsize Lane, Hampstead, where Hunter's Lodge (*c.* 1825) shows round towers with conical roofs, and again, ogival windows.

But the type of villa that breathes the Regency spirit more than any other is that which combines with the utmost freedom, frequently in a single building, the various elements of brickwork or stucco, curved window-bays, verandas, balconies, ironwork railings, trellis-work, classical porch, and either deep cornices with a parapet or broad eaves. Examples are found in every town possessing a Regency phase of building, but outstanding instances are Claremont Villa, Cheltenham; Kent Grange, Hampstead (already mentioned); and Rheola, Glamorgan, a house which John Nash built for his friend John Edwards, M.P., and now sympathetically used as a factory guest-house and offices. Halnaker Lodge, Coldharbour Lane, Brixton, and houses in Dulwich Village; at Twickenham, Strand-on-the-Green, Chiswick and Hampstead, at The Terrace, Barnes; Richmond Hill and the Park Villages East and West, Regent's Park, also finely represent the type.

The seaside town of Southwold in Suffolk deserves special mention for its medium-sized Regency houses of excellent quality, grouped mostly around the Gun Green and built about 1828. They form a delightful anthology of the favourite Regency styles from the severely non-columnar Grecian of Soane's inspiration (Pl. 9B) to stucco villas and houses with bows, balconies and verandas, while in the villages around are found plainer yellow-brick houses with porches of Doric and Tuscan and even, occasionally, Egyptian design.

The unconventional form of many Regency houses is not always due to fantasy, or the demands of the informal landscape, but to originality and experiment in planning to secure convenience in living, and the maximum admission of light and air. An early manifestation of this aspect of Regency thought is the astonishing Clare House at East Malling, Kent (1793), built by Michael Searles, architect of the Blackheath Paragon. In this house the intriguing circular form was determined by the planning of all living-rooms round a central hall. A similar house of a few years later is the charming villa at Havering-atte-Bower in Essex, where again the circular form ensured the procession of the sun through all the rooms of the house during the day. 'La Ronde'* near Exmouth is another example of a circular house, and contains astonishing decoration of shell-work.

The reticent manner of the post-Adam period which Holland showed in his houses at Sloane Street and Hans Place in the 1790's, persisted in the town terraces of the early Regency, as on the north side of Brunswick Square, London, where the houses, built about 1802, have a simple stucco ground floor, round-headed front-doorways, iron balconies, a flat stucco cornice, and first-floor windows within shallow arched recesses, flanking a central Wyatt-like segmental window bay rising through all floors to relieve the long façade. This terrace was part of the development of the Foundling Estate by James Burton, the remarkably capable London builder whose fame has been overshadowed by his more well-known son Decimus.

A transitional phase between this reserved early style and the more spectacularly palatial stucco Regency terrace of the years from 1815 onwards is marked by the terrace on the east side of Mecklenburgh Square, London, built in 1812 (Pl. 8A).

(A) JOHN NASH. Castellated Mansion. Knepp Castle, Sussex. 1806.

(B) Cottage Orné, Suffolk, in the manner of John Nash. *c.* 1815.

PLATE 5

(A) Verandah, with cast-iron railing, at Richmond, Surrey. *c.* 1815.

(B) Trellis verandah, with cast-iron railing, at Brighton. *c.* 1815.

PLATE 6

Villa at Brighton with bowed front, stuccoed, cast iron railings and canopy. *c.* 1820.

PLATE 7

(A) JOSEPH KAY. Town Terrace. Mecklenburgh Square, London. 1812–21.

(B) A small town-terrace. Montpelier Square, London. *c.* 1818.

(A) House in Sidmouth, with an especially original quality of fantasy in trellis work balconies and Gothic windows.

(B) Villa at Southwold, in the manner of Sir John Soane. *c.* 1815.

PLATE 9

(A) Balcony railing of cast-iron with a Grecian Doric porch at Brighton. *c.* 1820.

(B) Balcony railings of cast-iron, at Brunswick Square, Hove. *c.* 1826.

(A) Drawing-room with segmental window-bay and ceiling with shallow arches and groining in the manner of Sir John Soane. Sarsgrove House, Glos. *c.* 1815.

(B) John Nash. Knepp Castle, Sussex. 'Gothic' decoration in the form of miniature vaulting. *c.* 1806.

(A) Double staircase with cast-iron balusters, at Eastern Terrace, Brighton. *c.* 1824.

(B) DECIMUS BURTON. Doorcase, painted and gilt, and enriched modillion cornice, at The Holme, Regent's Park, London. *c.* 1818.

Cranbury Park, Hampshire. The Tent Room, formed when J. B. Papworth made additions. *c.* 1829–31.

PLATE 13

(A) JOHN NASH. The Royal Pavilion, Brighton. The East Front. 1815–22.
*Brighton Corporation.*

(B) JOHN NASH. Cumberland Terrace, London. 1826.

PLATE 14

(A) The Tower House, Park Village West, with villas of Park Village East in the distance, probably by James Pennethorne, under Nash. *c.* 1824–28.

(B) Italian Villa, at Park Village West. *c.* 1824–28.

PLATE 15

(A) C. A. Busby. Brunswick Square, Hove, Sussex. 1825.

(B) Decimus Burton. Adelaide Crescent, Hove. 1830–34.

(A) C. A. Busby. Brunswick Terrace, Hove. 1824.

(B) George Basevi. Pelham Crescent, London. *c.* 1829.

PLATE 17

(A) Belvoir Castle, Leics. The East Front by Thoroton, imitating James Wyatt's theme of deeply embrasured 'Norman' windows. *English Life Publications.*

(B) BENJAMIN WYATT. The Elizabeth Saloon, Belvoir Castle, Leics., using doorcases and wall-panels from a French *château*, and marking the origin of the Louis XV revival of the early 19th century. The ceiling was painted by Matthew Wyatt. *English Life Publications.*

(A) GEORGE BASEVI. Belgrave Square, London. 1825–40.

(B) JOHN NASH. The Royal Pavilion Salon. 1815–22.
*Brighton Corporation.*

PLATE 19

BENJAMIN WYATT. The Waterloo Chamber, Apsley House, London, 1828.

PLATE 20

This delightful design was the work of Joseph Kay, architect for the Mecklenburgh Square development in the Foundling Estate scheme with his master, Charles R. Cockerell, as consultant. A similar note on a more domestic level is struck by Trevor Square, Knightsbridge, London (1818), where again stuccoed ground storeys combine with severe brickwork, plain window-openings, and simple iron balconies to give a touch of smartness and gaiety.

The tradition of discreet design in the smaller house terrace (Pl. 8B) persisted right through to the end of the Regency period, and is seen in all its qualities of charm and reserve in Alexander Place, South Kensington, probably built about 1827–31, under the direction of George Basevi, who was responsible for Pelham Crescent and the Thurloe Square development. Here again are the shallow window bows, cast-iron balconies without hoods at the first-floor windows, and round-arched front doors. The ground storey is stuccoed and there is a moulded stucco cornice. A little-known, but enchanting *enclave* of simple Regency terrace houses is Edwardes Square, with Earl's Terrace, off Kensington High Street, London. This square was built between 1811 and 1819 by an unknown architect for a French speculative builder named Changeur. The long terrace of brick houses with stucco ground floors, where at No. 32 Leigh Hunt once lived, is approached past a tiny pedimented Doric gardener's lodge called The Temple.

From the middle of the eighteenth century onwards, as the popularity of sea-bathing developed, the idea of an annual holiday by the sea became more and more a national institution, and the demand for summer lodgings was enormous. At Brighton from 1795 onwards many new houses were being erected. Regency Square, begun in 1818, was the first of the Brighton squares on a larger scale, but still in the early tradition of yellow brick with rusticated stucco ground floors, bow fronts, and balconies with ironwork railings. These last owe much to the designs of the architect Busby and to the foundries for Sussex iron at Lewes nearby (Pl. 10A, B). The Brighton railings are almost invariably cast, not wrought, and exhibit a delightful variety of classical designs. One of outstanding fineness and delicacy, incorporating the honeysuckle motif, is seen not only throughout Brighton but in London, Cheltenham, Worthing and elsewhere.

Worthing, Hastings, Ramsgate, Margate, Weymouth and a host of other towns provide delightful examples in the earlier Regency seaside idiom of brick and stucco, bow windows and ironwork balconies, as well as important instances of the later phases of style. At Sidmouth the houses have an especially original quality of fantasy in trellis-work balconies and Gothic windows (Pl. 9A).

At Cheltenham, the pre-eminent Regency inland town, the first phase of its architectural development lasted until the advent of Papworth and Forbes about 1825. To this earlier period belong the stone-faced, bow-fronted houses Hygeia (once Vittoria) Lodge, *c.* 1813, and Claremont Lodge. This time saw also the creation of several works of monumental quality, favoured greatly by the existence of Cotswold stone, as well as many smaller buildings of high merit and individual character.

Royal Crescent, *c.* 1805–9, was the first of the large-scale groups, and still contains good interior work such as curved doors, fine plaster ceilings, and fanlights. An outstanding contribution is made to the quality of Cheltenham's Regency architecture by the remarkable beauty of its ironwork, based frequently upon generally available designs like those in Cottingham's *Directory*, but owing much to the fineness and delicacy with which the graceful linear Grecian detail has been executed by local craftsmen.

At Bath the Paragon (*c.* 1809–14) offers a striking example of individuality in terrace design, with its projecting semi-circular Grecian porches and double front-doors shaped to the curve. The great days of Bath were not in the Regency, but as well as having many pleasant domestic examples of the period, it provides a rather *triste* epilogue to the romantic adventure of Fonthill, in the shape of the classical Lansdowne Tower (1825),* built by Henry Edmond Goodridge (1800–63), where William Beckford ended his days.

*Interior design*

Just as the varied styles of Regency building resolved themselves into three or four basic types, so also interior architectural decoration ran in a few main currents. In the Picturesque house the spirit of interior design frequently bore no relation to the style adopted for the exterior. At Downton Castle, Richard Payne Knight deliberately retained a classical scheme as embodying 'the greatest convenience and progress' in interior arrangement. The Gothic Luscombe has classical rooms. Sezincote, the Gloucestershire villa in the Indian style, had a restrained classical interior. The Indian exterior of the Brighton Pavilion cloaks a *chinoiserie* decorative scheme.

The predominant trend in small and medium houses was towards greater simplicity, in whatever style was adopted. The style of Robert Adam, strictly modified in this direction, retained its popularity right through the period, from the latter half of the eighteenth century to the 1840's. In the smaller houses such decoration would be confined to a single circular garland of husks upon the ceiling with a small central ornament of leaves, a narrow frieze of delicate swags around the walls, and a similar frieze, or reticent decoration of an urn, vase or medallion gracing the chimney-piece, which might be of painted wood, composition or marble.

Fig. 3. The entrance to the Royal Pavilion, Brighton, from John Nash, *The Royal Pavilion*, 1826

The decorative style of George Basevi as expressed in the houses of Belgrave Square at the end of the Regency was modelled closely upon the manner of Adam and Wyatt, especially in the design of the chimney-pieces. His ceilings there are frequently plain, but with rich palmated coving and cornices. As at Bignor Park, Sussex, ceilings might be portioned out into squares or rectangles, with fine bead mouldings, another form of treatment, highly simplified, deriving from the Adam school of design. Frequently, cornices were of straight classical mouldings, sometimes called architrave mouldings, from their similarity to those used for the door-cases. Chimney-pieces were also designed in this way, with no other ornament except perhaps a fluted frieze or sculptured panel. This mode of interior design, restrained to the point of plainness, is frequently found in the houses of Nash, in the villas and terraces of Regent's Park and elsewhere, even in some of the private apartments of the Royal Pavilion at Brighton.

Nash delighted in the use of arched openings in doorways and corridors, usually of a flattish curve, with a simple torus moulding on the edge. It is a tendency he may have absorbed from Soane, who made the contribution of his distinctive Grecian style to interiors in a similar fashion to that he had employed at Aynhoe in 1804. There, and at Sarsgrove House, Oxfordshire (*c.* 1810), which was built, if not by him, then under his influence, a severely plain interior is relieved by shallow arched recesses in the walls, by arched door openings, and by ceilings of shallow vaulting, sometimes divided into four parts by blunt-angled groining (Pl. 11A). The chimney-pieces of Soane's style were of marble or fine stone, with plain jambs, and bearing his restrained incised Grecian ornament, the frieze probably incised with a full Greek key pattern design. Soane's interior method seems rarely to have been imitated other than by Nash, except occasionally in the provinces as by Foulston at Plymouth.

Despite stylistic divergencies, the integration of interior with exterior was frequently expressed in the endowment of rooms with beautiful curved shapes created by the rounded bays at the front or end of a house. These bays were often associated with the long French or, as they were sometimes called, 'Italian' windows, reaching down to ground level. The Romantic pre-occupation with nature, as well as the growing informality of manners, among women no less than men, may have stimulated the fondness for such windows, which enabled the occupants to move out upon the lawn at a single step, and filled the rooms with light and air. The windows of angular bays served the same growing aspiration. Malton wrote: 'In consequence of the inclined lights, the sides of the room ... are better lit than they possibly can be through square openings in the wall.' Even though, as at 'Northanger Abbey', the Gothic form of window was preserved, nevertheless 'every pane was so large, so clear, so light!'

The desire for informal living among the family or household continued the development of the open planning of rooms favoured by Adam, and just as the French windows broke down the barrier between house and garden, large folding doors abolished the distinction between one room and another.

A phase of severe archæological exactitude in the interpretation of Greek ideas was introduced by the wealthy banker and antiquary, Thomas Hope, at his house Deepdene, near Dorking, where he arranged a series of interiors not only in the Greek, but also in the Egyptian style, which the campaign of Napoleon in Egypt and Nelson's victory of the Nile had made fashionable. His work on *Household Furniture and Interior Decoration* was published in 1807, but his influence was limited. The Egyptian vogue manifested itself more in furniture and objects of art than in architectural decoration, though in a few interiors there were chimney-pieces with the tapering jambs of Egyptian pylons, and ornament of lotus design.

For the Gothic interiors of John Nash's domestic castles, such as Knepp Castle, and West Grinstead Park, Sussex, he evolved a Gothic decorative style of great delicacy, gaiety and charm, consisting of ceilings with light plaster ribs in the interlacing curvilinear or geometrical designs of the sixteenth century. The ornament of cornices or ceiling coves is especially charming, being in the form of Gothic arcading on a small scale with intersecting arches, or resembling miniature vaulting (Pl. 11B). Nash's assistant, George Stanley Repton, son of the landscape gardener, might have been responsible for the designing of this ornament, for his sketch-books indicate an interest in Gothic not possessed by Nash, who would complain that the designing of a single Gothic window took up more time than a whole house. But even in these Gothic interiors there were lapses into the classical, especially in the design of fireplaces, which were sometimes of simple architrave mouldings with a classical plaque in marble, or, if Gothic motifs were used, it was in the form of a Gothic arch, sketchily indicated on the fireplace jambs in the incised grooving of Soane's style.

Throughout the houses of the Regency, from the simplest to the most palatial, the tendency was for ceilings to be plain in the main portion. The sides were frequently coved, but although decorated centres are found in some of the great state apartments of the Regency palaces, even in these the plain expanse of ceiling is not unusual. Where chandeliers were used they frequently depended from a central ornament of leaves, sometimes composed in a swirling design (Fig. 4).

This kind of foliated ceiling ornament, which is found in every type of house from the smallest to the most elaborate, and which in a shrunken, enfeebled form survived all through the nineteenth century up to Edwardian days, descends from the magnificent central ornament of leaves in that

Fig. 4. A classical interior, from *Designs for Ornamental Villas* by P. F. Robinson, F.S.A., 1827.
An 'enriched' cornice and ceiling mouldings, but with a plain coving and ceiling, with small central ornament.

ceiling of the Temple of the Sun at Palmyra, which Flitcroft imitated at Woburn,* and Robert Adam paraphrased so gloriously in the ceiling of the Drawing-room at Osterley.*

If not plain, the ceiling might be given a compartmented form, but with plain shallow panels instead of the deep coffers containing rosettes as in the preceding years.

The fully Grecian villas of the Revival, such as those at Pittville and Bayshill, Cheltenham, or of Regent's Park, often had ceilings with flat borders or friezes of Greek key pattern, or of *guilloche* design resembling flat interlacing ribbon. The door-cases (Pl. 12B) frequently were given fluted architraves, with corner blocks carrying floral rosettes, a lion's mask, or a plain knob-like roundel. The frieze might be adorned with the *anthemion* design, in which the lotus flower alternates with palm leaves, the latter being frequently confused with honeysuckle, an equally popular motif. Other decoration might take the form of plaques of classical subjects on the walls of entrance hall or staircase. In wealthy houses, mouldings of doors, of skirtings and cornices were frequently 'enriched' with dentils – small block-shaped ornaments with narrow spacing – or with widely spaced modillions either of simple block-form or, in the richer examples, in the shape of a scrolled bracket carved with an acanthus leaf. In some of the smaller interiors, as at Luscombe, classical mouldings were frequently used of delicate and slender proportion, using tongue-and-dart, acanthus-tip, palm or bay leaf designs, often gilded (see figs., pp. 36, 92).

During the later Regency years interior ornament in some of the palatial houses, especially that of cornices, coves and friezes embodying scrolling of acanthus and other foliated or flower design, assumed a more sumptuous character, as in the work of Benjamin Wyatt described later, that was to become distinctive of this phase. The extreme delicacy which Adam had given this ornament, creating with it such eloquent shapes within the open voids of his borders, or the nervous vitality of James Wyatt's decoration as seen at Heveningham, was lost, and stalk, flower and leaf now assumed a luxuriant bold fulness, expanding to fill, almost to burst beyond, the confines of the frieze or coving it occupied.

The delicacy initiated by Robert Adam, refined and simplified by Henry Holland and James Wyatt, was, as in so many other features, the predominant influence in the design of staircases. The gracefully soaring curves, or elegant articulated angles of mounting treads, and the delicate line of handrail which they developed are the familiar marks of the Regency staircase (Pl. 12A). Much individuality was expressed in the patterning of iron balusters, in which the familiar classical motifs of acanthus and honeysuckle played restrained or florid parts, or in which pure linear designs of exquisite grace and subtlety were used, as by Soane in his staircases at Moggerhanger.

The lessened importance attached to the chimney-piece in Regency times was deplored by Papworth, who observed that greater decorative value had been transferred to immense gilt mirrors, which, as Britten remarked, were adopted 'to extend the apparent dimensions of our rooms', as in the dining-room at Uppark, Sussex,* remodelled by Humphrey Repton, and to create perspectives, as in his unfulfilled design for a flower corridor with mirrors at the ends at the Brighton Pavilion. John Nash used the same device in the mirror-faced doors at the ends of the Long Gallery in his own transformation of the Pavilion. It was a development again expressive of the Regency aspiration towards light and space.

The fondness for tents as part of the Picturesque equipment of park and garden in Regency times caused many designs for tented rooms indoors to be produced. One perfect room of this type was created at Cranbury Park, Hampshire,* designed in Adamesque style by George Dance (*c.* 1780–90), where J. B. Papworth formed the Library about 1831 (Pl. 13).

The Regency designers in their interiors, as well as externally, endowed their houses with gracious individuality, seemliness, and sunny charm, and reached a condition in architecture from which a sensible and agreeable modern style might well have emerged a century earlier than the Victorian obscurity allowed. It was the Brighton architect, Charles Busby, who remarked with justifiable complacency that 'the true impressions of cheerfulness, elegance and refinement are so well understood and so happily united in our modern domestic dwellings that I hesitate not to say we are rapidly advancing to a state of perfection'.

### *The Oriental episode*

Towards the end of the eighteenth century the place which China had occupied for nearly a hundred years as a land of romantic nostalgia had been taken by India, largely through the interest in Indian art and culture awakened by Warren Hastings when Governor of Bengal. Engravings made by William Hodges and by Thomas Daniell and his nephew of the buildings and scenery of India enthralled the English imagination with 'the splendour of the minarets and pagodas that shone out from the depths of its woods', and the Prince Regent's biographer Croly wrote of the mosques and palaces of Hindostan as the inspiration for 'a new poetic architecture'.

Thomas Daniell collaborated at Sezincote in Gloucestershire (1806), with the architect Samuel Pepys Cockerell, Surveyor to the East India Company, in rebuilding it as an India villa for a retired nabob. William Porden, who had been a pupil of

Cockerell, had built at the same time the Royal Stables and Riding House at Brighton for the Prince of Wales, and Humphrey Repton, who had been laying out the grounds at Sezincote, was summoned from there by the Prince to advise upon rebuilding the Pavilion in the Indian style, but his designs, which closely resembled Sezincote and seem to have been based on one of William Hodges' *Views*, were never carried out. It was not until 1815 that the Prince, then four years Regent, decided to go on with the project for rebuilding the Brighton Pavilion, but now with John Nash as his architect (Pl. 14A and Fig. 3).

Nash skilfully incorporated the original classical villa into the fabric of the new building, adding two great new State apartments to the ends, one a Banqueting Room, the other a Music Room, and gave unity to the whole by linking old and new parts with a long battlemented cornice, and rows of Indian columns along the eastern façade. Those outside the two great new rooms formed a screen linked by pierced stone-work lattice screens like Indian *jalis*, that give a delightful effect by casting dappled patterns of sunlight and shadow on the stucco walls. The roofs were crowned with Indian domes of exquisitely subtle contour, but remembering the essential character of a pavilion as a tent, Nash placed above the two large rooms not domes but spires, like the concave roofs of Crusaders' tents in a novel of Walter Scott's. Nash has wrongly been accused of plagiarizing Repton's designs, for there are no details which correspond.

The theme of the tent appears again in the interior, where Nash, with consummate skill, used drooping tented ceilings – in one room of black and gold and in another of bamboo – to form the transition from the low domestic scale of Holland's small rooms to the palatial height of the new great State Apartments. The palm-tree motif also persists throughout the Pavilion, in the design of the columns in the window-bays of the drawing-rooms, sometimes naturalistic, sometimes formalized. Even the cast-iron columns of the Great Kitchen become palm trees with fronds of sheet copper at the summit. And cast-iron is the stuff of the imitation bamboo staircases, exquisitely gay and light. The cast-iron of Functionalism underlies the fantasy of Romanticism, and makes the Pavilion doubly a monument of its age. Cast-iron forms the framework of the domes, and the tubular, bolted cores of the towering chimneys, minarets and pinnacles. With its long, reposeful, harmonious proportions, its classical symmetry, for all its oriental character, and the subordination of the small details to the main masses of the building, and in the graceful curves of dome and arch, the Pavilion embodies some of Nash's most brilliant work, and has been invested by him with more poetic beauty than any other of his designs.

### *Later Regency houses and terraces*

The principal factor which determined the character of the later Regency houses and terraces was the increased permeation of domestic architecture by the Greek Revival. It was a style having qualities of simplicity and sincerity that made it adaptable to the smallest private buildings, and provided inspiration for multitudes of villas and smaller town houses, from the Grecian villas of Regent's Park to those of Pittville Spa at Cheltenham.

The excitement of a mounting tide of victory in the wars against Napoleon and the sense of the beginning of a new historical epoch when George, Prince of Wales, was proclaimed Regent in 1811, found expression in the gigantic programme of public works carried out in London – the Metropolitan Improvements – between 1812 and 1828, the purpose of which was to provide much needed new housing in the north of London beyond what became Oxford Street, and to link this district by broad processional streets in place of squalid, mean alleys to the centre of government in Whitehall, and a great new Royal Palace to be built near St James's Park. It was a gigantic enterprise, which provided a city that had become the capital of Europe with many of the great monuments and landmarks that are the glory of London.

The scheme began in 1812 with the transformation of Marylebone Park from a tract of marshy farmland, with 'paltry cabins and monotonous cow-lairs' into a landscaped park with lakes, islands, villas and with the long ranges of palatial terraces that are its great glory. The designer was John Nash, who had been appointed as an architect to the Commissioners of Woods and Forests in 1806. On the death of Wyatt in 1813 Nash was given his place as Surveyor-General, though he had to share the post with Sir John Soane and Sir Robert Smirke. However, Nash was henceforth responsible for most of the Royal building programmes.

The planning of the terraces was based upon the principle of designing a row of houses to form a single magnificent palatial unit, usually with a central pedimented portico and flanking pavilions on the Palladian model. It was the principle, giving dignity and scale to a town area, that was first used in Grosvenor Square, London, by Edward Stephen in 1727, and which had inspired the Woods of Bath in the planning of their great unified street and square compositions.

In many of the terraces, so as not to mar the broad unity of design by a row of separate front-doors, the main entrances to the houses were at the back of the terrace. Further behind were stables and mews and rows of lesser houses, for tradesmen and artisans, devoid of ornament but nevertheless designed with seemliness and good proportions.

The terraces are not all of the same order of magnificence, and vary also in quality of design and execution. Nash's genius was for the dramatic, spectacular and picturesque in architecture and planning, but this gift was combined with impatience over detail, which caused him to be criticised for 'carelessness, sometimes degenerating to littleness, with a deficiency of elegance in the details' by James Elmes, who described the great schemes of the time in his volume on the *Metropolitan Improvements* in 1828.

The two chief entrances to the Park are on the south, and consist of two fine compositions: York Gate with Philip Hardwick's Church of St Mary-le-bone facing the Park between the two halves of York Terrace, and the entrance from Portland Place through the two curving wings of Park Crescent, with its beautiful ranges of coupled Ionic columns.

York Terrace (1822) stretching in two sections across York Gate is one of the most magnificent of the larger groups, having as Elmes said 'the semblance of the residence of a sovereign prince'. Like many of the Park compositions, the terrace is Palladian in conception, but with Grecian detail. Although on a smaller scale, Cornwall Terrace (1821), the first of the terraces to be built, has the richness of the Corinthian order, and is prettily detailed. Clarence Terrace (1823) is probably due to Decimus Burton. Sussex Place (1822), designed by Nash with ten melon-shaped cupolas, was condemned by contemporary critics, but is an exhilarating design, with the grand sweep of the two curving wings. Hanover Terrace (1822–3) is again on a splendid scale, but was regarded as 'more grammatical' in its rather dry Doric manner. Northernmost on the eastern side is Gloucester Gate, one of the most elegant of the terraces, with an Ionic façade, begun in 1827. Cumberland Terrace (1827) is the stupendous centre-piece of the great architectural panorama of the Park (Pl. 14B). The immense block of the central portico is crowned by a pediment containing a group of terracotta figures by J. B. Bubb, representing Britannia attended by the arts and sciences. On either side range the deeply recessed wings of the main building, with gigantic porticoes linked to those of further separate wings by triumphal arches leading into courtyards where cobbled ramps lead down to stables. The order is Ionic, and the balustrades and pediment carry statues. This brilliantly composed piece of dramatic scenery must be reckoned Nash's finest single classical work. The grandeur of Cumberland Terrace was difficult to challenge, but Chester Terrace (1825) next to it achieves its effect of splendour by the original device of triumphal arches forming the entrances at either end of the long façade.

Of the twenty-six villas originally intended, eight were built, so as not to spoil the rural character of the Park. Several, such as Hanover Lodge, St John's Lodge (now the Institute of Archæology), and Lord Hertford's Villa (now the American Ambassador's house) have been much rebuilt. The Doric Villa near York Terrace is severely Grecian. The Holme (1818), now part of Bedford

College for Women, was designed by Burton for his father, and is the prettiest villa in the Park, containing one of the most enchanting Regency rooms in existence (Pl. 12B). Behind the grand terraces are a number of smaller terraces of stucco designed with great simplicity, such as Munster Square (once York Square) built in the late 1820's, as houses for the lower clerical and artisan classes. Provision was made for middle-class families in a kind of garden suburb, Park Village East and Park Village West, which Nash conceived as a picturesque village similar to Blaise Hamlet, but the building was carried out by other architects. The delightful little houses display all the familiar devices of Picturesque Regency domestic architecture, fretted eaves-boards, trellised verandas, and canopied balconies. The Tower House in Park Village West is the most striking, with its charming octagonal tower and sculptured panel, a domesticated version of the familiar Temple of the Winds from Athens (Pl. 15A).

The new street leading to the West End was linked to the Park by Portland Place at York Gate, where Nash 'joined his bold style to the finicking finish of the Messrs Adams with good effect'. Of Regent Street itself nothing remains of Nash's except its noble sweeping curves, which, alas! no longer open up successive vistas of its varied original buildings, but only the drab façades which replaced Nash's work when it was demolished in 1922. Carlton House, which Holland had built for King George IV when Prince of Wales in 1783, was found to be in need of repair and was demolished in 1827. At the same time St James's Park, which had become a muddy swamp since its hey-day in the time of Charles II, was laid out by Nash as a landscaped park, much as it is today. Buckingham Palace was begun in 1825, but it was the least successful work of the ageing and heavily pressed architect. The death of the King in 1830 prevented its completion by Nash, who thus lost the baronetcy that was to have been his reward. It was finished in 1831–7 by Sir Edward Blore, but the present familiar east front was built in 1913 by Sir Aston Webb. Where Carlton House had stood the Duke of York's Steps were built to form an opening into the Mall, flanked on either side by the two massive ranges of Carlton House Terrace which make the broad avenue leading to Buckingham Palace one of the grandest processional ways in Europe.

A pupil of Soane, Sir Robert Smirke (1781–1867), whose Covent Garden Theatre of 1809 was the first Grecian building in London, designed one of the noblest works of the Metropolitan Improvements, the British Museum (1823–47), the dramatic Ionic colonnades of which have little of his usual pedantic dulness. It is doubly a monument of the Regency, since the eastern wing was built to house the King's Library, the collection of books once possessed by his father, that was given to the nation in 1821 by King George IV. William Wilkins (1751–1815), whose new buildings at Downing College, Cambridge (1807–20)* were the first major work of the Greek Revival, gave University College, London (1827–8)* what Professor Sir Albert Richardson has called the 'finest classic portico in England'. The National Gallery* was built (1832–8) on the site of William Kent's old Royal Mews, to house Julius Angerstein's great collection of paintings, which had been bought for the nation at the King's suggestion. Here, again, Wilkins created a magnificent portico, with an impressive arrangement of steps, using the entrance columns from Carlton House. In sentiment, and historically, no other use could have been more fitting. At Hyde Park Corner St George's Hospital (1827–8), designed by Wilkins, gives stolid support to two much-loved works nearby, the Ionic Screen and the Triumphal Arch at the top of Constitution Hill, both designed by Decimus Burton. Burton's greatest work was his superb contribution to the great club-building movement of the Regency, which came into being through the growth of the professional and learned classes. His Athenæum Club (1829–30) in Waterloo Place consists of a single block, of such eminently satisfying proportions that even the later addition of an attic did not spoil it. In deference to the Roman character of Nash's United Services Club opposite (now much rebuilt), Burton adopted the Roman Doric order for the coupled columns of the beautiful porch, which is surmounted by a gilded statue of

Pallas Athenae. This delightful adornment, and the sculptured frieze of the Pan-Athenaic procession, relieve the simple façade. In his massive treatment of buildings Burton seems to have absorbed some influence from Smirke, but in the Italian trend of his detail, as in such features as his deep cornices with console supports, he anticipates here the Italian phase of the years following the Regency era which was established by Sir Charles Barry.

*Edinburgh*

In Edinburgh, the 'Modern Athens', the Greek Revival established itself naturally where great works by Robert Adam and Sir William Chambers and others had been fostered by the classical trend of the city's culture during the later years of the previous century. With the ending of the Napoleonic struggle the building of the New Town was resumed, and a group of Scottish architects of great distinction came into prominence. Their work, however, took on some of the grimness of the Scottish stone even when the northern gravity of mind did not overwhelm the Regency sense of gaiety and elegance.

Archibald Elliott (1764–1823) carried out one of the earlier works of this phase, Waterloo Place, Edinburgh, begun in 1815. Eastwards, the vista of Waterloo Place is filled by the Acropolis-like eminence of Calton Hill, where it was intended should stand monuments to Scotland's greatness in war and in the arts, but the site was only a visual and not an organic social focus, and as interest waned, the erection of the buildings was delayed, curtailed, and eventually abandoned. But the unfinished portico of the National Monument (1812), which was designed by W. H. Playfair (1789–1857) with C. R. Cockerell, has a dramatic stark dignity that makes it a not unworthy memorial.

Playfair's plans of 1819 to re-organize the schemes for developing the New Town of Calton Hill resulted in little more than the building of one vast block, Royal Terrace, consisting of a single façade nearly a quarter-mile long. Regent Terrace, south of the hill, is less overwhelming, but St Bernard's Crescent, built in 1828 on land belonging to Sir Henry Raeburn, across the Water of Leith, plumbs the depths of portentous gloom. Playfair built also, in 1823, the severely plain Royal Circus. But in Ann Street, also on Raeburn's land, the houses are fronted by gardens and have intimate charm. Less scholarly, but dignified and pleasing in the Tuscan order, are Moray Place and Albyn Place, laid out in 1822 by James Gillespie Graham.

*Brighton*

The splendour and success of Nash's dazzling town-planning schemes in the Metropolis inspired great landowners, like Thomas Read Kemp in Brighton, and Pearson Thompson and Joseph Pitt in Cheltenham, to promote large speculative estate developments that would transform their towns with a similar grandeur.

In Brighton hitherto building had been on the modest domestic scale of the early Regency terraces and small squares like Regency Square. This was designed by the architect Amon Wilds, probably in conjunction with his son Amon Henry Wilds. From 1821 onwards they carried out extensive work with the architect Busby. These three men, frequently in partnership, but sometimes also separately, were to be responsible for the creation of the greater part of the squares, crescents and terraces of Regency Brighton.

Charles Augustus Busby was born in 1788. He studied at the Royal Academy and published two books of designs, *A series of designs for villas and country houses*, etc., 1808, and *A collection of designs for modern embellishments*, etc., *c.* 1810. This last included cast-iron balcony railings, and he is believed to have been responsible for designing most of the ironwork around Euston Square.

The first of the great Brighton architectural groups was Kemp Town in East Brighton, named after the landowner, who was M.P. for Brighton and Lewes. With Busby as architect, work began in 1823. The scale of Kemp's project was monumental, and although only half the number of houses originally intended were built, it is only exceeded in magnitude by Nash's scheme of

Regent's Park, and unlike this, which is broken up into separate units, Kemp Town is a single, immense closely-knit entity. It consists of Sussex Square opening on its seaward south side into the great sweep of Lewes Crescent with a span of 840 feet, 200 feet wider than the Royal Crescent at Bath. The Crescent is then flanked upon the sea-front by two great terraces, Chichester and Arundel Terrace. Despite sometimes ungainly modern additions, the whole architectural composition retains the impressiveness and beauty that are given by the lovely sweep of Lewes Crescent and the array of painted stucco fronts, shining in the brilliance of sea-coast sunshine against the background of deep blue sky.

From Kemp Town to Royal Crescent range the long groups of the stately terraces and smaller groups of enchantingly varied Regency styles that help to make the Brighton sea-front one of the most impressive in the world.

The second of the great monumental architectural compositions that distinguish the sea-front of Brighton and Hove is Brunswick Square and Terrace (Pl. 17A), built from 1825 to 1828 by the Wilds-Busby partnership. Although the square is smaller than Sussex Square, the architectural detail is more pronounced, and the two great flanking ranges of Brunswick Terrace are of impressive magnificence (Pl. 16A).

The third great architectural unit, which gives the western end of the sea-front such superb richness, is Adelaide Crescent, begun in 1830 but not finished till 1850. The architect was Decimus Burton, who was then working with his father, James Burton, upon the development of St Leonards-on-Sea. Only ten houses were built to Burton's design, but the Crescent retains the glorious double curve which gives it an extreme elegance and grace of line (Pl. 16B).

Right up to the opening of the Victorian period innumerable squares, terraces and streets of houses were built in Brighton, mostly by Busby and the Wilds, working either jointly or independently. They embody a multitude of delightful combinations of Regency features, and make that town one of the most fascinating architectural centres in the whole country.

### *Cheltenham*

The combination of landlord and architect that had been so fruitful at Kemp Town, Brighton, was to bring about no less interesting developments of later Regency architecture at Cheltenham. These have for long been, and always will be, indissolubly associated with the name of Papworth, but as Bryan Little has revealed, the influence of this most interesting architect upon Cheltenham is due less to the few buildings which it is certain he designed than to 'the ideas ... the philosophy, of development and town planning' that he inspired and which were carried into monumental effect not only by himself, but by other designers and builders who worked upon these lines.

John Buonarotti Papworth (1775–1847) had been trained in the office of William Plaw, the famous designer of picturesque cottages and farm-buildings. It was no doubt this experience that laid the foundation of his *Rural Residences* published in 1818. At Cheltenham Papworth was commissioned in 1825 to carry out developments upon the Montpellier and Lansdowne Estates, which belonged to the landowner Pearson Thompson.

The central improvement was the redesigning with a domed Rotunda of the Montpellier Pump Room, a charming early work (1817) of the local architect John Forbes. Although the banking crisis of 1825 prevented Thompson's magnificent ideas from being fully realized, the schemes that Papworth devised may very well have inspired the excellent work that was eventually carried out by others, especially the local architects R. W. and C. Jearrad. Outstanding among these works are Lansdowne Terrace and Crescent, built about 1828. The first is a noble composition in stone with elaborate pedimented porticos of coupled Ionic columns framing the first floor windows. The other is a restrained façade in plain stucco on a long graceful curve broken by simple projecting Doric porches. Each admirably expresses the character and proper potentialities of its own material.

It is perhaps in the villas of Bayshill Road that it is most difficult to deny the hand of Papworth, and one of them corresponds closely to a design he made of 'Montpellier Lodge' for Pearson Thompson himself. Each embodying some variation on the Grecian theme, all of considerable graciousness and beauty, these houses stand with those of Regent's Park in representing the Regency villa of the Greek Revival at the summit of its development.

At Pittville, Cheltenham, Joseph Pitt, a wealthy banker, aimed at an architectural and picturesque garden lay-out as the setting for a grand Pump Room surrounded by squares, terraces and villas. Pitt's architect was John Forbes, who created what was not only one of the grandest Assembly Rooms in the Kingdom, but one of the most beautiful monuments of the Greek Revival. The interior of the Pittville Pump Room has something of the splendour of one of Adam's great halls, but possesses the restraint in ornamentation and the subtlety in the handling of interior space that had been learned from Holland and Soane. Although the assemblies of the Regency were never held in a lovelier room, the Pittville Spa was just too far from the centre of the town to become part of its organic life. Mercifully it has been preserved, though its fate until recently was in the balance.

Around the Spa lie the Grecian villas of Pittville, smaller in scale than those of Bayshill Road, and less formal in their picturesque modelling. Arundel Lodge is the most individual of these. Thirlstaine House (1823), now one of the buildings of Cheltenham College, was one of the earliest and most accomplished manifestations in the provinces of the Grecian movement. It was almost certainly designed by the owner himself, J. R. Scott, a friend of Wilkins, Smirke and W. H. Inwood. The Entrance Hall has great dignity and serenity, modelled, as Bryan Little has perceived, upon the Great Hall at Kedleston, and containing twelve Ionic columns deriving from the Temple of Dionysos at Teos.

### *Other provincial towns*

Other notable examples of later Regency terraces are Pelham Crescent, Hastings, flanking the astonishing circular Regency church of St Mary in the Castle; Camden Crescent at Bath; Wellington Crescent, Ramsgate (1819–24), with its long Doric colonnade, and Spencer Square (1820), retaining the severer early tradition; and one of the most Nash-like of the provincial terraces, the delightful Crescent at Alverstoke, *c.* 1826.

At Tunbridge Wells Decimus Burton emulated the Regent's Park development by laying out the Calverley Estate on Mount Pleasant (1828–52). The Crescent has a severe classical elegance, but in the villas of the Park the ponderousness of Burton's Italianate manner is emphasized by the grey local stone.

The years following Waterloo saw accelerated progress in the development of great estates in London, chiefly through the immense undertakings of the great firm of Thomas Cubitt and his brothers, who introduced more highly organized methods of work into the building industry, and brought new standards of quality into material and construction. Their undertakings were scattered all over the metropolis, and later extended to provincial towns such as Brighton, where the firm completed the Kemp Town development, and Thomas Cubitt himself had a house. Polesden Lacey* near Dorking was rebuilt by him in 1824 and though altered since then retains its original beautiful Ionic colonnade.

In Tavistock and Gordon Squares the Cubitts built delightful houses of semi-Grecian design, linked by low screen walls. In Woburn Place this restrained treatment gave place to the use of the richer Roman orders for the columned façades. Their greatest enterprises in London, however, were the developments of Belgravia and Pimlico from about 1824 onwards, following the improvement in the character of the district caused by the building of Buckingham Palace.

The architect George Basevi (1794–1845) designed the houses of Belgrave Square (Pl. 19A), except for the large separate mansions at the corners. Basevi gave the main blocks of the square a palatial treatment of sumptuous richness presaging the ultimate floridity of classicism that was to appear later at the Fitzwilliam Museum, Cambridge. In 1829 Basevi became architect to the

Fig. 5. Eastnor Castle, Herefordshire, by Sir Robert Smirke, 1810–15. From *Jones' Views of the Seats of Noblemen and Gentlemen in England, etc.*, 1829.

A monumental example of Smirke's 'square' style.

Smith's Charity Estate and that of Mr Alexander adjoining, in South Kensington. Here he designed Alexander Place in the charming and simple early tradition, and Pelham Crescent which has a more sophisticated elegance (Pl. 17B).

In the final phases of Regency town house design there was a new reaching out on the part of architects like George Stanley Repton, once Nash's assistant, towards the regularity and restraint of the Palladian, possibly in reaction from the more absurd excesses of the Grecian and Picturesque. Through this impulse a number of terraces were built in London, Brighton and elsewhere from the late 1820's and into the 1840's, of severely classical character with porches of simple square columns, windows with moulded architraves surmounted by the segmental and triangular pediments that derive from Palladio and Inigo Jones, and flat, reticent façades with scrolled modillion cornices. But the instinct for the Picturesque had developed too strongly to be suppressed by this puritanical classicism, and the Italian characteristics displayed in so many villas of the time, like those designed by Decimus Burton at Tunbridge Wells, and even in his more formal Athenæum Club and his Hyde Park Lodges, became increasingly cultivated until the style attained full stature in the design of the Travellers' Club by Sir Charles Barry in 1829, and the Italian villa built by him at Queen's Park, Brighton in the same year. It was this kind of plain square house, with broad eaves and sometimes round-arched windows, somewhat simplified in the smaller examples, which became one of the standard types of English house from the end of the Regency right through the Victorian period (Pl. 15B).

Fig. 6. Lowther Castle, Westmorland, by Sir Robert Smirke, 1806–11. From *Jones' Views of the Seats of Noblemen and Gentlemen in England, etc.*, 1829

Smirke's medieval romanticism.

*Regency medievalism*

The romantic antiquarian nostalgia which had been fed by James Wyatt's graceful and refined Gothic creations such as Lee Priory in the later years of the eighteenth century had grown by the Regency to a thirst for more elaborate medieval pageantry. Wyatt's overwhelming fantasy of Fonthill, built for William Beckford, collapsed just before the opening of our period, in 1807.

Wyatt's Gothic designs for Plas Newydd, Anglesey, were not completed till 1826, long after his death, by his pupil Joseph Potter. Some of the original Gothic detail has been lost, and the house has reverted partly to the classical character of the 1790's that it already possessed in the Staircase Hall, the Drawing-room, Dining-room and Library, but the Gothic remains in the Entrance Front, charmingly fenestrated with large windows containing Wyatt's pleasant geometrical tracery. The Entrance Vestibule and Hall are also Gothic, with simple, graceful vaulting. The whole house breathes the unpretentious elegance and fine proportions that distinguish Wyatt's work, heightened by the dramatic beauty of the house's setting upon a wooded slope above the Menai Straits.

Like Wyatt, the other principal practitioners of Regency Gothic, William Wilkins and Sir Robert Smirke, were equally adept in the Grecian mode. The Battle of the Styles, which was waged with such bitterness in the field of religious and public architecture after the close of the Regency period, resulting eventually in the victory of the Gothic on moralist grounds, seemed in the realm of domestic architecture to become instead a gay, unwarlike pageant in which the contestants cheerfully mingled, and donned each others' clothes.

The 'square style' of Smirke's Grecian Doric was not required to change its nature for his Gothic Eastnor Castle, Herefordshire,* which has a central block rising out of the main rectangular mass (Fig. 5). The Gothic rooms are sombre, but there is a pleasant classical Octagon saloon. Lowther Castle, Westmorland (1806–11) (Fig. 6), is of similar design, but survives today only as a picturesque, empty shell. Panshanger, Hertfordshire (1806–22), for all its Grecian interior, was built on the rambling unsymmetrical lay-out of the medieval house. Its architect, William Atkinson (1776–1839), a pupil of James Wyatt, designed Thomas Hope's museum of frigid archæological eclecticism at Deepdene, Surrey (1806–22), and a house that is more truly a monument of Regency romanticism, Abbotsford, Roxburghshire (1822–3),* the home of Sir Walter Scott.

Eaton Hall, Cheshire (1804–12), was built by William Porden, architect of the Prince Regent's Royal Stables (The Dome) at Brighton. Some of his drawings for the rooms at Eaton remain at the Royal Pavilion. With its innumerable crocketed pinnacles and towers in 'Cathedral Gothic', the mounting ranges of terraced buildings, and the richly fan-vaulted ceilings of its rooms, it exceeded Fonthill in romanticism, and in its construction, including window-tracery of cast iron, surpassed Beckford's folly in durability. Eaton survives as a school, but was much altered in the 1870's by Waterhouse.

Arundel Castle, Sussex,* the home of the Earl Marshal of England, possesses as well as its truly Norman Keep and Barbican, and its convincing medieval stone scenery of the late nineteenth and early twentieth centuries, a 'Baron's Hall' remodelled in 1806 by J. Teasdale, and a Gothic Library also rebuilt in the Regency period.

The Regency castellated tradition attained its overwhelming climax at the end of the period in Penrhyn Castle, Caernarvonshire,* designed in 1827 by Thomas Hopper (1776–1856), who built the famous cast-iron Gothic conservatory at Carlton House for the Prince of Wales in 1807. The Great Keep has the severe Norman dignity of Castle Hedingham in Norfolk, from which it is copied. The round tower at the angle is reminiscent of Downton, but there is great character and beauty in the design of the round-headed windows. The interior carries the Romanesque style to a development never attained in the Norman era. The complexity and elaboration of the deeply cut mouldings of round arches, and heavy ribs of groined vaults, the small patterning of arcading round the gallery of the Great Hall, the writhing, interlaced ornament of the flat library ceiling, constitute as it were a 'rococo' phase of the Norman style far exceeding in exaggerated invention the mature richness of the Romanesque in the west towers of Ely, or the delicate fancy of the Galilee chapel at Durham.

As a background for the sophisticated life of nineteenth-century people, with their highly civilized and delicate clothes, manners and furnishings, this staggering phantasmagoria of Romanesque forms is incongruous, but it is redeemed as a successful artistic creation by the overwhelming vitality and robustness with which it has been carried out. It has its significance if only in expressing the overpowering force of the Romantic imagination in the Regency age.

### *Four great establishments*

The height of magnificence in Regency exoticism was reached in the Royal Pavilion at Brighton (Pl. 19B). The culmination of splendour in the classical style of the period may be studied in such great palatial establishments as Belvoir Castle, Windsor Castle, Apsley House and Londonderry House.

Belvoir Castle, Leicestershire,* is the fourth to occupy the site since its founding soon after the Norman conquest. Its present form is due partly to James Wyatt, who began rebuilding in 1800, and to the Rev. Sir John Thoroton, chaplain and friend of the 5th Duke of Rutland, and an amateur of architecture, who carried out his own designs after a fire in 1816. Wyatt had died in 1813. Towering high upon a wooded hill, Belvoir is one of the most beautifully and romantically sited of all castles. The south-eastern and south-western ranges are the surviving work of James Wyatt. The northern and eastern ranges are Thoroton's (Pl. 18A). His interior work is derived from Early English details at Lincoln Cathedral, and is in severer mood than Wyatt's more poetic interpretation of Gothic. The decorative work of the magnificent State Apartments was mostly designed by James Wyatt's own sons, Benjamin Dean Wyatt and Matthew Cotes Wyatt the sculptor. The most splendid room is the Elizabeth Saloon (Pl. 18B), so named after the 5th Duchess, herself a connoisseur of architecture, who decreed the adoption of the Louis XV style by having panelling brought from a French château of the period. The decoration of the ceiling, painted by Matthew Cotes Wyatt, makes the room one of the most sumptuous in the whole of the country, and displays for the first time that florid exuberance that is to be seen later at Apsley House, York House (now Lancaster House), and Londonderry House, all of which are Benjamin Wyatt's work. It is a manner representing the final opulence of the Regency outlook and is, as Summerson shows, the origin of that revival of French eighteenth-century decorative design that persisted throughout the nineteenth century and into the years of the Edwardian reign in the more lavish interiors of London.

Windsor Castle,* despite improvements in the direction of greater domestic convenience carried out by King George III, was at the opening of our period little more than a primitive, comfortless and straggling ruin. Transformed by Sir Jeffrey Wyatville (1766–1840) for his master King George IV, Windsor today is one of the most glorious monuments of the Regency age, a building nobly composed, with a skyline perhaps the most famous in the world, a symbol of the medieval romanticism that was among the invigorating influences of the period, and a palace worthy of the ancient lineage of our sovereigns. Under the direction of Wyatville the Castle was given unity and coherence of design. The principal improvements were the raising of the Round Tower by doubling its height, adding variety and interest to the skyline by the addition of lesser towers, and the construction of a broad corridor of two storeys round the inner side of the Quadrangle. By this means separate access was created to a large number of private rooms which previously could only be entered by passing successively through each. More than the building was transformed by the work. The architect was born Jeffrey Wyatt, but adopted his new name, more in keeping with the medieval atmosphere of the Castle, upon the laying of the foundation stone of the new King George IV Gate in 1824. He was knighted at the completion of the Royal quarters in 1828.

The Grand Reception Room, originally the King's Guard Chamber, was decorated for King George IV in the French taste of Louis XV, but with gilt ornament surpassing that of Belvoir in liveliness and delicacy. Wyatville gave St Stephen's Hall its present character, with a flat-arched timber-panelled ceiling of Tudor design. The most notable Regency apartment of the Castle is the Waterloo Chamber. This was built within an open space called Horn Court to contain the magnificent series of portraits which King George IV commissioned Sir Thomas Lawrence to paint of the sovereigns and leaders of the European nations which had been united with England against Napoleon. It is here that State Banquets are held in commemoration of the Battle of Waterloo.

Londonderry House, Park Lane, London (1825), represents consistently throughout its interior Benjamin Wyatt's sumptuously ornate mode of late Regency classicism, the Banqueting Room being an exceptionally fine example of his revival of the rococo manner. The Grand Staircase and Ballroom are richly palatial, the latter reminiscent of the Gallery at Belvoir, their magnificent coved ceilings coffered with rosettes, the friezes and pilasters of extreme florid splendour.

Apsley House, Piccadilly,* once the residence of the 1st Duke of Wellington, together with the magnificent collections it contains of paintings, silver, porcelain, furniture and other works of art, has been presented to the nation by the present Duke. As the Wellington Museum, administered by the Victoria and Albert Museum, it forms a national memorial to the life, achievements and taste in the arts of the Iron Duke, conqueror of

Napoleon. The house, originally built in the 1770's by Robert Adam for Lord Bathurst, was given its present Grecian exterior of Bath stone with a Corinthian portico when remodelled by Benjamin Wyatt in 1828–9 for the 1st Duke. Although the external appearance is severely plain and even pedestrian, the interior has an atmosphere of light, dignity and spaciousness. Adam's decoration of the 1770's survives in the Green Portico Room, and the delightful Piccadilly Drawing-room with its characteristic half-domed apse and barrel-vaulted ceiling. The striped Drawing-room and the Dining-room are of Regency character, with coved ceilings, that of the latter with a fine palmette frieze. Overlooking Hyde Park from the Western side of the house is the great Waterloo Chamber, which is rivalled in magnificence only by John Nash's State Apartments at Buckingham Palace, and in which Benjamin Wyatt displays his re-interpretation of the Louis XV style in its finest form (Pl. 20). It is in such monumental interiors that the decorative art of the Regency period attained its zenith of richness at its moment of historical triumph.

SHORT BIBLIOGRAPHY

John Summerson, *Architecture in Britain, 1530–1830*, Penguin History of Art, 1953.

John Summerson, *Georgian London*, 1945; *John Nash*, 1949.

Christopher Hussey, *English Country Houses*, Vol. 3, *Late Georgian.*

Donald Pilcher, *The Regency Style*, 1947.

H. M. Colvin, *Biographical Dictionary of English Architects*, 1954.

Bryan Little, *Cheltenham*, 1951.

Typographical borders from the 1821 Specimen Book of Vincent Figgins. These neo-classical motifs are similar to those found in friezes of classical Regency buildings and derive from the same sources. The anthemion (honeysuckle) motif occurs in the first two.

(A) Chair japanned in black and gold in the Chinese taste, *c.* 1810.

(B) Mahogany chair with lyre-shaped splat, *c.* 1800.

(C) Mahogany armchair with spiral reeding on the rails in back, *c.* 1810.

(D) Japanned chair with panel painted in the Chinese taste, *c.* 1810.

PLATE 21

*Facing page* 36

(A) Mahogany sofa table inlaid with brass; pedestal supported by a platform on splayed feet, *c.* 1815. *J. W. Evill Collection.*

(B) Mahogany pedestal library table, with ebonised stringing on the drawer fronts, *c.* 1815.

(A) Mahogany extending dining table, on a central pillar-and-claw; two of the reeded end legs swing out to give space for extra leaves, *c.* 1820.

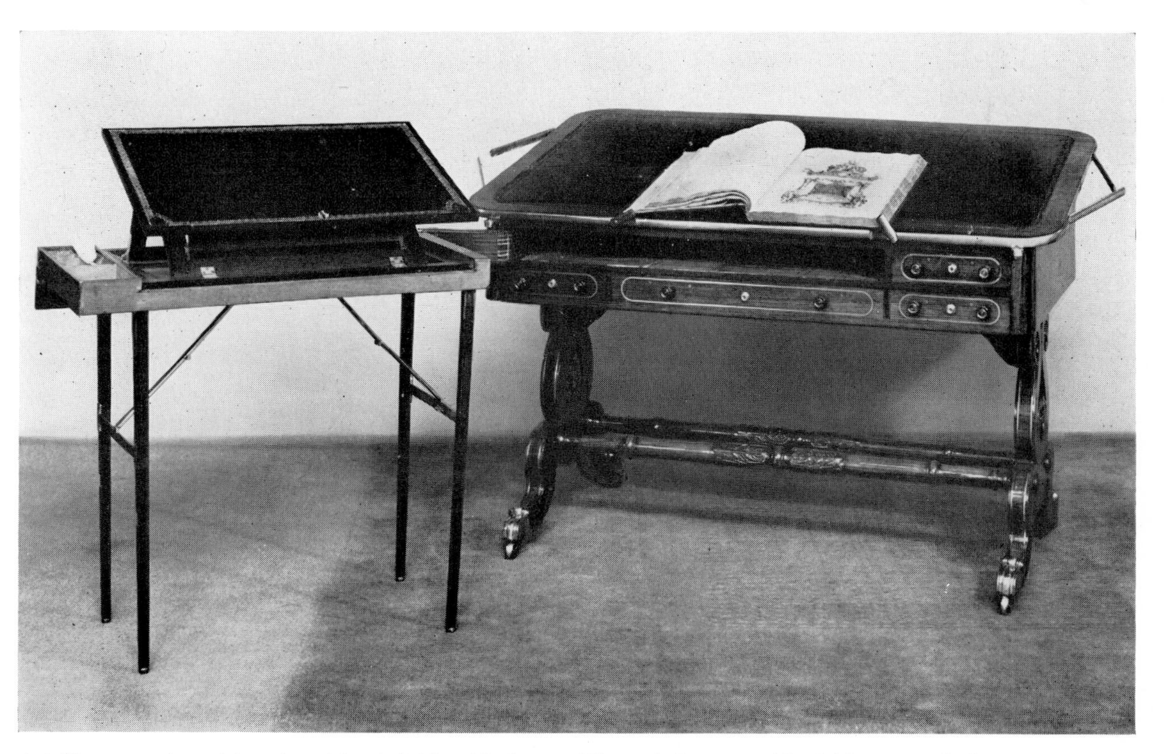

(B) Rosewood architect's table, inlaid with brass. The miniature table folds up and shuts away as a drawer, *c.* 1810.

(A) Mahogany circular pillar-and-claw dining table, showing method of adding leaves, *c.* 1815–20.

(B) Mahogany side table inlaid with brass, supported by lion monopodia, in the Egyptian taste, *c.* 1810.

PLATE 24

(A) Rosewood side table, with ormolu mounts, marble top, and supports in the Egyptian taste, *c.* 1810.

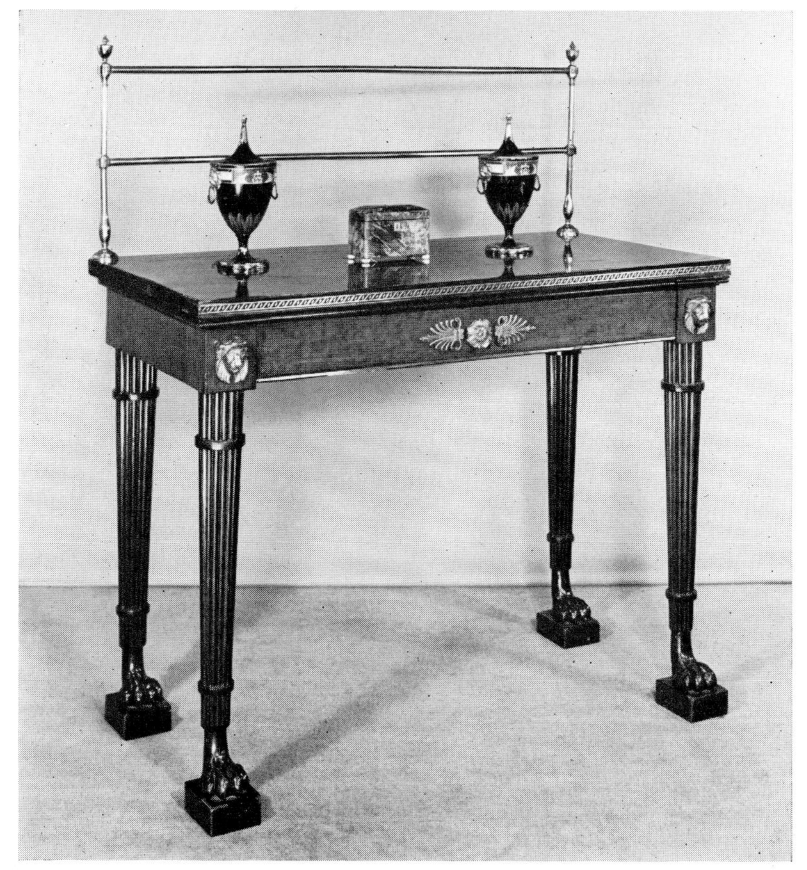

(B) Mahogany side table with carved paw feet, ormolu mounts and brass gallery, *c.* 1810.

The Chinese taste: two stands, painted ivory, with mounts of ormolu and carved wood, gilt, and white marble tops. Made for the Saloon at the Royal Pavilion, Brighton, about 1822. (*On permanent loan to the Royal Pavilion from H.M. the Queen*).

PLATE 26

Painted and gilt sofa, with brass paw feet on the outward-curving legs, *c.* 1810. *Victoria and Albert Museum.*

PLATE 27

(A) Rosewood cabinet with marble top, lion masks and feet and brass trellis doors and sides, *c.* 1810.

(B) Mahogany music stand ('Canterbury'), *c.* 1810.

PLATE 28

# *Furniture*

D

# Furniture

E. T. JOY

The furniture of any given period is a reflection of what Horace Walpole called 'the history of the manners of the age', and this is particularly true of the two decades 1810–30 which saw the important social and economic changes occasioned by the upheaval of the long wars with France (1793–1815) and the increasing tempo of industrialization. The wars had 'doubled the cost and trebled the difficulty of genteel living',[1] with the result that the long and salutary domination of good taste in furniture by the upper classes was now drawing to a close. Their place was gradually being taken by the new middle classes, who owed their wealth and position to industry; they lacked the high standards, based on many generations of classical learning, of their predecessors, and they sought fresh styles in the belief that experience and knowledge were no longer necessary to judge decorative forms. Thus the Regency period (which in furniture overlapped the nine years – 1811–20 – when the Prince of Wales was Regent) saw the last phase of the classical development in furniture design which had begun in the seventeenth century. The transition to new forms was made easier through the gradual abandonment of traditional decorative methods like carving and inlay, and through the growing influence of machinery on furniture-making. Wood-working machines, able to carry out almost all the processes which are known today, had been patented by Sir Samuel Bentham between 1791 and 1793, and already in 1807 Thomas Hope in his *Household Furniture* was warning his readers against the debasement of furniture design 'through the entire substitution of machinery to manual labour'.

It was symptomatic of the changing ideas of the time that much of the formal grace which had distinguished the interiors of great houses in the eighteenth century was disappearing. Louis Simond, visiting Osterley House in 1811, wrote that 'Tables, sofas and chairs were studiously *dérangés* about the fire places, and in the middle of the rooms, as if the family had just left them ... Such is the modern fashion of placing furniture, carried to an extreme ... that the apartments of a fashionable house look like an upholsterer's or cabinet-maker's shop.'[2]

The best furniture of the period was still, of course, of a high standard in both design and workmanship, and it should always be related to its setting, which conformed to a carefully-thought-out scheme of decoration. But while this is true of the finest pieces, in others the deterioration in standards is all too evident, heralding the decline of the early Victorian era.

## *The Regency Style*

In general terms the Regency style in furniture may be described as a close reproduction or adaptation, carried out in a strong antiquarian spirit, of Græco-Roman types of furniture and forms of decoration. It was inspired by (but was not a close version of) the contemporary French Directoire and Empire styles, and for that reason was for long

[1] *The Lady's Keepsake and Maternal Monitor*, 1835.

[2] L. Simond, *Journal of a Tour and Residence in Great Britain 1810–11*. (1817).

known as 'English Empire'. In view of the war period it may seem surprising that English designers should have been influenced by artistic movements in France. This, however, is to look at wars through modern spectacles. France had been too long the arbiter of Europe's taste for war to destroy her prestige, and in any case the connexion of ideas was maintained through the many French craftsmen who took refuge in England from the revolution in their own country. When peace came in 1815 an English writer acknowledged the relationship in these words: 'The interchange of feeling between this country and France, as it relates to matters of taste, has not been wholly suspended during the long and awful conflicts which have so greatly abridged the intercourse of the two nations, and as usual the taste of both has been improved.'[3]

The chief spokesmen for the style in France were Charles Percier and Pierre Fontaine, whose *Recueil de Décorations Intérieures*, 1812, coinciding with Napoleon's widespread conquests, had a great influence throughout Europe. They regarded the study of the decoration of antiquity, with its 'simple lines, pure contours and correct forms', as the most fruitful source of inspiration for architects, designers and craftsmen, whose work, they considered, had an essential unity. 'Furniture', they wrote, 'is too closely allied to interior decoration for the architect to remain indifferent to it. Decoration separated from construction will lead to all sorts of absurdities and misinterpretations.' They were at pains, however, to warn against too slavish an imitation of the models of antiquity; these should be 'followed, not blindly, but with the discernment allowed by modern manners, customs and materials'. Such, then, were to be the principles to be observed: inspiration and admiration tempered with discrimination; the avoidance of mere imitation; the unity of all forms of decoration; and due acknowledgement of modern processes and habits.

In this country the origins of the Regency style in furniture can be clearly seen at the end of the eighteenth century in the work of the talented architect and designer, Henry Holland (1745–1806). With delicacy and a sure touch, he adapted ancient forms into a unified system of decoration without losing the spirit of antiquity or falling into the error of copying contemporary French work. The furniture which he designed for the Prince of Wales at Carlton House (1784) and for Samuel Whitbread at Southill (1795) established his reputation and encouraged imitation. The new style is foreshadowed in Sheraton's *Drawing Book*, 1791–4, and *Cabinet Dictionary*, 1803. But after Holland's death in 1806 the designing of furniture was soon to become an antiquarian pursuit, missing the spirit of antiquity, and seeking to reproduce the actual forms of ancient furniture.

Holland's immediate successor in the field of furniture design was Thomas Hope (1768–1831), whose *Household Furniture and Interior Decoration* was published in 1807. Hope, a man of wide interests and sound scholarship, had been trained as an architect and had travelled extensively throughout the eastern Mediterranean, where he had spent some eight years studying architectural remains. He was a friend of Percier and an admirer of his work. With this background Hope aimed to give the public a range of furniture designs which would 'cultivate a new description of art, so urgently wanted and hitherto so rarely possessed'. At Deepdene, his house in Surrey, furniture of his own design had been made for the rooms where he kept his collection of antiquities, 'forming', he wrote, 'the entire assemblage of productions of ancient art and modern handicraft, thus intermixed, into a more harmonious, more consistent and more instructive whole'.

These words echoed the sentiments of Percier and Fontaine, but it was too much to expect Hope's and Holland's scholarly approach to be shared or understood by the many craftsmen and designers who now took up the new mode wholeheartedly. Hope was well aware of the dangers of imitation, for he could already see them at work: 'extravagant caricatures, such as of late have begun to start up in every corner of the capital, seem calculated for the sole purpose of bringing this new style into disrepute'.

The main features of Regency classical furniture were extreme simplicity of outline, large un-

[3] R. Ackermann, *The Repository of the Arts*, Feb. 1815.

interrupted surfaces emphasizing horizontal and vertical lines, subordination of ornament to a minor role, and a stress on solidity – characteristics which Brown summarized in 1820 as 'bold in outline, rich and chaste in the ornaments, and durable from the rejection of little parts'. The favourite methods of decoration were metal inlay and reeding. At first Greek, Roman and Egyptian antiquities were the models, but as time went on 'Grecian severity' became the rule. Interest in Greece was intensified when the Parthenon sculptures were bought by public subscription in 1816, and when the Greeks revolted against the Turks in 1821. Wherever possible, from vase-paintings and similar sources classical Greek furniture was copied, as in the fashionable Grecian sofa and chair; when this could not be done, antique forms were adapted to modern usage. Simple straight lines and bold curves marked this quest for severity. 'Grecian' now became a much-favoured word among furniture craftsmen and designers; and in 1836 Loudon's *Encyclopædia* could still describe the 'Grecian or modern style' as 'by far the most prevalent'.[4]

### *The design books*

As in the eighteenth century, the current furniture trends were set out in several design books intended for the trade and the general reader. George Smith's *A Collection of Designs for Household Furniture and Interior Decoration* appeared in 1808 and popularized the new style. Smith was a cabinet-maker who described himself as 'Upholsterer Extraordinary to His Royal Highness The Prince of Wales', and his book contained 158 plates in colour 'studied from the best antique examples of the Egyptian, Greek and Roman styles' with some Gothic and Chinese designs added. Many of the plates showed a somewhat extravagant treatment of the new fashions. In 1820 Richard Brown published *The Rudiments of Drawing Cabinet and Upholstery Furniture*, which had a second and revised edition in 1822. He claimed to be giving craftsmen not only designs for furniture but also the principles which lay behind them (which, he said, the 'trivial compositions' of men like Chippendale and Sheraton had omitted to do). His book was a version of the designs of Hope, Percier and Smith, to whom he paid full acknowledgement. In 1826 many coloured designs, with much Greek detail, appeared in *The Practical Cabinet Maker, Upholsterer and Complete Decorator* by Peter and Michael Angelo Nicholson. In the same year George Smith, now styling himself 'Upholsterer and Furniture Draughtsman to His Majesty', issued *The Cabinet Maker's and Upholsterer's Guide, Drawing Book and Repository*. He stressed the 'perfection of Greek ornament', but included plates of Egyptian, Etruscan, Roman, Gothic and French interiors. He seemed to sense the growing poverty of ideas. About chairs he wrote that 'the necessity for economy urged by many at the present day is in itself sufficient to check and weaken the spirit for design, and thus we see nothing but a monotony of character in this article of furniture'. Of a different nature from the above books was R. Ackermann's *The Repository of the Arts*, published in monthly parts between 1809 and 1828. Each issue had a section devoted to fashionable furniture illustrated by coloured plates, providing an interesting record of contemporary taste.

### *Other styles: Gothic*

The Regency period was marked by a restless search for new forms. So rapid were the changes in design that we find Thomas Martin in 1820 suggesting 'were it practicable, it would be necessary that cabinet, like female fashions, should be published monthly'.[5] Smith in his *Guide* of 1826 confessed that the designs which he had submitted in his *Household Furniture* of 1808 had become wholly obsolete and inapplicable owing to the changes in taste during the last twenty years. It was thus natural that the search for novelty did not stop at Græco-Roman furniture; other styles were attempted, including the Gothic, Chinese and Egyptian.

There was, of course, nothing new in the application of Gothic motifs to furniture. The 'Strawberry Hill' Gothic of Horace Walpole extended

[4] J. C. Loudon, *An Encyclopædia of Cottage, Farm and Villa Architecture and Furniture*, 1836.

[5] T. Martin, *The Circle of the Mechanical Arts*, 1820.

its influence long after the rococo period of the mid-eighteenth century which gave it birth. The Romantic Revival in literature added to the strong interest in medieval antiquities, with its stress on the picturesque. But both these trends had been aristocratic in origin and remained subordinate to the classical tradition of the upper classes. Now two new tendencies were at work: one was the growing partiality of the middle classes, shortly to be the final arbiters of taste, for the Gothic; the other was the belief that the Gothic was an essentially English style, with a robust vigour which had a strong emotional appeal. Furniture with Gothic motifs, often in the form of window tracery and pinnacles, was increasingly made for the now fashionable villas and '*cottages ornés*'. In 1836, when Loudon was noting the predominance of the Grecian style, Sir Samuel Meyrick voiced the opinion that Grecian forms were no longer suitable for English residences, and that support for the Gothic was growing.[6]

At this time the Gothic was divided into the Tudor (or Perpendicular) and the Elizabethan. The former was held to be the improved style introduced by Henry VII and Henry VIII, and the latter was the English version of the Renaissance. 'Elizabethan' furniture was to have a growing appeal to the popular imagination, despite criticisms of its spurious character.

### *Chinese*

The revival of the Chinese taste was partly due to the Prince of Wales. Carlton House, his London residence, had a Chinese drawing-room which is illustrated in Sheraton's *Drawing Book* and for which Henry Holland designed some furniture in 1790. In 1802 the Prince had a Chinese gallery made at Brighton Pavilion to show some beautiful Chinese wall-paper which had been presented to him. But the most important work of this kind at Brighton took place between 1815 and 1821, when extensive improvements were made to the Pavilion under the direction of John Nash, and the interior was decorated in the Chinese manner, mainly by Frederick Crace and Robert Jones.[7]

Chinese furniture of this period made free use of dragons, pagodas, mandarins, and other oriental motifs. Much of it was japanned, especially the cheaper sort intended for the general public. Another characteristic was the use of imitation bamboo on chairs and small tables. Like the Gothic, the Chinese taste can be considered as part of the cult of the Picturesque; the justification for such styles was said to lie in the train of romantic and agreeable ideas which they produce (Pls. 21A, 21D, 26, 31).

### *Egyptian*

Unlike the Gothic and Chinese revivals, the Egyptian revival was a novel development of this period, and one that will always be associated with Regency furniture. Egyptian antiquities had already been attracting some attention among European artists in the later eighteenth century, and this interest was considerably quickened in England and France after 1798, the year in which Napoleon began his Egyptian campaign and in which the French fleet was destroyed by Nelson at the Battle of the Nile. Napoleon took with him a team of French scholars, one of whom, Dominique Vivant Denon, later Director-General of the Museums of France under the First Empire, published in 1802 *Voyage dans la Basse et la Haute Egypte*. This book, with its many illustrations of Egyptian ornament, was soon available in an English translation, and was destined to have an important influence on furniture design. Egyptian motifs were used by Thomas Chippendale the younger in some of the furniture which he made for Sir Richard Colt Hoare at Stourhead, Wiltshire, in 1804–5. The new style was taken up by Thomas Hope, and his *Household Furniture* contains an engraving of the Egyptian decoration and furniture which he had designed for the room containing his collection of Egyptian antiquities at Deepdene. He had many imitators, despite his warnings against indiscriminate use of the style. The vogue was per-

[6] Sir S. Meyrick, *Specimens of Ancient Furniture*, 1836.

[7] C. Musgrave, *The Royal Pavilion*, 1948, and p. 25, above.

haps at its height about 1810, encouraged by the incorporation of Egyptian motifs in Smith's design book of 1808; but it by no means died out rapidly. Ackermann's *Repository* of May 1812, for example, illustrates a library table with supports in the form of sphinxes, although an earlier issue, that of August 1809, had declared that 'the barbarous Egyptian style' was already on the wane. Brown's *Rudiments* of 1820 shows examples of decoration with the 'Egyptian lotus, or water-lily of the Nile', and similar Egyptian ornament was still being advocated by the Nicholsons and Smith in 1826.

Among the Egyptian motifs found on furniture were the lotus leaf, sphinx heads, lion supports, and, in the more extravagant examples, crocodiles and serpents (Pls. 24B, 25A, 28A). The style could easily get out of hand, especially when it was injudiciously mingled with the Gothic and Chinese. The resulting confusion is satirized by Miss Mitford in her account of a visit to Rosedale Cottage:

> 'Every room is in masquerade: the saloon Chinese, full of jars and mandarins and pagodas; the library Egyptian, all covered with hieroglyphics, and swarming with furniture crocodiles and sphinxes. Only think of a crocodile couch and a sphinx sofa! They sleep in Turkish tents, and dine in a Gothic chapel.... The properties are apt to get shifted from one scene to another, and all manner of anomalies are the consequence. The mitred chairs and screens of the chapel, for instance, were mixed up oddly enough with the squat Chinese bronzes, whilst by some strange transposition a pair of nodding mandarins figured amongst the Egyptian monsters.'[8]

### *Woods and decoration*

The emphasis on plain lines and unbroken surfaces led to the use of dark and glossy woods, such as mahogany and rosewood, and of woods with boldly striped figure, such as amboyna, calamander and zebra-wood. These gradually replaced the lighter-coloured woods which had been fashionable in the Adam period.

Mahogany remained the established favourite in the library and dining-room. Rosewood, zebra-wood and kingwood all came from Brazil, whence direct trade with Britain had been opened during the Napoleonic Wars. Rosewood, which was also imported from the East Indies, was in great demand; it was a hard, heavy wood marked with dark streaks. Kingwood was finer in the grain than rosewood and generally lighter in tone. Zebra-wood took its name from the streaks of deep brown and white; it could be highly polished and was very fashionable until supplies began to run short after about 1815. Calamander, imported from India, Ceylon and the East Indies, had a hard and fine grain and was of a light brown colour mottled with dark brown and black. Amboyna from the East and West Indies was distinguished by a figure of small knots and curls, resembling bird's-eye maple, on a warm brown ground. It was the practice of the time to obtain some of these fashionable colours and figures by staining other woods, and this was done even in the case of good furniture. Rosewood, for instance, could be closely simulated by staining wood with logwood and marking the streaks with vitriol. Much furniture was also japanned to accord with the Chinese taste.

At the end of the war with France, French polish was introduced into this country and quickly became popular. It was described by Loudon as by far the best polish 'for bringing out the beauties of the wood and giving it a brightness and richness of colour which nothing else hitherto invented can produce'. Much old furniture was stripped and the polish, consisting of shellac disolved in spirit, was then applied. The grain had first to be filled and the substances used for this purpose have subsequently bleached, thus spoiling the furniture.

Both the economic effects of the war period and the changes in taste caused the gradual abandonment of the two decorative processes of inlaying and carving which had been used in the late eighteenth century. The former was found to be too expensive and the latter was fast becoming a decaying craft. According to Martin in *The Circle of the Mechanical Arts*, 1820, only eleven master carvers were then at work in London, and though the old title of 'Carvers and Gilders' appeared over the doors of many shopkeepers, it could be 'proved that hundreds of the latter never saw a carving

[8] M. R. Mitford, *Our Village*, 1824–32.

tool in their lives'. In 1835 the architect C. R. Cockerell asserted that a very great dearth of carvers had existed for fifty years.[9]

The principal new decorative medium was brass, which was both cheaper and more durable than the former methods, and also showed up handsomely against dark woods. It was used in a variety of ways on almost all types of furniture: inlays of delicate lines or of more ornamental scrolls and floral and classical motifs; galleries on the tops of sideboards and similar pieces; colonnettes to support galleries and shelves; ornamental beading; wire trellis in the doors or sides of cabinets, bookcases, cupboards, etc.; lion feet on tables; castors on chairs and tables; and ringed, lion mask handles on drawers (Pls. 22A, 23B, 24B, 25B, 28A, 29A and B and p. 52). Brass inlay was a specialized craft centred in London in the area of St Martin's Lane, and good work of this character found on furniture of the period is a sure indication of its London origin. Chased ormolu work, on the other hand, was a French speciality, and when it is found on English furniture it is most likely that it was done by immigrant craftsmen. A certain amount of the furniture of this time was also decorated with boulle work – inlay of metal and tortoiseshell – at the 'Buhl factory' established by the Frenchman, Louis le Gaigneur, in the Edgware Road about 1815, and at other workshops where English craftsmen carried out this traditional French decoration (Plate 30).

At its best, metal ornament was used in a restrained and delicate fashion, but there was inevitably a tendency to extravagance. In 1820 Brown warned cabinet-makers that a very important part of their skill lay in 'harmonizing metals with woods, so as not to overload the articles with buhl, bronze or ormolu, which is too frequently to be seen'.

### *Fashionable furniture: chairs and other seat furniture*

There was so much variety in chair design during this period that Brown declared that it baffled 'the most skilful artist to produce any new forms'.

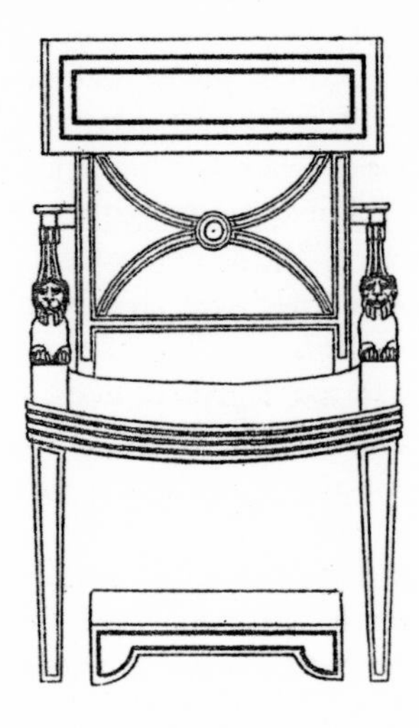

Fig. 1. Armchair from Hope's *Household Furniture*, 1807.

Typical of Hope's influence was the fashionable Grecian chair, which figures prominently in the interior scenes of Henry Moses' *Designs of Modern Costume* (1823). On this kind of chair the rear legs and the back formed a bold continuous curve, balanced by a forward curve of the front legs. The cresting rail, following the fashion of the beginning of the century, was a wide board set at shoulder height, generally over-running the uprights. In the case of armchairs, the arms, which usually had supports coming straight up from the front legs, often swept upwards to join the back uprights near the top, though in some examples, favoured by Hope and Smith, the arms were straight and joined the back about half way up (Figs. 1, 2, 3).

By about 1830 something of this form was still preserved in the backs and rear legs; the cresting rail, however, was now to be found slightly curved in shape and resting on the uprights; while a more noticeable change was in the front legs, which were straight and turned, often ornately.

The bergère continued to enjoy favour; the best examples were made of mahogany and had the

[9] Examination of C. R. Cockerell before the Select Committee on Arts and Manufactures (1835–6).

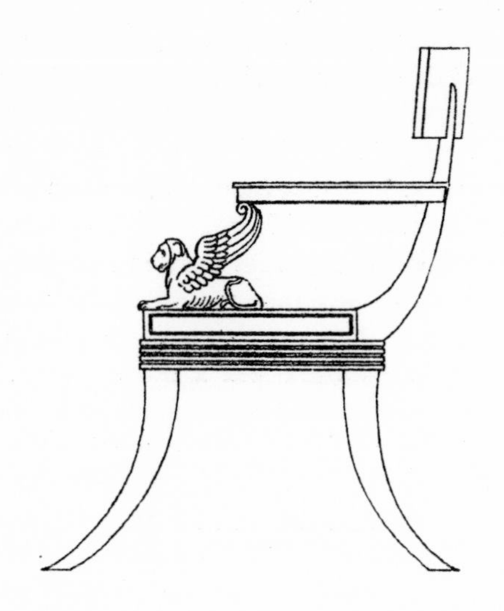

Fig. 2. Armchair from Hope's *Household Furniture*, 1807.

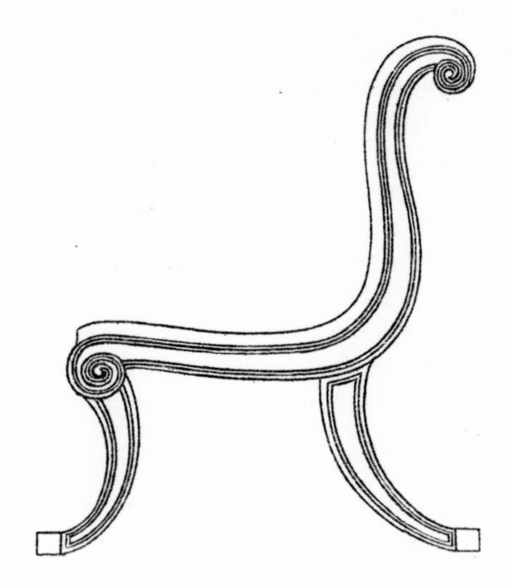

Fig. 3. Chair from Hope's *Household Furniture*, 1807.

seat, back and sides of cane-work. Among other decorative features of the chairs of this period were spiral reeding (Pl. 21C), lion feet and lyre-shaped splats, the latter being a revival of a fashionable motif of the later eighteenth century (Pl. 21B). What were termed 'fancy 'chairs were often made of beech and painted or japanned (Pls. 21A, 21D), or had turned framework to imitate bamboo. Gothic chairs had their backs carved and fretted to represent tracery, and sometimes had small pinnacles on the back uprights.

The sofa or couch was a prominent piece which now became more fashionable than the settee. The Grecian sofa is described in Ackermann's *Repository* (1811) as 'adapted for the library, boudoir or any fashionable apartment'. Where the couch form was employed, based on classical models, there was usually a boldly curved head-piece and a similarly scrolled end, and as the couch was intended for reclining, there was normally a short arm-rest on one side of the larger end. The legs were of various shapes: lion feet, or outward curving, or turned in the form of tops. Other kinds of sofas had upholstered backs, curved end-pieces of the same height, and usually short feet which curved outwards (Pl. 27). Ottomans (or 'Turkey sofas') were also in fashion. They had no backs or sides and were chiefly intended, according to Brown, 'for music rooms and picture galleries', though he presented some modified designs for boudoirs and cabinets. The circular ottoman, on which the sitters were back to back, was a novelty, and was used in rooms which had bow windows or circular ends.

Stools were a familiar part of Regency interiors, for window recesses, or to accompany elegant sets of chairs. The X-shape cross frame was in vogue, often with lion feet.

### *Tables*

It was customary in the larger houses to have large dining-tables made up of sections which could be fastened together as required, and several varieties of these were to be found (Pls. 23A, 24A). In the later eighteenth century what was known as a 'set of dining-tables' had three units – a centre table with rectangular flaps supported on gate-legs, and two end tables with rectangular or semi-circular tops. After 1800 sectional tables frequently had their supports in the form of pillars and claws, generally, as Sheraton wrote in 1803, 'four claws to each pillar, with brass castors'. Tables of this kind could be made up to any required length, for the sections, each with pillar and claws, were bolted together with metal clips. For calculating the length of table for a dinner-party, two feet for each diner was the accepted rule. The method of fitting separate tables together had its disadvantages, and a number of patents for single extending tables were taken out, notably by Richard Gillow (1800), Richard Brown (1805), and George Remington (1807). They showed much ingenuity of construction. The description, for example, of Brown's table, which had straight turned legs, states that 'the end rails of the table frame are connected by pieces of wood so jointed together as to form what are commonly called lazy-tongs'.

Though pillars and claws were so fashionable, they seem to have caused a certain amount of inconvenience. *The Repository* in 1810 illustrates a patent sideboard and dining-table (given the name 'Trafalgar' because one was supplied, it is claimed, to Nelson) in which the table could be pushed into the sideboard and extra flaps kept in the drawers; the advantage being that the 'feet of this table are completely out of the way ... in this particular they far excel the claw tables'. It was for this same reason that Smith in 1808 recommended the use of the circular dining-table supported on a pedestal or circular base, and this type came into wide use, especially as it had the additional advantage of avoiding invidious distinctions among guests when seated at dinner.

The sofa table was also in general demand after 1800. The table-top, when its two small end-flaps were extended, was some five to six feet long, and about two feet wide, and it was supported either by two end supports linked by a stretcher, or by a pedestal on a small platform with splayed feet (Pl. 22A). This attractive and useful table was often fitted with two drawers in the frieze and was intended for the library, drawing-room, boudoir or any ladies' apartment, for reading, writing or drawing. It was a development of the smaller Pembroke table, which it did not, however, supersede, for the latter was still fashionable and now often had, like the sofa table, rectangular end flaps with rounded corners.

Small tables of all kinds were placed about the living-rooms. Sometimes nests of tables were found, expecially little sets of four, known as 'quartetto' tables. Ladies' work-tables were in constant use, and many varieties of these were made by the cabinet-makers in their search for novel designs. A pouch for needlework was a usual feature, together with a lifting top over a small compartment or set of drawers (Fig. 4). Combined work-and-games tables were also popular; an example made by Morgan and Saunders in 1811 and illustrated in *The Repository* was in the fashionable 'Brazil wood' (i.e. zebra-wood), and was fitted for 'seven different accommodations', including reading, writing, needlework, chess and backgammon. Tables of this kind, and other sorts of combined games-and-card tables, tended to oust the old-established card-tables, for fewer of these were now made; one does find, however, 'loo tables' specially made for the popular card game of the period.

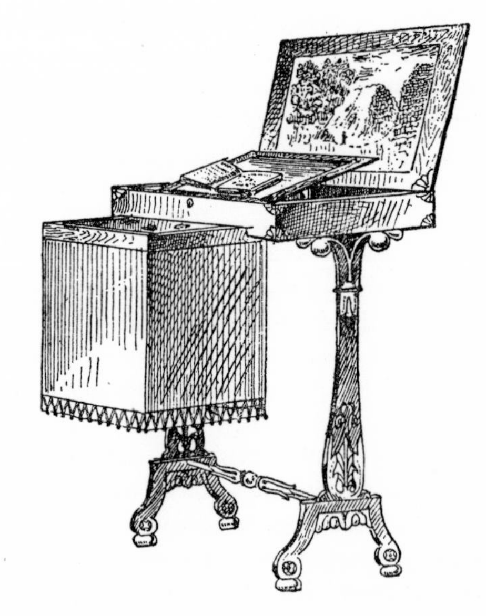

Fig. 4. Work Table, from Ackermann's *Repository*, 1811.

In libraries the pedestal table with knee-hole and flanking drawers or cupboards followed the traditional form (Pl. 22B), except for the addition of details like lion feet and Egyptian figures to accord with changing fashions. A more novel type was the Carlton House writing-table, which made its appearance at the end of the eighteenth century. This had a superstructure of small cupboards and drawers running round the back and sides of the top, and drawers in the frieze. The reason for its name is a mystery, as there is no evidence to connect it with Carlton House.

Side or pier tables continued in use in dining-rooms, often supported by lion monopodia or Egyptian figures. Some examples had a low platform at the base and were occasionally fitted with silvered glass on the inside and back, 'to produce', in Smith's words (1826), 'a reflecting effect from the china objects which are usually placed in such situations'. The tops of some of these tables were of solid marble (Pls. 25A, 28A, 29A).

*Bookcases*

For larger libraries cabinet-makers continued to make the traditional type of bookcase in two stages, in which the lower stage of cupboards was surmounted by rows of shelves enclosed by glazed doors. Classical proportions were maintained, with some concessions to prevailing decorative changes. Thomas Hope, for instance, designed a bookcase of this kind for Deepdene which had carved sphinx heads on the pilasters separating the four glass doors, and four lion monopodia on the lower stage.

A distinctly new piece in fashion in the early nineteenth century was the dwarf bookcase, the doors of which were either glazed or fitted with a trellis of brass wire. It was made purposely low to leave 'an ample space on the wall above for the placing of pictures' (Smith, 1826). Several varieties were found, in use in the sitting-room and boudoir as well as in the library. One type shown by Brown in 1820 was a lady's bookcase with cabinet, the object of the latter being 'to contain ladies' jewels, ancient medals and precious stones, with other valuable curiosities' – an interesting reminder that the hobby of collecting curios, which had stimulated the production of cabinets in the late seventeenth century, was still very much alive among richer people.

The revolving circular bookcase was an innovation of this period. One kind was patented by Benjamin Crosby in 1808 and was described as 'a machine or stand for books, which may be made either circular, square or any other convenient shape, and which may be turned or moved at pleasure, with cases to receive books, as well as various other articles and things'. This type and others of the same kind followed the general principles of a central shaft to which cylinders holding the shelves were screwed.

The trend towards lightness in bookcases produced one of the most attractive of the smaller Regency pieces, the little set of portable open shelves which could be carried by ladies about the room, or from one room to another. The sides of the shelves were often made of brass wire. There were many other kinds of small bookcases (Pl. 29B).

In large libraries, for reaching the books on the upper shelves, library steps were indispensable, and some of these were in the form of folding steps ingeniously fitted into chairs, stools and tables; the back of a library chair, for example, could be swung over to the ground, disclosing a small set of steps (Figs. 5, 6).

*Sideboards and other dining-room furniture*

In the early years of the nineteenth century the lighter kind of sideboard associated with Hepplewhite and Sheraton went out of favour, and there was a revival of the sideboard table fitted with pedestal cupboards which had been developed from the designs of Robert Adam. This was the type favoured by Smith in 1808. It soon became a commodious piece of furniture and lost its former graceful proportions. The pedestal cupboards, which often tapered slightly almost to floor level, were used as cellarets and plate-warmers, and on them often stood knife-boxes of similar tapering shape, in place of the urns which had been found in the Adam period. All these fittings were necessary, as the servants still washed the glasses and cutlery in the dining-room between courses. A characteristic feature of the later sideboards of this type

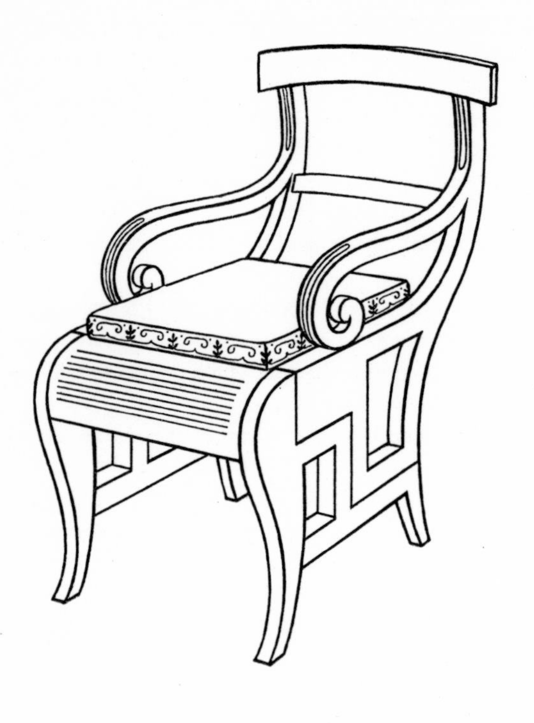

Figs. 5 and 6. Combined library chair and steps, from Ackermann's *Repository*, 1811.

was the high back-piece rising above the table-top (Fig. 7).

Sideboard tables, without the pedestal cupboards, were also in use. These tables were large, and sometimes had animal supports which stood on a plinth. A cellaret or wine-cooler, commonly of sarcophagus form at this time, stood in a central position beneath the table, and drawers with brass lion-mask handles were often found in the frieze. An elaborate brass gallery usually ran along the back of the table.

Several other accessories were necessary in the fashionable dining-room. Dumb waiters continued in use, but with rectangular tiers and supports of pillars and claws instead of the circular tiers and tripod bases of the earlier varieties. One of the two pieces called a 'Canterbury' (the other was a music-stand) was a plate-and-cutlery stand described by Sheraton as 'a supper tray, made to stand by a table at supper, with a circular end and three partitions cross wise, to hold knives, forks and plates at that end, which is made circular on purpose'.

### *Chiffoniers, chests of drawers, etc.*

The French-inspired commode of the later eighteenth century, with its curved surfaces and decoration of fine inlay and painting, did not lend itself to the bold outlines which were now in favour, and its place was taken by the chiffonier. This was not a new name, for it had been in use in Chippendale's time, but the chiffonier of the eighteenth century seems to have been modelled on the French chiffonière, which was a small case of drawers on legs, whereas the Regency chiffonier was a low open cupboard with shelves for books (Pl. 29A). It held the books which were in constant use, and was found in both the drawing-room and the library. Sometimes a small set of shelves stood on the top.

The chest of drawers retained its traditional form, and continued to be straight- or bow-fronted. Since the end of the eighteenth century, however, new features were spirally reeded columns at the front corners (about 1810 spiral reeding began to replace the plainer vertical reeding), and a deep frieze above the top drawer. Also characteristic of the period were lion-mask handles. The old-estab-

One of a pair of commodes in veneered rosewood *c.* 1820-30 which owes much of its design to the French Boulle tradition. *H. Blairman and Sons Ltd.*

lished tallboy or chest-on-chest was only occasionally made at this period, owing to the inconvenient height of the upper drawers.

*Other small pieces*

Among the newer pieces of the period were the what-not, a portable open stand with four uprights enclosing shelves for books and ornaments, and the music Canterbury, a small stand usually mounted on castors, with partitions for music books, and sometimes small drawers for sheets of music (Pl. 28B). The fire- or pole-screen, necessary to give protection from the intense heat of open fires, was not, of course, a novelty, but it now underwent two distinct changes: the former tripod base gave way to a solid base, and the screen took the form of a banner hung from a bar on the upright. The teapoy, a small three- or four-legged table or stand which was not originally associated with tea, was also in use in drawing-rooms at this time (Fig. 8).

*Mirrors*

Shortly after 1800 the circular convex mirror, made in varying sizes from a foot to perhaps three feet in diameter, became very popular in this country after a vogue of half a century in France. The gilt frame had a hollow moulding for which a filling of evenly-spaced gilt balls was a common form of decoration; the outer edge was usually reeded, with a reeded ebonized fillet on the inner edge next to the glass. This type of mirror, surmounted by a carved eagle with outstretched wings, or by acanthus foliage, and sometimes fitted with candle branches, was a prominent feature of Regency interiors.

In the living-rooms of the wealthier houses large mirrors continued to be fashionable. The chimney-glass, set over the chimney-shelf and extending for most of its length, was in a gilt frame which normally had a pilaster at each end and a straight cornice above. Beneath the cornice a hollow moulding was often found, decorated, like the frame of the circular mirror, with a row of balls. The glass did not always extend over the whole area of the frame, for sometimes there was a deep frieze below the cornice, and this was decorated with classical figures in low relief, or with a painting. Large pier-glasses were also found, extending in some cases up to the ceiling.

Mirrors were deliberately placed to catch the reflections within a room or between rooms. 'A pier-glass', wrote Loudon, 'placed opposite the chimney glass always has an agreeable effect, as they reflect one another; so that the size of the room is doubled, from whichever end the spectator directs his view.' And at night time mirrors gave added attraction to the much-improved illumination provided by the large cut-glass chandeliers suspended from the ceiling. The angularity of the many small pieces of faceted glass in the great lustres was noted by Archibald Alison, whose *Essays on the Nature and Principles of Taste* ran into six editions between 1790 and 1825, in the following words:

> 'In a Lustre, one of the most beautiful productions of this manufacture, all is angular. The Form of the Prism, one of the most regular and angular of all Forms, obtains everywhere, the Festoons even are angular, and instead of any winding or waving Line the whole surface is broken into a thousand little Triangles.'

One of the favourite kinds of smaller mirrors was the cheval or horse dressing-glass, a toilet mirror in an upright rectangular frame on four legs. The glass frame pivoted on screws set in the uprights, or could be moved up and down by means of a weight within the frame ('the same as a sash-window': Sheraton).

*Other furniture*

The search for novelty was reflected in the number of patents which were taken out in this period for furniture, fittings and upholstery. Whereas between 1620 and 1799 thirty-three patents altogether were registered under these headings, no less than sixty-eight were taken out between 1800 and 1830, fifty-three during the years 1810–30.[10] They included invalid furniture, extending tables (to which reference has been made) and chairs, adjustable screens and bed-frames, and

[10] Patent Office, Old Series of Abridgements of Specifications relating to Furniture and Upholstery 1620–1866 (1869).

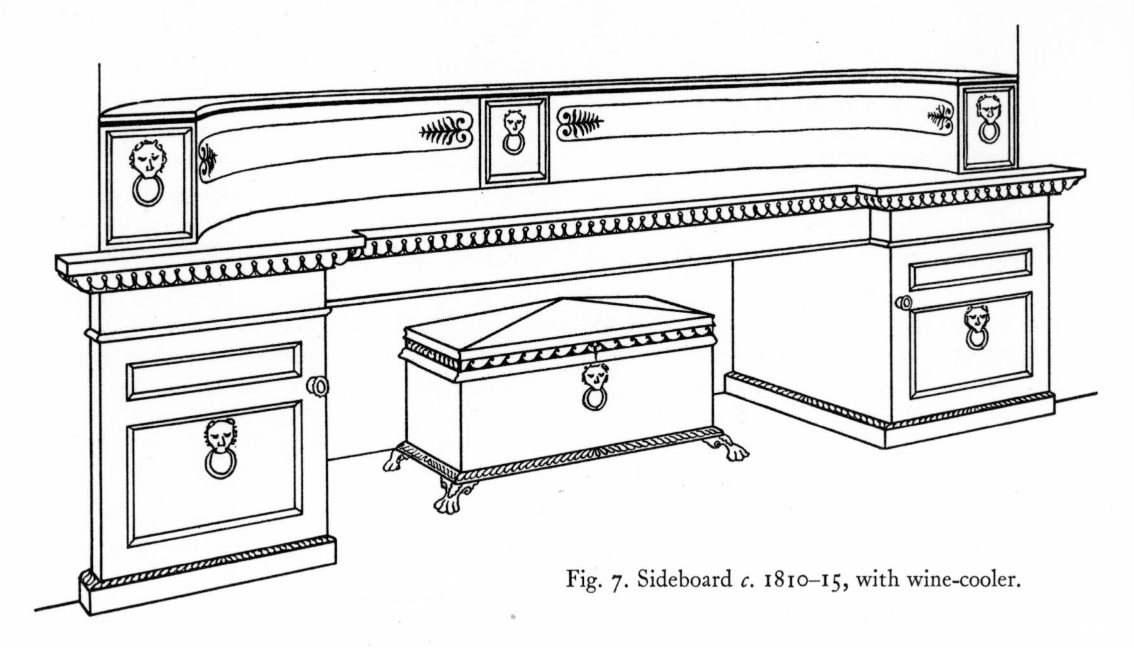

Fig. 7. Sideboard *c.* 1810–15, with wine-cooler.

several kinds of castors. These last were an indication of the growing massiveness of furniture.

It was at this time that High Wycombe in Buckinghamshire became an important manufacturing centre of Windsor chairs. For at least a century previously these chairs had been made in the woods around the town. 'Bodgers' turned the legs, stretchers and sticks on their pole lathes; benchmen made the seats, bows and splats; and framers saw to the assembling and finishing. Local woods were used, mainly elm for the 'dished' seats, ash, yew and willow for the bows, and beech and ash for the legs and sticks. In 1805, according to local tradition, Samuel Treacher, a farmer, started chair-making as a winter occupation for his hands on Marlow Hill. Thomas Widginton came to High Wycombe to teach these men how to assemble the chairs from parts supplied by the rural craftsmen, and about 1810 he set up the first furniture factory in the town. It is known that by 1837 Widginton was a substantial property-owner with his own Chair Manufactory.[11] Windsor chair-making was not, of course, confined to High Wycombe or to Buckinghamshire; it was an old rural craft which continued in other parts of the country. In fact Loudon referred to Windsors as 'one of the best kitchen chairs in general use in the midland counties of England'.

Other cottage furniture varied considerably both in quantity and quality. In poor homes in out-of-the-way areas such as Devonshire and Cornwall only the most rudimentary kind might be found. But more comfortable furniture could be seen in those places where it could be supplied cheaply from London (perhaps by sea) or from other convenient sources of supply; or else the cottage might occasionally have pieces from the local manor house which had got rid of them to make way for a re-furnishing.

Where the farm-house had profited from the rising food prices of the war period the opportunity was often taken to replace the old furniture with something more up-to-date. This excited the indignation of William Cobbett, who regarded the change as aping one's betters. He described a Surrey farmhouse in 1825 in these terms:

[11] F. Roe, *Windsor Chairs* (1953).

'Everything about this farmhouse was formerly the scene of plain manners and plentiful living. Oak clothes-chests, oak bedsteads, oak tables to eat on, long, strong and well supplied with joint stools.... One end of this once plain and substantial house had been moulded into a 'parlour': and there was a mahogany table, and the fine chairs, and the fine glass, and all as bare-faced upstart as any stock-jobber in the kingdom can boast of.'[12]

It was an interior of this kind which Gillray showed in his etching of 1809, 'Farmer Giles and his wife showing off their daughter Betty to their Neighbours' (shown as Plate 27 in Trevelyan's *Illustrated English Social History*).

[12] W. Cobbett, *Rural Rides*, 1821–32.

SHORT BIBLIOGRAPHY

For general study, the best work is *The Dictionary of English Furniture* by P. MacQuoid and R. Edwards (3 vols., revised edition by R. Edwards, 1954). For more detailed study of the period, M. Jourdain's *Regency Furniture* (revised edition, 1948) is indispensable. See also Brian Reade's *Regency Antiques*, 1953, which contains records of some 340 London cabinet-makers and furniture firms of the period. Among the contemporary sources quoted in the text, the works of Smith, Hope, Sheraton, the Nicholsons, Brown, Loudon and Ackermann all contain interesting illustrative material. The quotations from Sheraton in the text are from his *Cabinet Dictionary*, 1803.

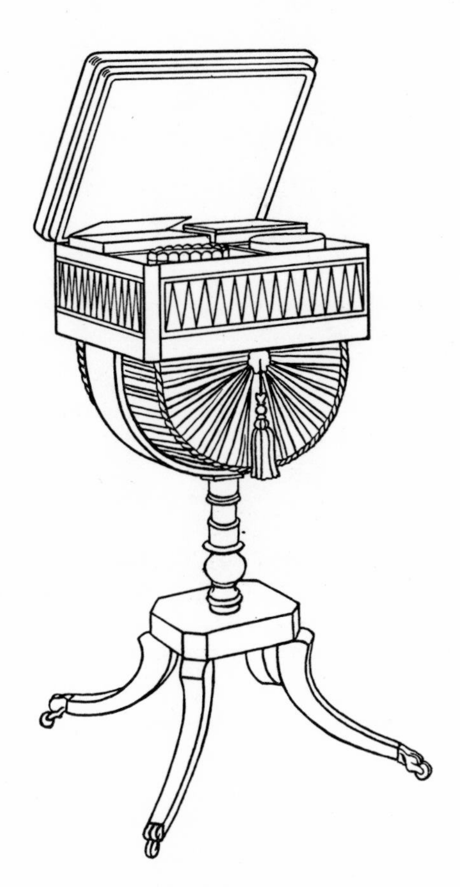

Fig. 8. Teapoy, rosewood with parquetry decoration, *c.* 1820
*Victoria and Albert Museum.*

Brass chair ornaments, from a brass-founder's pattern book *c.* 1820. *Victoria and Albert Museum.*

(A) Chiffonier, ('used chiefly for such books as are in constant use', G. Smith, 1808). Lotus and anthemion decoration, paw feet and brass trellis door, *c.* 1810.

(B) Small rosewood bookcase on stand, showing characteristic turning and brass decoration, *c.* 1810.

PLATE 29

English commode with marked French influence; boulle work panels, *c.* 1800–10.

Mahogany side table with imitation bamboo decoration in the Chinese taste, *c.* 1810.

PLATE 31

One of a set of four painted satinwood armchairs with panels of flowers and cupids and with cane seats, *c.* 1810. *In the collection of Mr and Mrs Frederick Poke.*

PLATE 32

(A) JOHN SCARLETT DAVIS. The Interior of the British Institution Gallery. *Courtesy Lt.-Col. A. Heywood-Lonsdale.* (*Canvas* $43\frac{3}{4}'' \times 55''$).

(B) C. R. LESLIE. The Grosvenor Family. *Courtesy the Duke of Westminster.* (*Canvas* $46'' \times 64''$).

PLATE 33

(A) THOMAS PHILLIPS, R.A. Lady Caroline Lamb. *The Trustees, the Chatsworth Settlement.* (*Canvas* $36'' \times 27\frac{1}{2}''$.)
(B) RICHARD WESTALL. Lord Byron. *National Portrait Gallery.* (*Canvas* $29\frac{1}{2}'' \times 24\frac{1}{2}''$).
(C) SIR HENRY RAEBURN. Self-Portrait. *National Gallery of Scotland.* (*Canvas* $34\frac{1}{2}'' \times 26\frac{1}{2}''$).
(D) ANDREW GEDDES. The Artist's Mother. *National Gallery of Scotland.* (*Canvas* $28\frac{1}{4}'' \times 23\frac{1}{2}''$).

PLATE 34

(A) JOHN CONSTABLE, R.A. Malvern Hall, Warwickshire, from the Garden Side. *National Gallery.* (*Canvas* $20\frac{1}{4}'' \times 30''$).

(B) JOHN CROME. Moonrise on the Yare. *National Gallery.* (*Canvas* $28'' \times 43\frac{3}{4}''$).

(C) J. M. W. TURNER. Somer Hill, Tonbridge. *National Gallery of Scotland.* (*Canvas* $25'' \times 47''$).

(A) HENRY EDRIDGE. Robert Southey. *National Portrait Gallery.* (*Pencil and chalk*, 11″ × 8¾″).

(B) WILLIAM ETTY. Self-Portrait. *The Ashmolean Museum, Oxford.* (*Pen and brown ink*).

PLATE 36

*facing page* 53

# *Painting and Sculpture*

E

# Painting and Sculpture

BERNARD DENVIR

A few days after the publication of the Order in Council appointing him Prince Regent, the future George IV attended a banquet given by the Royal Academy at its headquarters in Somerset House. He behaved with noticeable affability, proposing the toast, 'Prosperity to the Fine Arts and the Royal Academy'. The remaining ninety years of the century were to see the ample fulfilment of this wish, a fact which must be attributed in part at least to the efforts of the extraordinary person who so felicitously voiced it. The Prince Regent, however much he differed from his father, resembled him at least in his warm feeling for the visual arts. Constantly attending exhibitions, a collector of works by old masters – and in this he relied on the advice of several *virtuosi* including Sir Charles Long (later Lord Farnborough) – the younger George was an enthusiastic, kindly patron of contemporary artists. His commissioning of Lawrence to paint the series of portraits which now adorn the Waterloo Chamber at Windsor Castle was prompted no doubt by that sense of England's historic grandeur which warmed many imaginations after the defeat of Napoleon, but he had well-defined, less official, more personal inclinations. From Wilkie he bought and commissioned on a scale which was almost lavish. He was one of the main supporters of that distinguished animal painter Ben Marshall (1767–1835), who rivalled, if he did not excel, the masterpieces of the great George Stubbs (1724–1806); and in the very Academy banquet speech referred to above, he paid 'high compliments' to J. M. W. Turner's *Mercury and Herse*, a fact which, according to an account in the contemporary press, 'became the source of much embarrassment to the ingenious artist, as two of his earliest and warmest patrons have been so eager to possess it, that rather than disoblige one of them, he has resolved not to part with it at all'.

On the walls of Carlton House there hung, beside the old masters, works by Stubbs, Ben Marshall, and Sawrey Gilpin (1733–1807), whose main contribution to the art of the *animalier* was the addition of wild, romantic landscapes. There were also: Gainsborough's *Diana and Actæon*, which had been bought for the Prince in 1797; six or seven Spanish and Italian scenes by Wilkie, as well as the famous *Blind Man's Buff* and *The Penny Wedding*, both of which had been commissioned by the Prince in 1813; Mulready's *Interior of an English Cottage*, and Sir Joshua Reynolds' *The Death of Dido*, which had been bought on his behalf by David Seguier, a dealer and restorer whose brother William became Keeper of the National Gallery.

The very diversity of these paintings suggests the curious fact that, although in the social and decorative arts there is a distinct and recognizable 'Regency style', the painting and sculpture of the period are not marked by the same well-defined characteristics. It is perhaps illogical to expect that it should have been so, for the evolution of style is in the 'fine arts' a slower and more involved process than in the sphere of the decorative arts, where the pressure of social and economic factors compels speedier adaptation to the dictates of that nexus of influences which we call 'fashion'. Even more baffling to the historian, however, is the refusal of English art during the period between 1810 and 1830 to allow itself to be coaxed into the category of 'romantic'. Between the works of Lord Byron and Coleridge there are stylistic affinities which cannot, by any stretch of the imagination, be detected as linking the works of Mulready with those of Constable. The dominant type of portraiture was still founded on the formulæ perfected by Lely and Kneller and polished up by reference to that international 'grand style' which had found its popular exemplar in the Roman Pompeo Battoni. It is significant, however, of the underlying 'romantic' temper of the time that Lawrence, its most successful portraitist, offered, as his diploma piece on election to the Royal Academy, an immense and horrific image of Lucifer. This was not only influenced by Fuseli, but was virtually cribbed from that impressive Swiss, who for most of this period was Professor of Painting at the Royal Academy schools, a position from which he exercised a great influence on the outlook, if not on the style, of many of the younger generation.

Although it is difficult to impose a stylistic label on the works of those painters and sculptors who flourished during the period of the Regency, a list of the works at Carlton House alone suggests the emergence of the pattern which was to characterize English art throughout the nineteenth century. The popularity of animal paintings, the overwhelming vogue for *genre* pictures,[1] a tendency to pay lip-service to the iconography of classical art, and a penchant for exotic and picturesque scenery, wherever it was to be found, provided the main themes upon which exhibitors at the Royal Academy's Summer Exhibitions were to supply variations until well into the twentieth century. When John Hoppner (born 1758) died in January 1810 the vacancy created in the Royal Academy was filled by Augustus Wall Callcott (1779–1844), who had been his pupil. Hoppner had been thought of as the peer and the rival to Reynolds; Callcott's name suggests the Victorian era.

In the decorative arts the period between 1810 and 1830 saw the last great statement of the ideals of the eighteenth century. In the fine arts it saw the establishment of those relationships between art and society which have prevailed ever since. The artists of the twentieth century can look back to Turner, Constable, Blake, and to many others who were at the peak of their powers between 1810 and 1830, as their lineal ancestors. Those of the preceding century belong to the remoter branches of the family tree.

### *The artist and the public*

Whether or not Turner's *Mercury and Herse* did place him in the awkward position suggested by the newspaper report quoted is, in a way, irrelevant. The interesting and suggestive fact is that it should have appeared at all. Artists had always been aware, to varying degrees, of the benefits to be obtained from 'puffs' and publicity, but the circumstances of the early part of the nineteenth century demanded of them a more extensive acquaintance with this kind of guile. The rapid increase in population, the diffusion of literacy, and the steady expansion of fluid wealth promoted an increase in the size, variety and quality of the periodical press. *The Times*, which had been erratic in the quantity of its art criticism, felt itself in 1818 driven to apologize for the fact that:

> 'If we have not been accustomed to notice in our journal the proceedings of the Royal Academy, and especially its periodical displays of the works of genius, it is not because we are indifferent to the welfare of the Royal Academy, or insensible to its claims, but because our observations have been chiefly directed to objects yet higher in respect to National Importance, the great concerns of civil society, of legislation, trade and commerce.'

In other daily or weekly papers there was throughout the period a great increase in the amount of space devoted to the visual arts.

Still more important was the influence of the less frequently issued periodicals, the editors of which must often have been hard pressed for material. William Hazlitt, himself a painter, wrote extensively and inspiringly on art in the *Morning Chronicle*, the *Champion*, the *Examiner*, the *Edinburgh Review*, the *Encyclopædia Britannica*, and other publications. He also produced guides to

[1] This subject is treated by Mr John Woodward in Vol. 6 of this series.

various art collections and other miscellaneous writings about art. He was one of many, and in addition to this ephemeral literature, each year more books about art and about artists were published. Many of these were written by artists and were biographical or autobiographical; others expounded theories of aesthetics or revealed unknown aspects of the art of the past, or of other cultures. The Napoleonic campaigns had focused on Egypt an attention which was largely tinctured with æsthetic preoccupations, and from Italy, Greece, Asia Minor, as well as from Egypt itself, there came a constant flow of antiquities. The most spectacular of these were the Elgin Marbles (removed to the British Museum in 1813) and the sarcophagus of Seti I which was bought by Sir John Soane the architect from Giovanni Battista Belzoni in 1824 for £2,000.

Art was 'news' to an extent unknown in Britain before, and the æsthetic experience of the nation was sharpened by the increasing ease of foreign travel. The poetry of Byron and Samuel Rogers, no less than the prose of countless others who rushed into print to record their experiences before the Acropolis or the Colosseum, did more than anything else to lift art out of the category of a craft, and establish it as a branch of polite learning.[2] Even more important perhaps was the fact that actual visual experience of works of art was being brought within the reach of thousands. For every single person in Great Britain who had seen a 'real' painting in 1720, there must have been at least ten thousand in 1820.[3] A growing sense of national pride had led in 1824 to the opening of the National Gallery, after a long and painful period of gestation. Ten years earlier the Dulwich Gallery had been made accessible to the public, and though the Soane Museum did not become one, in the formal sense, until the death of its founder in 1837, access to its treasures had never been difficult. The popularity of the British Museum was increased by the disputes about the aesthetic value of the Elgin Marbles, and its importance in the world of art was considerable, since art students were permitted to draw from the antique in its galleries. An interesting record of the new role which was played in the world of culture by museums and galleries is provided by John Scarlett Davis (1804–44), whose style was closely allied to that of Bonington. He became a specialist in the painting of the interiors of the Louvre, the Uffizi, and other famous art galleries (Pl. 33A).

Of even greater importance, as far as artists themselves were concerned, was the attitude of great collectors, who not only made their treasures available, but were prepared, from time to time, to lend artists certain works for study. Between 1810 and 1830 men such as Sir George Beaumont, the Marquis of Stafford, Dr Monro, Sir John Leicester and many others took a positive view of the functions of patronage, helping and advising their protégés, and offering them support on levels other than the merely economic.

Nor should it be forgotten that during the period immediately following the Napoleonic wars, London was rapidly becoming one of the more important centres of the art-selling world. The political and economic turmoil which followed the French Revolution broke up many of the great collections of France, Italy and Spain. In England a generation of art dealers, more alert, more adventurous, and more discriminating than any this country had known, scoured the Continent whenever opportunity offered. Men such as Buchanan, Fagan

[2] By the 1820's the guide-books of John Murray, with their fairly exhaustive treatment of the fine arts, had begun to flood the market.

[3] In 1720 the only public exhibitions of pictures were those which took place at auctions and sales. By 1820 there were at least four annual exhibitions of pictures in London, one at the Royal Academy, two at the British Institution (one of contemporary paintings in the winter, one of old masters in the summer) and two of water-colours. Various dealers, such as the enterprising Bullock, not only showed paintings in London, but toured them (e.g., Géricault's *Wreck of the Medusa*) around the British Isles. Large collections brought to the London market for sale (e.g., those of Orléans, de Calonne, Truchsess) were put on public exhibition before being disposed of, and many artists (e.g., Wilkie and Haydon) held what we would now call 'one-man exhibitions' of their works. There were also regular public art exhibitions in towns outside London, including Edinburgh, Liverpool, Glasgow, Norwich and Bristol.

and the Woodburn brothers brought to London works of art which are still among our most important national assets. At the same time too, the reputation of the auctioneers, led by James Christie, ensured that several important collections, notably those of the Duc d'Orléans and of the French politician de Calonne, were sold here. The influence of these movements in the art market was considerable; it is doubtful, for instance, whether Constable would have developed as he did, had it not been for the influx of a great number of works by Claude and many other European landscape painters between 1800 and 1820.

The machinery of buying and selling had improved beyond all expectation. Contemporary artists could now sell their pictures, at open auctions, at their own galleries, or exhibitions (as Turner did), at any of the large mixed exhibitions, or at the premises of the ever-increasing number of dealers who were prepared to traffic in the work of the living. Above all, the Royal Academy had become so firmly entrenched that it was now, to mix a few metaphors, a shop-window, a sounding-board and a market. It was now difficult to succeed without its support and impossible to maintain success without becoming an academician.

### *Portraiture*

Throughout most of the eighteenth century, artists had been complaining about the necessity of painting portraits when they should have been devoting themselves to the claims of 'high art'. By 1820 it was becoming apparent that their agitations had succeeded. Portraiture was never to lose its popularity, nor to be displaced as one of the most certain ways of making a large income; but it was never again to hold the near-monopoly of the art market which it had enjoyed in England between 1680 and 1780.

Yet by a curious irony England had produced in Thomas Lawrence, who died in 1830, a portrait painter who reached a European eminence which was only to be rivalled by that of Winterhalter half a century later. A biography of Lawrence by Douglas Goldring is entitled *Regency Portrait Painter*, and of all the artists who flourished during this period he is the one who has been most closely identified with it. The son of an innkeeper, his is one of the most baffling personalities in the history of British art. A superb, though occasionally a meretricious technician, handsome, a courtier to his finger-tips, fêted from one end of Europe to the other, he was able to charge for his services prices which even now seem very high. A scholar, and the owner of one of the finest collections of old master drawings ever known, he was harassed by the most atrocious, and largely inexplicable financial difficulties, and his habit of accepting half-fees on commissioning led him to undertake far more works than he could ever finish. Many of these uncompleted portraits have a charm and beauty of their own, and it is a tribute to Lawrence's exacting artistic conscience that he never scamped a work, preferring to leave it unfinished. If a portrait painter's success is to be measured by the degree to which he satisfies the needs and demands of his clientèle, Lawrence was pre-eminently successful.

His technical innovations were so slight that it is difficult to describe any of the many artists whose works were similar in some ways to his own as followers. The word may justly perhaps be applied to William Owen (1769–1825) and to Richard Rothwell (1800–68). The point was of course that few others were able to contact such influential clients. Sir William Beechey (1753–1839) had owed his success to the support of George III and Queen Charlotte, and his work seems to us now sufficiently embedded in that period to excuse our thinking of him rather as looking back towards Reynolds than forward to Millais and Leighton.

Of the other portraitists of the period Richard Cosway (1742–1821) is the one who, after Lawence, is most typical of the spirit of the Regency. This was due rather to his personal friendship with the Prince of Wales, and to his extravert, even eccentric, social behaviour than to any qualities peculiar to his art. He was indeed essentially a miniature painter, and his style reflects the brittle elegance which that kind of work implies.

By far the most interesting portraitist of the period apart from Lawrence is the Edinburgh-born Andrew Geddes (1783–1844) who had much to do with the revival of interest in etching, and whose works in every medium which he used are marked by strong personal characteristics. He was one of the many artists of the period who asserted the prominence of Scotland in the artistic history of the period (the Regent himself was partial to tartans and had an ambivalent passion for the Stuarts). More famous than Geddes, and usually described as the rival of Lawrence, was Sir Henry Raeburn (1756–1832), whose work, at first sight anyway, more rugged than that of his English contemporaries, suggests at times the influence of Hogarth. On the whole, artists from north of the Border tended to look towards Flanders rather than towards Italy for their exemplars, and the troubled history of the Netherlands was directing towards Britain an increasing number of works from those countries.

The subdued richness of colour which marked the works of John Jackson (1778–1831), whose career reflected the patterns of the eighteenth century in that it was based on the patronage of such north-country aristocrats as Lord Mulgrave and the Earl of Carlisle, suggested the influence of Rembrandt, and there were similar features to be detected in the work and career of Henry Howard (1769–1847), who was also known for his historical and classical subjects. Few artists confined themselves to the exclusive practise of portraiture; Wilkie, Haydon, and Etty,[4] for instance, all produced important portraits, and achieved varying degrees of fame in that genre. Among the less exalted, the idea of having one's portrait painted was widely accepted as a social necessity. Certain artists specialized in certain types of sitter. Thomas Phillips (1770–1845), who was born at Dudley and trained as a glass painter, changed to portraits and tended to specialize in those of members of the literary world, whilst Samuel de Wilde (1748–1832) dealt with personalities of the stage.

The success of Henry Edridge (1769–1821), who produced successful tinted portrait drawings, was symptomatic of the wide demand for portrait painters, who by now counted among their ranks such female professionals as Margaret Carpenter (1793–1872).

During the years 1810–30 it became evident that there would be no dearth of efficient portrait painters for some time to come, and it would be outside the scope of this work to discuss them all. One may note, however, the names of George Richmond (1809–96), David Scott (1806–49), George Henry Harlow (1787–1819) and Sir William Allan (1782–1850).

The *réclame* of men such as Beau Brummell, with their insistence on sartorial uniformity, ensured that the general tone of portraiture would be a good deal more restrained than it had been in the past. Ideals were domestic rather than official; the parlour table was succeeding the Roman arch; the dress-coat, the toga. Wealth had come to be considered more important than station. As we look at it in retrospect, it is not surprising that the Prince Regent, who was by way of being a sponsor of lost causes, should have preferred himself to be painted in rather spurious armour. Nor is it unforgivable that he should have detailed a sergeant in the Scots Guards to pose to artists for those portions of his own Royal anatomy below the neck-line.

### *Landscape and water-colours*

The major hypothesis of all romantic art is that it should be engendered by emotion and feeling. In the late eighteenth century the attempt often resulted in a note of false theatricality, a fact largely due to the absence of a suitable vocabulary and of a suitable medium. Feeling and emotion become stale when they are over-polished. The phenomenal development of water-colour provided for painters a solution to this problem.

Between 1810 and 1830 there were still living and flourishing representatives of the older style of water-colour. John Smith (1749–1831) had been on the Grand Tour with the Earl of Warwick, and his topographical drawings and paintings were always slightly redolent of Hadrian's Villa, but he lived to become, between 1814 and 1817, President of the Old Water-Colour Society. This had been formed to combat the neglect, real or imagined, which the Royal Academy showed of the

[4] William Etty is dealt with in detail in Vol. 6 of this series.

medium. John White Abbott (1763–1851) was so entrenched in the older practise of the art that in his copying of paintings and drawings by the old masters he might have been emulating the earlier activities of a Vertue or a Mrs Beale.

Men such as these were, however, exceptional. The new attitude towards water-colour was voiced early in the nineteenth century by Edward Dayes (1763–1804), the teacher of Girtin: 'The nearer a drawing (i.e. a water-colour drawing) can be brought to a picture (i.e. an oil painting) the better.' Water-colour made possible an immediacy of expression and spontaneity of feeling impossible before. It permitted of open-air painting; it cleared from the palette those 'chiaroscuro' effects which had led Sir George Beaumont (1753–1827), himself a respectable amateur practitioner in the older styles of landscape art, to suggest that a good painting should be as brown as an old violin. It permitted a new devotion to those topographical and landscape subjects which fascinated the age, and having set off with the desire to emulate the grandeur of oil painting, it had come, by 1830, to impose its own standards on that more viscous medium.

So closely had landscape art become interlinked with the discoveries of water-colour painting, that it is almost impossible to consider them apart. Our current sensitivity to the charm of Constable's sketches derives very largely from the fact that they are, as it were, water-colours in oil. Less expensive than oils, more readily adaptable to the decorative schemes of the medium-sized 'villa', water-colours introduced a feeling for art into new social regions. There were many less famous than John Ruskin, who discovered the ease of execution and satisfaction of accomplishment which the actual exercise of the art entailed. Foreign scenes, hitherto accessible only to the accomplished traveller, were revealed to those whose previous experience of them had been limited to monochrome engravings. The facile art of Samuel Prout (1783–1852) made the inhabitants of Denmark Hill or Putney as familiar with the Gothic façades of Rouen or Chartres as they were with those of their own parish churches. Prout's vast, widely disseminated output would have been impossible in oils. The necessity to 'feel' opened up new fields of observation for artists, and though some followed the tradition of Fuseli and Martin in exploring the realms of the horrific, others achieved this end by more familiar means. The sea appeared for the first time as an important subject, igniting the genius of Turner, and stirring the imaginations of Francia, Bonington, Copley Fielding and George Chambers, to name but a few.

The experience of water-colour, whether it was visual or practical, endowed the eye with that kind of artistic honesty which Wordsworth and his literary peers valued so highly. It gave the final blow to the persistence in landscape art of those classical accessories which may be thought of as the graphic equivalents of the Latinised metaphors and similes of Pope and Dryden. It destroyed that sense of theatricality so obvious in the work of an artist such as Philip James de Loutherbourg (1740–1812), who in 1767 had become a member of the French *Académie*. He indeed had some excuse, for, settling in London in 1777, he devoted much of his time and attention to devising elaborate theatrical exhibitions and devices, which influenced his work even when he came to devote his attention to the industrial landscapes of the north.

The development of topographical art gave landscape painters an inclination towards regional fidelities. The Norwich School was one of the main nurseries of genius, and the variable talent of John Varley (1778–1842), whose activities as a teacher forced him into exorbitant mannerisms, was at its best when it contemplated the mountains of Wales. Art clubs flourished in Liverpool, Birmingham and elsewhere. Artists frequently became associated with some particular spot. In 1820, 1821 and 1823 Constable stayed with the Fishers at Salisbury, producing that cycle of views of the great cathedral which forms a contrast to his usual preoccupation with the part of Suffolk which has now come to be known as 'Constable's country'.

Such allegiances were noticeable in the work of lesser men. Luke Clennell (1781–1840), a farmer's son, born near Morpeth, became an apprentice of the famous Bewick,[5] and though he came

[5] See 'Painting and Sculpture' by Hugh Honour in preceding volume: *The Late Georgian Period.*

JOHN CROME. Castle Eden Dean.
*National Gallery of Scotland.*
(*Water-colour on buff paper*, $16\frac{5}{8}'' \times 14\frac{3}{4}''$.)

PLATE 37

*facing page* 60

(A) AUGUSTUS CHARLES PUGIN. A Room in the Royal Pavilion.
*Courtesy C. Musgrave, Esq.* (*Water-colour*).

(B) DENIS DIGHTON. The Third and Last Challenge by the Champion during King George IV's Coronation Banquet in Westminster Hall. *Royal Collection, Windsor Castle. Reproduced by gracious permission of Her Majesty the Queen.* (*Water-colour* $16\frac{3}{4}'' \times 21\frac{1}{2}''$).

PLATE 38

SIR FRANCIS LEGATT CHANTREY, R.A. Mrs Jordan and her family. *Courtesy the Earl of Munster.* (*Marble 72″ high*).

PLATE 39

(A) William Behnes. Samuel Woodburn.
*Ashmolean Museum, Oxford.*

(B) Samuel Joseph. Lady de L'Isle and Dudley.
*Courtesy Viscount de L'Isle. (Marble 31" high).*

(A) ANDREW ROBERTSON (1777–1845). An unknown lady.
*Victoria and Albert Museum.*

(B) FREDERICK CRUICKSHANK (1800–68).
Mr W. H. E. Pattisson. Sketch for a miniature portrait. *Victoria and Albert Museum.*

(A) John Linnell (1792–1882). An unknown man, signed. *Victoria and Museum.*

(B) Henry Collen (worked 1820–72) Captain Octavius Vernon-Harcourt, signed, and dated 1838. *Victoria and Albert Museum.*

(C) Alfred Edward Chalon, R.A. (1781–1860). An unknown lady, signed, and dated 1828. *Victoria and Albert Museum.*

PLATE 42

SIR WILLIAM CHARLES ROSS, R.A. (1794–1860). Mrs Bacon, signed, and dated 1841. *Victoria and Albert Museum.*

Simon Jacques Rochard (1788–1872). Miss Mary and Master Patrick Stirling, signed, and dated 1826. *Victoria and Albert Museum.*

PLATE 44

*facing page* 61

to London in 1805 and eleven years later won a prize for a sketch of *The Life Guards charging at Waterloo*, the roots of his art were, in the best sense of the word, provincial. The only pity is that his frequent attacks of insanity make it difficult to evaluate his full potentialities. John Glover (1767–1849), also a farmer's son, from Leicestershire, moved in 1794 to Lichfield, where he taught painting and drawing and made his first essays in oil. He did not reach London till eleven years later, and after some time there, during which he helped to found the Royal Society of British Artists, migrated to Tasmania, where he managed to combine being a successful *rentier* with the exercise of his profession.

Glover's Tasmanian paintings did not make any impact on the English art world, though they were admired by Louis Philippe. Many of his contemporaries did, however, base their reputations on a skilful exploitation of the exotic. George Chinnery (1774–1852) claims our attention if only because he was the first English artist known to fame whose dislike of his wife drove him to migrate, first in 1802 to Madras, then, being followed by his spouse, to Calcutta in 1807; finally to Canton and Macao in 1827. A facile yet distinguished painter, his delightful paintings and drawings of oriental scenes and subjects are among the more fascinating by-products of English art.

Although men like Frederick Catherwood were prepared to endure endless discomfort depicting the landscape of remote Mexico, most artists found the exotic nearer home. David Roberts (1796–1864) and William James Müller (1812–45) shared a penchant for Spain and the Near East; and it is impossible to enumerate the artists whose views of France, Germany, Switzerland and Italy perpetuated for those who had visited the places the memory of one of the highlights of their lives. The Grand Tour had become a mass-produced pleasure, and whereas a century earlier the aristocracy had been accompanied by their tame painters who recorded their experiences for them, in the nineteenth such relics were purchased subsequently.

France was in a special position, and it was during this period that the artistic relations between the two countries were at their most cordial. England had come to be looked upon as one of the main progenitors of romanticism, and the *Salon* of 1824 was known as the *Salon des Anglais* because of the impression created by the works of Constable, Bonington and Copley Fielding. The precocious Richard Parkes Bonington (1802–28), born at Arnold near Nottingham, was the son of a local portrait painter who had been Governor of Nottingham Gaol. He accompanied his father to France in 1817, and studied for some time at Calais under Louis Francia (1772–1839), who had spent much of his life in England, and who was to be largely responsible for introducing into French art the lessons of the English water-colour tradition. Later Bonington worked at the Louvre and the Institut de France under Baron Gros. His work, brilliantly lucid, clear, and spontaneous, was produced almost entirely in France and dealt with French subjects. He also worked in lithography and, after 1824, in oils. After his early death his paintings were much publicized by his father. Anthony Vandyke Copley Fielding (1787–1855) was also, as his names might suggest, the son of an artist, and though he achieved great popularity in his own lifetime, he is now less highly esteemed.

The main developments of water-colour painting had been made possible by the work of men who almost entirely specialized in that medium. Peter de Wint (1784–1849), who was of Dutch extraction, is mainly responsible for an immense widening of the visual and technical horizons of water-colour, for a startling vindication of its powers of expressing mass and volume, and for his expressionist freedom of handling and technique.

John Sell Cotman (1782–1842) was born in Norwich, and was for some time an employee of Ackermann (cf. *Engraving and Illustration*, *passim*). He was one of those employed, if that is not too ponderous a word, by Dr Monro, the far-seeing patron of many artists. His greatest works were connected with the landscapes of Wales, Yorkshire and Norfolk. From 1810 to 1824 he was much preoccupied with the exhibitions and activities of the Norwich Society of Artists, producing illustrations for various archaeological books. After various tours in France, he was appointed in

1834 Professor of Drawing at King's College. Throughout his life he was much afflicted with nervous and economic troubles.

John Crome, known as 'Old Crome' (1768–1821), was also a native and resident of Norwich. Like many of his eighteenth-century predecessors, he had been apprenticed to a coach-painter, but through the good offices of a local collector, Thomas Harvey of Catton, he became acquainted with the works of Hobbema and Gainsborough, which, with those of Richard Wilson, were to be the main influences on his subsequent development. He was the guiding spirit of the Norwich School, and painted in both oil and water-colour, bringing to the delineation of landscape and architectural subjects a bold simplicity of handling and a sensitivity to atmosphere which foreshadow many of the attitudes of later artists.

It seems absurd to think of Turner and Constable as 'artists of the Regency', yet that fact alone suggests how remote from the accepted pattern of the times painting in effect was. Between 1810 and 1830 both these artists produced some of their greatest works. But though we think of them in the same breath, their contemporaries did not. In 1810 Turner, who was thirty-five, was a popular and well-established artist, and on 17 August of that year he held £7,216 16*s*. 2*d*. in the funds. The critics and the general public saw nothing difficult in his works, and Hazlitt's earlier description of them as 'containing the very elements' was a formula which won fairly widespread acceptance. During this period he was consolidating his gains, establishing his reputation, and making possible those post-1830 forays into fields of expression where few of his contemporaries could follow him.

Constable, a year younger than Turner, at the beginning of the period, had yet to become an Associate of the Royal Academy, and at the end of it had just managed to attain that full membership which he was to enjoy only for seven years more. The French critic Charles Nodier had hailed *The Haywain* (1821) as a painting which could compare with the finest of the works of the old masters, but Constable's English contemporaries were obsessed with the 'coarseness' of his handling and saw him merely as a minor landscape artist, precluded from greater successes by a lack of technical expertise. Yet during these twenty years he produced, among other works, *Dedham Vale* (1811), *Boat Building* (1815), *Hampstead Heath* (1827), *The Leaping Horse* (1825), and the Salisbury Cathedral cycle (1821–4).

In style David Cox (1783–1859), though not of the same stature, merits comparison with Constable. Although he worked his way up the social and artistic ladder, having spent some time in the profession of scene-painter, he was an articulate and sophisticated artist, who published a book on water-colour painting, and for some time taught drawing to the senior officers of the Military College near Farnham, a knowledge of the rudiments of landscape art being then considered essential for warfare. Cox greatly enriched the technique of water-colour painting, producing by means of wet colours and broken tints a richness and complexity which allowed the medium to assume the textural intricacy of oil-painting in the expressionist tradition.

### *Engraving and illustration*

The period of the Regency may be looked upon, as far as the arts of illustration and engraving are concerned, as a golden age. Hand-processes and mechanical processes were in a state of equipoise, and a greater number of first-rate artists applied their talents to these arts than was ever the case before or since. It was a honeymoon period in the chequered history of the matrimony of art and industry.

Originally the outlook had not been propitious. The wars of the Napoleonic period had dealt a serious blow to English engravers who had dominated the European market. In 1787 it had been asserted that 'the export of our engravings to France far exceeds the trade at home, and of the more costly works, the French exceed by three to one the buyers in England'. The cessation of this trade forced into bankruptcy men such as Alderman Boydell, who had been responsible for its existence.[6]

[6] See 'Painting and Sculpture' by Hugh Honour in preceding volume: *The Late Georgian Period.*

This position, however, was only temporary. By the second decade of the century other factors were coming into operation which stimulated trade in the home market, and opened up new fields of exploitation in places as far away as Mexico and China. Aquatint had first been used in 1775,[7] and the cheap use of colour which it facilitated produced a revolution in taste and in the art-buying habits of the public, the effects of which became increasingly obvious during the next half-century.

Close on the heels of aquatint, with its variations in tone and texture, and its influence on both book-publishing and print-production, came lithography. This was introduced into Britain in 1808 by Philip André, and extended still further the fields in which artists and printers could co-operate.

The potentialities of lithography were brought to the attention of Rudolph Ackermann (1764–1834), who in 1817 published in that medium *Albert Dürer's Designs of the Prayer Book*. In so doing he discovered weaknesses in the process as it then stood, and two years later crossed over to his native Germany to meet the actual inventor, Senefelder. As a result he published Senefelder's *A Complete History of Lithography* (1819), and presented a portable lithographic press to the Royal Society of Arts. The implications of lithography were not at the moment fully realized, and Ackermann used it mainly for the many text-books on the art of drawing and painting which he published. These, of course, in themselves, promoted an active and a fruitful interest in art.

Had it not been for Ackermann, who did for English art in the first half of the nineteenth century what Boydell had done in the eighteenth century, it is doubtful whether either aquatint or lithography would have produced such startling results in so short a time. Ackermann was born in Germany: his father was a coachbuilder, one of the aristocrats of the craft tradition, and he himself was concerned with the design of Nelson's funeral car. But he was primarily interested in publishing and bookselling, and established in the Strand the *Library of the Fine Arts*, which was at once a bookshop, a print shop, a library, a place for the sale of artist's materials and a social centre. *Conversazioni* were held there on Wednesday evenings, and the place served as a kind of *salon* for the 'middling and mercantile classes', where they could hear about art, meet artists and buy, in a reasonably cheap form, their productions.

The inventive and enterprising Ackermann represented the best type of artistic impresario, and the appearance of his name on a print or title-page indicates artistic excellence. Perhaps the most spectacular of his publications was the *Microcosm of London*, published between January 1808 and May 1810, with letterpress by William Combe, author of the famous 'Dr Syntax' tours; and hand-tinted plates, the joint work of Rowlandson (see previous volume) and Augustus Charles Pugin (see below). It was a perfect combination; the neat, laborious accuracy of the Frenchman complementing the vital social reportage of the great caricaturist, and the *Microcosm* was one of the most magnificent publications of its kind ever to appear, its immediate success being no less than the approbation subsequently accorded to it by posterity. It propounded for the first time a theme which the illustrators of the period were to make popular, the pictorial possibilities of the urban scene. Similar publications, especially those dealing with Oxford and Cambridge, appeared and very soon other publishers adventured into the same field.

The success of these publications emphasized a revolution which had been taking place in the respective positions of artist and engraver. The increased demand for works of a certain kind meant that the artist was now the dominant partner, for he had become not merely a commentator and a provider of visual beauties, but an illustrator of current events. That chain of causation had begun which was to lead to the *Illustrated London News* and the pictorial journalism of the nineteenth century.

Sir Charles Eastlake (1793–1865), later to become President of the Royal Academy, Director of the National Gallery, and one of the most impressive cultural tycoons of the century, achieved his first success by hiring a boat to row out to the *Bellerophon*, when it anchored off Plymouth.

[7] See below, p. 170, note.

There he did a painting of Napoleon, and so brought his name before the public in the most advantageous way.[8] Turner was equally aware of 'news value'. This is evident not only in the *Battle of Trafalgar*, but in the work with the now innocuous title of *Ships Dropping Anchor* which was in fact a record of the arrival in home waters of two captured Danish frigates. He changed the title because of the outcry aroused by this hostile act against a neutral nation. Artists had begun to realize that if they could record an interesting event, the completed work would first of all be exhibited in London, then, possibly, in the provinces, and that some publisher or engraver would probably buy the reproduction rights.

There were few artists who did not, at some time or another, come into contact with Ackermann, for in addition to his publishing activities, he maintained a circulating library of prints and drawings for the use of artists and 'amateurs'. In 1809 he also started publication of the famous *Repository of the Fine Arts*, a monthly journal which created new standards of presentation and production in the world of periodicals. Finely printed, with a wealth of illustrations and with such novelties as insets of new dress materials, it was intended to appeal to the tastes of both sexes and all classes, adding the sugar of fashion to the pill of art. Exhibitions, books, cattle prices and social gossip jostled each other in the lively pages of a magazine which employed, even for its fashion plates, artists of distinction. Chief among these was Thomas Uwins (1782–1857), who, having commenced his career as an engraver, attended the Royal Academy Schools, and by 1813 was secretary of the Old Water-Colour Society. As a result of the employment given to him by Ackermann he was able to embark on a series of foreign tours from which he derived the material for his popular and picturesque water-colours of Spain and elsewhere.

Ackermann catered for the middle classes, but the higher ideals of Regency sartorial culture were expressed by the drawings of Niklaus Wilhelm von Heideloff (1761–1839), whose *Gallery of Fashion* is an outstanding achievement of its species.

*The Repository of the Fine Arts*, with its wide range of interests, indicated the way in which the work of the illustrators tended to give a unity to all the various art manifestations of the age, encouraging the application to decorative and architectural uses of themes and motifs evolved in the realm of the graphic arts. A great step had been taken towards the standardization of taste, for the middle classes, with their rising incomes and their empirical tastes, untouched by traditions of patronage, could now be kept abreast of the latest trends. The wives of Birmingham and Liverpool business men could have their clothes cut to the latest Parisian styles, and their husbands could exhort their architects to follow the latest innovations of Mr Nash or Mr Papworth.

The magazine was also used to publicize Ackermann's productions and artists, thus establishing a closed circuit of patronage and interest. When John Martin (1789–1854) first came to London from his native Newcastle, where he had been apprenticed to a coach-painter, he took three of his drawings along to Ackermann, who bought them for 12*s*. 6*d*. Twenty years later, however, when he came to add up his accounts, he recorded that between June 1826 and December 1827 he had received £691 18*s*. from Ackermann, £476 from Moon, £87 from Colnaghi, and £259 2*s*. 3*d*. from Agnew and Zanetti of Manchester. Martin, who in 1816 won the British Institution's prize and secured a great reputation in 1821 with his apocalyptic *Belshazzar's Feast*, had a talent which was especially inclined towards literary illustration, but the sums which he received from these four printsellers may be taken as presenting a reasonable picture of the extent to which an artist of his calibre depended on reproductions (cf. Thomas Balston, *John Martin*, London 1947, p. 91). Significant too is the appearance of Manchester as a point of sale. Ackermann indeed told Martin on one occasion that the small engravings of his works which he published were very popular in China.

There was a growing awareness of the new forms of beauty produced by the industrial Revolu-

[8] Eastlake procured a signed statement from one of the officers in the *Bellerophon* that he had produced a good likeness of Napoleon.

tion: in 1831 Ackermann published what has come to be considered a classic of railway art, Thomas Talbot Bury's *Coloured Views on the Manchester and Liverpool Railway*. Visual standards of beauty were now applied to objects which had hitherto been judged by purely functional considerations. The taste of the nineteenth century was to be dominated by pictorial sensibility, and the foundations of this sensibility were laid by the print-makers and illustrators of the Regency period.

That feeling for the 'Picturesque' which had been evolving throughout the eighteenth century received a powerful stimulus from the literature of the early nineteenth. Improvements in transport and means of communication, both at home and abroad, fostered the spread of sensitivity among those sections of the population who had hitherto had little opportunity of venturing beyond their own immediate neighbourhood. The *Tours of Dr Syntax* (including one *In Search of the Picturesque*) were half-serious parodies of a craze for books of this nature. One of the finest was *A Vogage round Great Britain* (1814–25), with exquisite coloured aquatints by William Daniell (1769–1837), who is also known for his fine Indian views, executed there when he was working in collaboration with his uncle, Thomas Daniell (1749–1840). A taste for the Oriental was yet another aspect of the picturesque which was to be popularized during this period.

Even though these luxurious publications were produced in instalments, their price necessarily restricted their circulation, and in 1823 Ackermann produced his *Forget-me-not*, a stout little volume, $5\frac{1}{2}'' \times 3\frac{1}{2}''$, which was destined to release an avalanche of similar publications. These were to dominate the artistic habits of an entire generation, and give employment to a multitude of artists, ranging from Turner to gifted female amateurs. To be found on every dressing-table and in every parlour, they brought a taste for art within the range of many whose outlook would in an earlier age have been uninfluenced by such matters. The mere fact that their titles were so overtly æsthetic as *The Landscape Annual* gives some indication of the extent to which interest in them gradually shifted from the letterpress to the illustrations. Single proof impressions of particular plates were soon fetching higher prices than those of the original volumes.

The predominant public interest in landscape was fostered still further by publications such as Cooke's *Picturesque Views on the Southern Coast of England*, the first four parts of which were published in 1814. William Bernard Cooke, who undertook the series with the assistance of a syndicate of publishers, including John Murray, was a professional engraver. Turner, who had been commissioned to provide twenty-four drawings for the book, eventually produced thirty-nine, for which he was paid ten guineas each. Each part contained, in addition to the letterpress, three full-page engravings and two vignettes. This was Turner's first experience of this kind of work, and it was to be for some considerable time one of his main occupations, and an incentive to many of his major landscapes.

It may well be that the extent to which artists came to rely on the engraver had a cumulative influence on their style, making for that clear definition of colour and form which was to be a characteristic of 'high Victorian' painting. Normally, however, it was considered to be supplementary to an artist's activities, and there were few who specialized in work for the engravers. One who, however, is chiefly remembered for his work in this field is the architectural draughtsman, Augustus Charles Pugin (1762–1832), a refugee from the French Revolution, who was much employed by Ackermann and others, and whose most characteristic work was carried out in conjunction with John Nash. The folio *The Royal Pavilion at Brighton* was prepared at the command of the Prince Regent. A drawing and a water-colour were needed for each plate, and Pugin exhibited these at the Old Water-Colour Society's exhibitions.

Several artists directed their attention to the production of flower paintings for reproduction, and Francis Bauer (1758–1840), who settled at Kew in 1790 and remained there for the rest of his life, has been described by Mr Wilfrid Blunt (*Flower Books, an Exhibition at the National Book League*, 1951) as 'perhaps the most brilliant horticultural draughtsman of all times'. An outstanding compilation of floral prints was *The Temple of Flora*, edited by Dr Robert John Thornton (1768–1837), which contained reproductions of works by all the finest practitioners of the time, and resulted in the editor's financial ruin.

Another remarkable development of the time, and one which is hard to associate with our usual preconceptions of the period, is the development of wood-engraving in the hands of the group of of artists associated with William Blake (1757–1827).[9] In 1820 Blake cut seventeen remarkable woodcuts for a new edition of Ambrose Philips' *Pastorals*. These had a great influence on the work of Edward Calvert (1803–83), whose pastoral and poetic subjects, produced in the period 1827–9, have an extraordinary charm and fascination. Equally remarkable was the work of Samuel Palmer (1805–81), who in the period 1826–33 was producing at Shoreham paintings, water-colours and engravings of one kind or another the reassessment of which during the last twenty-five years has been one of the more fruitful artistic experiences of our time.

[9] See 'Painting and Sculpture' by Hugh Honour in preceding volume: *The Late Georgian Period*.

NOTE: It is clearly impossible in a work of this kind to enumerate all the artists whose work in the fields of engraving and illustration are of value or importance. In addition to those mentioned above the following are notable.

*Etching*: J. M. W. Turner, John Crome, John Sell Cotman, Edward Thomas Daniell, Andrew Geddes.

*Line-engraving*: William Miller, J. T. Willmore, W. Radclyffe, Robert Brandard, John Pye, R. Wallis, J. B. Allen, E. Goodall.

*Mezzotint-engraving*: John Raphael Smith, William and James Ward, S. W. Reynolds, Charles Turner, George Dawe, R.A.

*Stipple-engraving*: Peltro William Tomkins, Thomas Cheesman, John Ogborne, Robert S. Marcuard, Luigi Schiavonetti, Giovanni Vendramini.

*Aquatint*: J. C. Stadler, Thomas Sutherland, J. Bluck, Daniel Havell, C. V. Fielding.

# Sculpture

'Of all the arts', said Théophile Gautier, 'the one which least lends itself to the expression of the romantic ideal is sculpture, which seems to have recieved its definitive form from antiquity'. The history of that art in England bears witness to his words. At one point in the nineteenth century there were few forms of life, from 'what-nots' to prayer-book covers, untouched by the Gothic Revival. Architects were prepared to cut each others' throats over the respective merits of the round and pointed arch; painters grew agitated as to whether Raphael marked the beginning or the end of artistic excellence. The major problem which exercised sculptors, however, was whether trousers were to be preferred to togas. Works of art in stone and marble enjoyed a comparative freedom from the social exigencies of the time, and though the nude was looked upon as a medium for the indulgence of the baser passions, young men and women frozen into permanent poses exposed their chiselled forms to view in the most public places, without exciting anything but æsthetic comment.

Sculpture, indeed, retained many of the characteristics of the eighteenth century. By its very nature the profession tended to exclude amateurs, demanding of its practitioners an almost menial skill. Men such as Gibson and Chantrey came from lower-class backgrounds; they began their careers as apprentices, and it was not unusual for a sculptor such as John Bacon to 'inherit' his father's practice.

Patronage was ample, finding its fullest deployment in the commemoration of political and military achievements, in funerary monuments, and, of course, in portraiture. The practitioners of sculpture ranged from wax-modellers such as the famous Catherine Andras, who modelled the funeral effigy of Nelson, to national figures of the stature of Chantrey. One may note, as typical of the general run, the names of Matthew Cotes Wyatt (1777–1862) and George Garrard (1760–1826). More successful than either of these was William Behnes (1795–1864), the son of a Hanoverian piano-tuner, and the unlikely preceptor of G. F. Watts. Commanding the ability to display a Roman verism in his portraiture, Behnes, who received much patronage from the royal family, fell on evil days, and died suddenly in the streets, of a stroke. He was also a draughtsman of very considerable powers, and there is a large and impressive collection of his work in the Department of Prints and Drawings at the British Museum.

John Bacon (1777–1850) began as a precocious youth, winning the Royal Academy's silver medal at the age of sixteen and its gold medal a year later, but his subsequent career did not quite live up to this promising beginning. A more interesting figure is that of Samuel Joseph (1795–1850), whose seated figure of Samuel Whitbread is a remarkable creation.

By constant application to the demands of those who indulged in the current passion for the trappings of death, Richard Westmacott (1775–1856) did better for himself than his father had done as a painter, and won a knighthood in the process. One of his main claims to our attention, however, was that it was he who was responsible for the almost embarrassingly unadorned statue of Achilles in Hyde Park, made out of French guns captured at Waterloo, and commissioned in 1826 by the Women of Britain to commemorate the achievements of the Duke of Wellington.

Sir Francis Legatt Chantrey (1781–1841) first achieved fame by his portrait bust of Horne Tooke, the famous radical and scholar, and by an emotionally expressive monument in Lichfield Cathedral based on a design by Stothard. Starting off as a jack-of-all-trades, prepared to turn his hand to anything from portrait painting to woodwork, Chantrey, who died worth £105,000, foreshadowed in his career the ideals which were later to be enunciated with such compelling force by Samuel Smiles. Running his own foundry at Pimlico, and employing many assistants, Chantrey applied to his art many of the principles which were winning acceptance in the fields of industry and commerce. Our own romanticized conception of the artist's role has often allowed these facts to blind us to the real merits of his work. In the history of sculpture he represents a period marked by the dependence of all the arts on the graphic ones. He was the supreme exponent of the pictorial.

When, in the discussion of any of the art forms of early nineteenth-century England, one refers to classical ideals, it must be understood that these ideals are derived from Italianate prototypes, and that it was to the studios of Canova and Thorwaldsen rather than to the workshops of ancient Greece that most sculptors directed their attention. There were always sculptors of Italian birth or descent working in England as assistants or independent artists, among whom were Pietro Cingolnelli (1760–1825), one of Flaxman's assistants, and John Charles Felix Rossi (1762–1839), the son of an Italian doctor who practised in Nottingham. Rossi was apprenticed to G. B. Locatelli in London, and became an R.A. in 1802.

The peak of the Romanizing tendencies – and one must not forget that in the background hovered the slightly sententious figures of Mengs and Winckelmann – was John Gibson (1790–1866), the son of a market-gardener of Conway, who was apprenticed to a monumental mason in Liverpool. He attracted the attention of that fascinating banker, collector and scholar William Roscoe (1753–1831), and eventually made his way to Rome, where he worked with Canova and Thorwaldsen, and built up an almost mystic reputation for himself. Although Gibson, whose work is to be seen in abundance in the gallery devoted to it at the Royal Academy, was mostly known for his 'high art', posterity tends to look with a more favourable eye at his portraits.

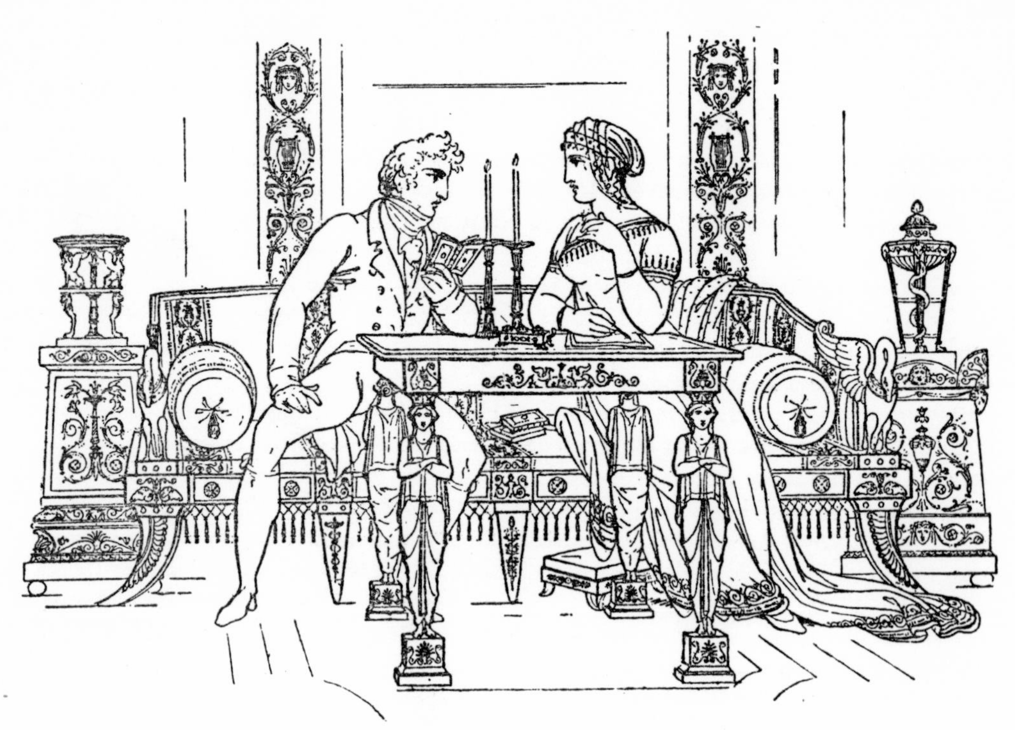

The poet reads his Works. From a drawing by Henry Moses, *Modern Costume*, 1823

*Miniatures*

F

# Miniatures

JONATHAN MAYNE

In 1801, as readers of Volume 4 of these Period Guides may remember, the young Scottish miniaturist Andrew Robertson (1777–1845) (Pl. 41A) surprised and delighted the *cognoscenti* of London with a large, elaborately-wrought copy which he had made after a portrait by Van Dyck. Painted solidly, as though in imitation of oil (so that Cosway, when he saw it, could not at first believe that it was a water-colour miniature at all), Robertson's copy seemed at that time to point the way towards an enhanced seriousness in the status of the art; and today it may conveniently be considered as marking an important stage in the transition between the elegant, aristocratic style of the late Georgian age and the heavier, more bourgeois climate of the succeeding period. Although it would be a mistake to suppose that the transition was a sudden one – indeed, at the turn of the century Cosway and Engleheart had still many years of activity ahead of them – it is with the 'new style', consciously initiated by Robertson and adopted by the majority of his contemporaries and pupils, that we shall be primarily concerned in our consideration of the Regency and Early Victorian miniature.

### *Andrew Robertson*

Andrew Robertson was born in Aberdeen in 1777. When about sixteen he went to Edinburgh to study landscape and scene-painting under Nasmyth; but far more influential for his future career was his meeting at this time with Raeburn. According to Robertson's own account, Raeburn received him kindly and gave him permission to copy one of his portraits; he also allowed him to be present on occasions during his portrait-sittings. The result was a stylistic influence that can be discerned in Robertson's work throughout his career. His system of lighting and modelling, his feeling for three-dimensional structure, and above all his concentration on characterization may all be attributed in some degree to his study and admiration of Raeburn. From the outset of his career in London, in 1801, Robertson showed an almost puritanical conscientiousness: 'I *shall* draw well', he wrote in a letter to his brother, 'and go more to the bone than any other artist – shall study anatomy, the driest part, many say it is a bugbear. Miniature painters study no more than the head. *I* must do much more.' And again, of the miniatures of Cosway he wrote, 'They are pretty things, but not pictures. No nature, colouring, or force. They are too much like each other to be like the originals.'

This second remark throws additional light on Robertson's aims. The miniature, hitherto regarded as, in some sense, an article of adornment, was to become a picture in its own right. Already in the last years of the eighteenth century, as has often been observed, miniaturists had begun to explore the possibilities of larger sheets of ivory. Robertson and his contemporaries were consciously to exploit this tendency, and to combine with it a seriousness of craftsmanship, amounting almost to a moral earnestness, which may seem to be an implied criticism of the style of their predecessors. 'I have done some things lately in Cosway's style', wrote Robertson in 1802, 'and I see it does not require a conjurer to succeed in it – a *little* genius

– knowledge of the figure and drapery is all that is necessary.'

From all this it might be expected that Robertson's finished works would be estimable but academic, and it comes perhaps as a surprise to find him capable of such a degree of sympathetic understanding and charm of colouring in his best portraits. The seal was set on his early success by his appointment in 1805 as miniature-painter to the Duke of Sussex; and in 1807 he was at Windsor, engaged in painting portraits of the Royal princesses. By this time his style was fully formed, and he was launched on a lifelong career of official distinction.

### *Sir William Charles Ross*

Robertson's most eminent pupil was undoubtedly Sir William Charles Ross, R.A. (1794–1860) (Pl. 43), who today seems to represent his age as completely as did Cosway the late Georgian or Hilliard the Elizabethan periods. After a precocious youth, during which he won a succession of prizes at the Society of Arts, Ross entered the studio of Robertson in 1814 as assistant, and as a result of this employment his original desire to make a name for himself as a history-painter became deflected into another channel – though it is interesting to note that as late as 1825 he was exhibiting at the Royal Academy a large oil-painting, with life-size figures, of 'Christ casting out the Devils from the Maniacs of the Tombs'. Ross's status as a leading miniaturist of his time was confirmed by his appointment as miniature-painter to the Queen in the year of her accession, and in the following year he was elected an Associate of the Royal Academy; in 1842 he became a full Academician, and was knighted. He continued to work until he suffered a stroke in 1857, three years after which he died.

Ross's style represents a consolidation of the developments initiated by Robertson. The Redgraves, in their *Century of Painters*, point to indications of his study of Reynolds, but to the twentieth-century eye this is discernible no more than would be expected in the work of any portrait painter of his generation. Rather we would tend to think of Lawrence or even of Winterhalter when examining a series of miniatures by Ross; Reynolds' epic distinction is already giving way to a type of good-natured, domestic elegance, and in spirit, if not in style, we are at a long distance from the great portrait-machines of the eighteenth century. The Redgraves go on to observe that Ross 'possessed the great power of combining a faithful resemblance and individuality of character and expression with art of a high class', and with this praise one would not quarrel. 'His drawing was refined and accurate', they continue, 'his composition and grouping agreeable, his colouring of the complexion, hands and arms of his female sitters admirable, and the draperies, accessories and background painted and arranged with great taste and skill.' Ross was capable both of a high degree of finish and of a bolder, sketchier manner, either of which he employed at will. In composition his works are sometimes of a telling simplicity, and at others strikingly intricate. In one important respect Ross showed a marked difference from his master, Robertson; this was in his fluency and speed of execution. As may be remembered, Robertson records that an early miniature-portrait took him well over thirty hours – 'a week's hard labour' – to complete; and although he was doubtless able to improve on this time-table as his skill developed, he can have come within no distance of rivalling the total of over 2,200 miniatures, many of which were on a large scale and of great elaboration, with which Ross is credited. In the recent past Ross's work has been insufficiently appreciated; already, however, in 1929 Basil Long, in his *British Miniaturists*, was looking forward to a juster estimation of his powers, and today it is already possible to regard him as among the great artists of our school of miniaturists.

### *Newton and Cruickshank*

If Robertson and Ross represent as it were the mainstream of miniature-painting during the first half of the nineteenth century, a number of lesser artists may be considered as roughly grouped around them and as sharing to some extent their stylistic atmosphere. In his time probably the best-known of these was Sir William John Newton (1785–1869), who enjoyed a career of considerable success. While good miniatures by Newton are not infrequently met with, they can seldom provoke comparison with the works of his two greater contemporaries, and today he is perhaps best remembered as the author of two of the largest miniatures ever painted – each about 27 by 37 inches in size – representing the marriage of Queen Victoria and Prince Albert, and the Christening of the Prince of Wales. A more interesting artist, who painted both miniatures and water-colour portraits, was Frederick Cruickshank (1800–68) (Pl. 41B), a pupil and fellow-countryman of Andrew Robertson. He exhibited regularly from 1822 until within a few years of his death, and as a rule his work reflects the influence of his master. The example reproduced here, which is a sketch rather than a finished work and which is executed almost entirely in tones of grey and brown, with a little pink in the face, is particularly interesting for its controlled freedom of brushwork. Very little is recorded concerning the biography of Cruickshank, but it appears that he was able to build up a successful professional connexion in London, and he also lived – and presumably worked – in Manchester. According to family tradition he was unstable and erratic of temperament, and towards the end of his life he suddenly packed up and left his wife and family, 'in very much the same way, and for the same reason, that caused him to "down tools" when the spirit moved him'.

Others who may be said to come within the Robertson–Ross orbit were such artists as Henry Collen (worked 1820–72) (Pl. 42B), G. L. Saunders (1807–63), Alfred Tidey (1808–92), Annie Dixon (exh. from 1844), Reginald Easton (1807–93), and Robert Thorburn, A.R.A. (1818–85). John Linnell (1792–1882) (Pl. 42A), the friend and disciple of William Blake, who is far better known as a landscape-painter, nevertheless executed a number of interesting miniature-portraits during the early part of his career, and two examples in the Victoria and Albert Museum give a flattering impression of his powers in this medium. He developed a strongly personal manner, in which an emphatically linear definition of forms is combined with a type of free stippling which is familiar from his water-colour landscapes.

### *A. E. Chalon*

In spite of the dominant influence exerted by Robertson and his 'new style' during the first decades of the nineteenth century, one other small, and to some extent independent succession of miniaturists remains for consideration. The leader of this succession – if something so loosely organized can be so described – was Alfred Edward Chalon, R.A. (1781–1860) (Pl. 42C), an artist of French descent, whose family came to settle in England in 1789. Chalon received instruction in miniature-painting from the Genevan artist L. A. Arlaud, who was in London in the 1790's, and began to exhibit water-colour portraits and miniatures in 1801. Thus, professionally speaking, he was an almost exact contemporary of Andrew Robertson. But stylistically the two artists had little in common beyond a fondness for painting on a fairly large scale. Chalon's particular gifts led him to specialize in the portraiture of elegantly dressed women, and in this he achieved a brilliant, fashionable success. Writing some years later, a friend observed that Chalon was 'so fond of painting ladies in flowing silks and airy laces that some of the artists published an advertisement in one of the morning papers to the effect that "muslins and laces would be done up equal to new at 19 Berners Street" ' – which was his address at that time. And towards the end of his life, when Queen Victoria remarked to him that she feared that photography would ruin his profession, Chalon is said to have replied, '*Ah non*, Madame, photographie can't *flattère*'. But it would be a mistake to suppose from anecdotes of this kind that Chalon was a mere 'society painter' – a kind of Laszlo of his time. Quite apart from an acute and delightful sensitivity to the vagaries of fashion and a Gallic appreciation of female beauty, his work shows a firmness of drawing and a vivacity of colour which themselves would entitle him to serious consideration. Chalon is also well known today for his entertaining caricatures of opera singers.

### *The Rochards*

The arrival in London in 1816 of the French miniaturist Simon Jacques Rochard (1788–1872)

(Pl. 44) and, a year or two later, of his younger brother, François Théodore Rochard (1798–1858) is a further indication that the Robertson school was not alone in the field. The Rochards, whose individual styles it is often difficult to distinguish one from the other, worked in a manner not far removed from that of Chalon, though the general influence of Lawrence's bravura is sometimes more noticeable in their work. Like Chalon, they were masters of a brilliant, flickering brushwork, and were particularly skilled in the depiction of elegant female beauty. S. J. Rochard is said to have been a pupil of Isabey, and though nothing is recorded of his younger brother's training, it is reasonable to suppose that he was brought up in the same tradition. Between them the Rochards established a successful practice, which lasted until 1846, when the elder brother left London to settle in Brussels; four years later François Théodore retired.

With the working lives of Chalon, the Rochards, and the pupils of Robertson we have already been taken beyond the Regency period and into the reign of Victoria. But while it is a fact that good miniatures continued to be painted at least until the death of Ross in 1860, it is also true that the last significant developments in the art occurred during the first three decades of the century; and because of this it has seemed natural to include in our survey some artists whose training and formation took place in the earlier period, but many of whose best-known works belong to the later. The precise reasons for the decline and exhaustion of the art of miniature-portraiture about the middle of the nineteenth century are difficult to define; but the invention of photography and the substitution of a diffused, tonal vision for one more properly linear must be held to a large degree responsible. Although miniatures were still to be painted, in dwindling quantities, throughout the century, and although more recently attempts have been made to infuse new life into the art by a conscious return to earlier traditions, the recorded death-bed lament of Ross that 'it is all up with future miniature-painting' must seem to most students today to have been only too accurate a prophecy.

Mr and Miss Wilkinson, a cut-paper silhouette by Augustin Edouart, 1829. Reduced from 12 ins. wide. *Victoria and Albert Museum.*

# *Silver and Plate*

(A) DIGBY SCOTT and BENJAMIN SMITH, 1805–6. Pair of double-lipped wine-glass coolers, embossed each side with classical subjects on a matted ground. *From the Royal collection at Windsor Castle, by gracious permission of H.M. the Queen.*

(B) PAUL STORR, 1812–13. One of a pair of highly rococo silver-gilt soup-tureens and stands resting on the backs of tortoises. The arms of George III are applied each side of the body. Weight 1,073 oz. (the pair). *From the Royal collection at Windsor Castle, by gracious permission of H.M. the Queen.*

PLATE 45

(A) JOHN BRIDGE. Silver-gilt tureen. One of a set of four made for George IV in 1826. Height 15¼ in. *From the Royal Collection at Windsor Castle, by gracious permission of H.M. the Queen.*

(B) WILLIAM PITTS, 1809. One of a pair of silver-gilt dishes, with shaped edges, the centre panel embossed with a scene of Jupiter in the clouds taking vengeance on the earth, the panel surrounded by swans and bulrushes. *Courtesy the Marquess of Londonderry.*

(C) WILLIAM PITTS, 1810. One of a pair of silver-gilt dishes, with escalloped edges, the broad rim embossed with sprays of different flowers in panels. In the centre is a Tudor rose encircled by a wreath of husk design, with an outer floral border. Diam. 15¼ in. *Courtesy the Marquess of Londonderry.*

(D) PAUL STORR, 1814–15. Circular dish of silver-gilt depicting the Triumph of Dionysus (Bacchus) and Ariadne. The Bacchic emblems seen on the broad rim are largely taken from the Warwick Vase. The royal arms of George IV were added later. Designed by T. Stothard, R.A. Diam. 31 in. Weight 374 oz. 15 dwt. *From the Royal Collection at Windsor Castle, by gracious permission of H.M. the Queen.*

(A) The Warwick Vase, in its restored state, with a Latin inscription on the pedestal recounting its history and the part played by Sir William Hamilton in its restoration. *Warwick Castle.*

(B) PAUL STORR, 1812–13. One of a pair of silver-gilt wine-coolers in the form of the Warwick Vase, the rims chased with vines on a matter ground. The Harewood coat of arms is applied to the square plinth. Fitted with fruit dishes to match. Height 18 in. *Collection of H.R.H. The Princess Royal and the Earl of Harewood.*

(C) Details of one side of the Warwick Vase showing the eighteenth-century female head on a modern background. The head to the left is original, and that to the right is also eighteenth-century work. *Warwick Castle.*

PLATE 47

(A) PAUL STORR, 1809–10. Candelabrum—silver-gilt—designed by John Flaxman, R.A., depicting the Three Graces gathering the apples of the Hesperides. Height 60 in. Weight 1,386 oz. *From the Royal Collection at Windsor Castle, by gracious permission of H.M. the Queen.*

(B) and (C) PAUL STORR, 1810–11. Pair of silver jugs, based on Roman originals by John Flaxman, R.A. to which spouts, handles and lids have been added. Height 7 in. Greatest circ. 16½ in.

*Courtesy Charles Oman, Esq.*

PLATE 48

# Silver and Plate

N. M. PENZER

### *Regency silver*

In the present volume the term Regency Period is used to cover the years 1810–30, but such dates are clearly employed more as a designation of convenience than as covering the entire period to which such a term can reasonably be applied. The previous volume – *The Late Georgian Period 1760–1810* – will make this appear obvious. There the silver section will be found to include much that is Regency, for the dates cover not only the Nelson victories, but also the Indian and Portuguese campaigns of Wellington. Thus though George, Prince of Wales, did not become Regent until 1811, by then the Regency Period, as the term is popularly understood, had practically reached its peak, a fact we must realize in the present volume. We may, however, consider for a moment the difficulties which arise in attempting to date the so-called Regency Period. A term which has to cover, apart from its historical significance, not only architecture, painting, sculpture, furniture, plate, textiles and ceramics, but all the minor arts and crafts as well, is bound to receive many interpretations so far as its duration is concerned. Thus some writers, such as Margaret Jourdain in her *Regency Furniture*, begin at 1795, the date of the marriage of the Prince of Wales to Caroline of Brunswick, and end in 1820 with the death of George III. The Victoria and Albert Museum, in their excellent series of 'Small Picture Books', prompted by the fact that by 1800 the Adam style had lost its original vigour and those who sought to guide public taste were looking out for fresh sources of inspiration, place the commencement of the Regency as 1800, and its end as 1830 with the death of George IV.

Writing on the architecture in his *Regency Style*, Donald Pilcher also chooses 1800–30 in order to include the 'formative period' which dates roughly from the beginning of the century.

In one point alone everybody appears to be agreed – that the Regency Period in art in no way coincides with the political Regency, which extended only from February 1811 to January 1820. It refers, rather, to the period affected by the personal tastes of George Augustus Frederick as Prince, Regent and King. Whether such tastes are regarded as beginning in 1783, when the Prince became of age and paid his first visit to Brighton; about 1790, when his father introduced him to the firm of Rundell and Bridge; or in 1800, when the Adam style had greatly declined in popularity, seems to be largely a matter of opinion. We must leave it at that.

It is by no means easy to determine when one style ends and another begins. Styles often overlap and the gradual change is almost imperceptible. Yet a new style is sometimes occasioned by a reaction to the existing one – as with neo-classic following Rococo – and a period of temporary vacillation, a kind of art interregnum, may exist before some definite 'movement' shows the way. Such a lead may be afforded by some trenchant utterance of the sovereign, some political or military crisis at home or abroad, or some important archæological discovery which, by its very innovation, fires the imagination of the public. Any or all of these things may contribute to a new style, but more often it is the publication of a work by an architect, goldsmith, furniture-maker or designer that is of far greater importance. As the Classical Revival is equally manifest in both the Adam and Regency styles, it can be claimed that the latter was but a culmination of the former. It must not be supposed, however, that when a style changes such a change is complete and absolute. Far from it, as the repeated occurence of the Rococo in both the above styles proves. Politically, the Regency covers a period of glory, triumph and progress which, save for the Elizabethan age, stands alone in English history. As far as the goldsmiths' craft is concerned, the glory and triumph showed itself chiefly in the imposing and massive presentation plate made to celebrate the long series of victories, both naval and military, which started with that of Lord Howe on the 'Glorious First of June' in 1794, and ended with Waterloo in 1815.

The 'progress' appeared in the rise of the factory, the commercial and industrial activities of men like Matthew Boulton, the ever-increasing output of machine-made component parts of plate – especially in Birmingham and Sheffield, and the consequent speed with which the growing middle classes could be supplied with silver articles which their prosperity now permitted them to enjoy. The retail goldsmith was taking the place of the individual plate-worker, and it was now possible to see the finished article in the shop windows of the leading firms before an order was given. Even the finest plate, such as that required for the royal services, or by the ruling noble families, was usually ordered from one of the great retail houses.

In studying Regency plate it is necessary to consider to what extent the Regent himself was responsible for the style implied by that term, to what degree the royal collections benefited during the period in question, and the debt, if any, that English art as a whole owes to his personal taste and patronage. It will be generally agreed that Regency art is largely neo-classical in concept, although Chinese, Egyptian, Gothic and especially Rococo styles are also found. Such eclectic features may make the study of the period difficult and somewhat confusing, but at least by their variety of form and decoration they contribute to what has, with good reason, been called the Age of Elegance.[1]

The first opportunity the Prince had of satisfying his personal taste was when in 1783, the year of his coming of age, he was presented with Carlton House as his separate establishment. It was sadly in need of renovation and enlargement, and so offered ample opportunity for self-expression and the releasing of those inhibitions which the restrictions of life at Buckingham House had imposed. In choosing Henry Holland (1745–1806) as his architect, the Prince had selected a man who, shunning the Adam school, followed the contemporary Whig taste of French neo-classicism. The Louis XVI style was selected as having the necessary dignity and restraint, and Frenchmen were employed for the decoration and furnishing. J. P. T. Trécourt was Holland's leading assistant, Guillaume Gaubert his foreman who supervised the architectural ornament of the rooms, and Dominique Daguerre, late 'marchand privilége de la Cour' of Louis XVI, the art dealer who supplied most of the furniture. It was, however, not in the stately rooms that we find any trace of the Prince's love of the fantastic, the bizarre and the exotic. For this we must turn to the Gothic additions to the lower storey and the Chinese drawing-room of yellow silk filled with Chinese furniture and porcelain.

There is no need to give further details of this strange house with its varying styles embodying the luxury of East and West. It was merely a sample of the eclectic tastes of the Prince which were to be developed further in that Oriental fantasy at Brighton, the Pavilion.

Before considering the plate in detail, it is necessary to appreciate the situation at the time when the Prince moved into Carlton House. As every-

[1] There is no better way of coming to appreciate the Age of Elegance than looking through the forty volumes of Rudolph Ackermann's *Repository of Arts, Literature, Commerce, Manufactures, Fashions and Politics*, published in monthly parts from 1809–29. The coloured plates are of remarkable quality. Brian Reade (*Regency Antiques*, p. 22) rightly calls the *Repository* the 'Key to the life and works of the Regency period'. Both the British Museum and Victoria and Albert Libraries have complete sets.

body knows, at the Restoration the royal collection of plate was non-existent, or very nearly so, and even the coronation of Charles II had to be postponed partly because there was no regalia to complete the ceremony. Gradually the collection was built up and the palaces supplied with ample plate, so that by the time of Anne it was necessary only to supplement the domestic items. In 1721 George I ordered an inventory to be taken, and this MS is now at the Public Record Office (Treasury Board Papers (T.I.) bundle 235, No. 25). From its 266 items, which include plate at all the palaces as well as at the Tower, we note, especially, a generous supply of sconces and andirons in nearly every room at St James's, Kensington and Windsor – the very type or article which was soon to become 'old fashioned', and so doomed to extinction. Records exist at Windsor, however, which show that a considerable number of these discarded pieces were sent to Hanover. The ewry, spicery, scullery, kitchen, confectionery, pantry, etc., were well supplied with all that was necessary, and we find the usual salts, bowls, cups, dishes, ice-pails, and an 'Aparn' recorded. But what we do *not* find is any mention of important ceremonial pieces with which Tudor inventories abound. We can only conclude that they had never been replaced, owing chiefly to the fact that the first two Georges hardly ever entertained. So, too, the retiring disposition of George III left matters very much as they were. Such plate as he did buy was for ordinary domestic use, although after he had transferred his patronage from Thomas Heming to the goldsmiths Rundell and Bridge of Ludgate Hill, his interest in plate considerably increased, and had it not been for his repeated illnesses it seems probable that substantial additions to the royal collections would have been made. But as things turned out this was reserved for the Prince Regent. What plate was sent to Carlton House in 1783 we do not know, but it would never have been sufficient in quantity or importance to cope with the receptions and banquets held there. As was usual on such occasions, it was doubtless hired for the evening and often left on display for several days after. The Prince's interest in plate dates from about 1789, when George III returned to Windsor from Weymouth, where he had gone to recuperate after his first serious illness. True to his nickname, Farmer George, in discussing local agricultural matters, decided to visit a farmer named John Bridge who lived near Bridport. The meeting was highly successful, and a mutual respect and understanding followed. At one of their many meetings Bridge mentioned that his cousin, of the same name, was a partner in a firm of goldsmiths on Ludgate Hill and begged of the King his gracious support and recommendation. On his return to London, George III sent for Bridge, and was so pleased with him that he not only appointed Messrs Rundell and Bridge to the office of Jewellers, Gold and Silversmiths to the Crown, but obtained a similar warrant from the Prince of Wales and the entire royal family. It appears to have been from this time that the Prince of Wales began to show an interest in plate, a taste which John Bridge took every opportunity to cultivate. With the enormously increased orders from both royalty and the nobility which his firm was now receiving, it was found necessary for Rundell and Bridge to improve their stock very considerably. A great opportunity to do this was afforded by refugees from the French Revolution, whose sole remaining wealth lay in what jewellery and plate they were able to bring with them. The renewal of the war with France in 1803 caused rents to rise, and the landed gentry put their unexpected profits into plate. It was about this time that the Prince of Wales discussed with Bridge the manufacturing of a service of silver-gilt plate of sufficient size and importance for use on State occasions. There was now adequate stock for the Prince to select the styles which most appealed to him – not only the neo-classical vases, centre-pieces, and candelabra, but also the Rococo of Meissonier and his school, the table-services of Thomas Germain and his son François, Jacques Roettiers, Henri Auguste and many others. According to a MS account of the history of Rundell, Bridge and Rundell by one of their former employees,[2] sufficient pieces of the royal

[2] This MS is in the Baker Library of the Graduate School of Business Administration, Harvard University. A photostat copy can be seen at the Victoria and Albert

service were finished by 1806 – the date of the building of a new show-room to the premises – for an exhibition of them to be held for three days of every week during the spring of 1807. Invitation was by ticket only, and 'all the Rich, the great and Noble of the Land' flocked to see the wonderful display, while Ludgate Hill became blocked by their carriages until seven o'clock each evening. Thus the fashionable world was able to see the personal taste of the Prince, and the Regency style was about to be established.

With one exception, all the plate exhibited in 1807 was made either by Digby Scott and Benjamin Smith, by Benjamin Smith alone, or with James Smith.[3] The one exception was the four large soup tureens of Egyptian design made by Paul Storr[4] in 1803 and 1805.[5] This apparently formed the first item of the 'Grand Service' to which George IV was to add continually for the rest of his life. Between 1802 and 1807 Storr was fully occupied with the 'Nelson Plate'. No wonder other work had to be put out to associated firms such as Scott and the Smiths. After 1807, however, Storr was able to devote himself to the Grand Service, and his production, especially in 1809–15, was enormous.

Reverting to the soup tureens, they are of interest for several reasons. The use of Egyptian *motifs* at this particular time – the Battle of Alexandria and the surrender of the city having occurred in 1801 – had a special significance. Storr had already (1799) made the Nile Cup presented to Nelson by the Governor and Company of Merchants of England trading in the Levant Seas, and cornucopia handles had been used in both cases, although it must be admitted that the sphinxes issuant from those of the Nile Cup are much more 'Egyptian' than the winged Ephesian Dianas (Artemis) of the tureens.[6] Digby Scott and Benjamin Smith also used Egyptian *motifs* for their two dozen round chased salts made for the Grand Service in 1802 (another dozen was added later), and twelve helmet-shaped sauce-boats made in 1804. The use of Egyptian *motifs* at this time[7] was only sporadic and never became popular. It should be noted that the large circular stands for the tureens were French in design, having been copied by Storr from a pair made by Henri Auguste in 1787 and subsequently purchased by George III at the sale of the effects of a Neapolitan Ambassador.[8] Turning to some of the other pieces shown at the 1807 exhibition, we find several examples with classical *motifs*, which were later to be used much more generously. Thus the twelve bottle-stands, made in 1805, are richly chased with boys, tigers and vine-leaves; a bread-basket is ornamented with grapes, vines and tendrils with goats' heads at the hinges of the handles and a lion's mask at the centre.

In some of the candelabra the tapering shafts encase the attenuated bodies of Greek maidens, *Korai*, whose heads with long tresses falling over their bosoms appear as capitals, while their bare feet and edges of their plaited garments protrude below to rest on a plain circular base.[9]

Of considerable interest and beauty is a set of

Museum library (86.DD.27). The writer was a man named George Fox, who was with the firm from 1806 to 1833.

[3] Digby Scott and Benjamin Smith entered their joint mark on 4 October 1802, and Ben. and James Smith on 23 February 1810.

[4] Storr did not join Rundell, Bridge and Rundell (which it had become in 1805) until 1807. Previously he had worked for the firm from his own place in Air Street, Piccadilly. The Royal Inventory, prepared by Garrard and Co. in 1914, includes articles by Storr from 1794 to 1802, but several of these dates need checking.

[5] This dating is according to Jones, *Gold and Silver of Windsor Castle*, p. 166. Garrard gives the dates as 1802 to 1803.

[6] For the Nile Cup see N. M. Penzer, *Paul Storr*, Pl. XIV; and for the tureens see Jones, *Gold and Silver of Windsor Castle*, Pl. LXXXIV.

[7] This was no *introduction* of Egyptian *motifs*. Such elements had been used in European Arts, from time to time, since the Renaissance, and both Piranesi in Rome and Tatham on his return to England had published Egyptian designs. See further Hugh Honour, 'The Egyptian Taste', *Connoisseur* May, 1955 pp. 242–6.

[8] See E. Alfred Jones, *op. cit.* Pl. XLVIII, and No. 15 of the Victoria and Albert *Royal Plate* 'Small Picture Book', No. 37, 1954.

[9] See E. Alfred Jones *op. cit.* Pls. LXIV and LXXX, and Storr's seven-light candelabrum from the Londonderry collection here reproduced (Fig. 1).

double-lipped wine-glass coolers, described as 'Verriers'[10] in the inventory of William IV prepared by Rundell, Bridge & Co. (as it was then) in 1832 (Pl. 45A). They are embossed on either side with a classical subject in relief on a matted ground framed by a narrow acanthus border. One shows a muscular youth (*not* Hebe, daughter of Zeus, as Rundell's inventory says!) seated on a tree-trunk feeding an eagle, while the other represents a Naiad feeding a long-tailed sea-horse. The projecting lateral lips of the vessels are supported by double-tailed mermen. An egg-and-dart moulding runs round the edge. They were made by Digby Scott and Benjamin Smith in 1805–6. In the years 1809–12 many additions were made to the 'Grand Service', most of which were in a strictly classical style, for Rundell had employed Flaxman to make the designs. We shall return to him later.

On the other hand, we find highly rococo pieces, such as the soup-tureen and stand shown on Pl. 45B, being added to the royal collection at this time. The tureen, one of a pair, was made by Paul Storr in 1812 and clearly betrays its French inspiration. It may, indeed, have been inspired by similar *soupières* acquired by Rundell from the French refugees. The massed fish and vegetables on the lid, the extravagant use of the foliated acanthus for both handles and legs, the tortoise feet to the stand, and the rich effect obtained by the introduction of lobing, fluting and gadrooning – all can be found on French pieces of the eighteenth century by such designers and goldsmiths as François Germain, Juste Aurèle Meissonier, Edme-Pierre Balzac, Jacques Duguay, Jean-Baptiste Chéret, and François Joubert.[11] The

Fig. 1. Seven-light candelabrum, silver-gilt, the tapering shaft encasing three Greek maidens whose feet protrude on a plain circular base. The base is in the form of a tripod of three lions' feet with acanthus decoration. The central light socket is surmounted with the Londonderry crest. Height 34½ ins. Paul Storr, 1814–15. *From the collection of the Marquis of Londonderry.*

[10] This word is not English, but represents the French *verrière* which means both a monteith and, as here, an individual wine-glass cooler. Double-lipped coolers usually accommodated glasses for champagne and hock, those for red wines being placed on the table.

[11] For these see Henry Nocq *Le Poinçon de Paris*. As some of the finest examples are in Russian and Portuguese collections reference should be made to A. de Foelkersam *Inv. de l'Argenterie ... des Palais Impériaux*, St-Petersbourg, 1907, Vol. I, Pls. 24–8 (particularly for Louis Lenhendrick) and C. G. Bapst, *L'Orfèvrerie français à la Cour de Portugal au XVIII^e^ siècle*, 1892, Pl. V, fig. 19, and Pl. VI, fig. 27, elaborate centre-piece by F.-T. Germain, and Pls. VII, VIII and IX for rococo soup-tureens.

objects depicted on the lids vary, but include lobsters, broccoli, artichokes, peas, cauliflowers, pomegranates, mushrooms and vine-leaves. Some craftsmen, such as Louis Lenhendrick, preferred to use *putti* both for the lid and handles, and magnificent examples are in the Russian collections. We may well ask if such sumptuous pieces as the 1812 tureen, so reminiscent of French plate of some fifty years earlier, can be regarded as true examples of a rococo type characteristic of the Regency period, or are merely copies. Such a doubt is by no means lessened if we consider some of the tureens produced in England during the first half of the eighteenth century – especially those by De Lamerie. We may take two by way of example. The first, made in 1736, was in the Swaythling collection (P.A.S. Phillips, *Paul de Lamerie*, Pl. CVIII), and can be described as wildly rococo. The cover is overlaid with dead birds, flowers, foliage, weeds and scrolls surmounted by a large crowned lion passant as a handle. The fluted body is enriched with scroll- and basket-work, shells, quatrefoils and beaded shields, the border being of reed-and-ribbon design, exactly as in Storr's tureen of 1812. Beneath the double voluted scroll handles are lobsters modelled in the round and free from the body giving the appearance of, quite unnecessary, secondary handles. The legs are formed as dolphins' heads.

The second, made in 1747, was in the J. P. Morgan collection,[12] and bears the arms of Lord Lichfield[13] enclosed within spreading floral branches and ears of wheat, below which is the mask and pelt of a ewe, a conceit repeated above the four scrolled feet. The distinctive feature, however, is the finely wrought spread eagle, with its talons embedded in dead game, which forms the finial to the highly decorated cover. It has a silver liner which was made by Storr in 1806. Many examples of less ornate mid-eighteenth-century tureens could be quoted, but sufficient has been said to show that those which appeared in Regency days were but a revival of French and English types which had been popular in the reigns of Louis XV and George II.

The extravagant and exotic tastes of the Prince Regent clearly found satisfaction in such rococo pieces which suited the French and Chinese decoration of Carlton House better than those of the more austere neo-classical type, and they again became fashionable with the upper classes. All kinds of plate, besides soup- and sauce-tureens, were affected, including candlesticks, ice-pails, coasters, tea equipage, salvers, dishes, épergnes and centre-pieces. Usually the work was pure rococo, but *rococo chinoiserie* is also found, especially on tea-caddies and occasionally on borders of salvers. Mention should also be made of what we might call the marine Rococo, possibly inspired by Nicholas Sprimont of Liège, silversmith and manager of the Chelsea porcelain factory from 1750 to 1770. The chief object used was, of course, the shell, which varied in shape and size according to whether it was for mere decoration, when it mingled with coral, seaweed, lobster claws, etc., or was for use as a container – as a salt-cellar, sauce-boat or soup tureen. In this case large decorative bivalves, such as the giant clams, were more suitable (Pl. 46A). In the latter years of George IV's reign John Bridge made several such pieces, including the great wine-cooler of 1829.

In view of all this evidence, it is clear that we must regard the continuance of Rococo into the early nineteenth century as an important part of the eclectic whole which we call Regency.

To return to the subject of classical *motifs* in Regency plate, a most necessary piece for the dining-hall, chiefly for purposes of display, was what the royal inventory lists under the heading 'Sideboard Dishes'. A prominent maker of such dishes in the early nineteenth century was William Pitts,[14] who executed several orders for the Prince of Wales and members of the nobility between 1810 and 1812. He also made eighteen dishes as

[12] See E. Alfred Jones, *Old Plate of J. Pierpont Morgan*, pl. XLV, and the Parke-Bernet Galleries sale catalogue, 1947, lot 474.

[13] i.e. George Anson (1697–1762), admiral, circumnavigator and reformer of the Navy.

[14] What relation he was, if any, to Thomas Pitts whose premises at 20, Air Street, Piccadilly, were taken over by Paul Storr in 1796, appears to be unknown.

his share in the enormous silver-gilt service ordered in 1814 by the Duke of Wellington on his appointment as Ambassador to Paris. He usually enriched the centre of his dishes with some familiar classical scene in high relief, such as the Feast of the Gods, the Battle of the Giants, the Rape of the Sabines, etc., and surrounded it with a broad border either of marine monsters and grotesque masks; or else, inappropriately enough, with a peaceful scene of swans and bulrushes (Pl. 46B). In one instance[15] he used small plaques bearing hall-marks of the time of Charles II depicting the tale of Daphne and Apollo, and enclosed them with wide scalloped borders divided into panels filled with various flowers embossed and frosted on a matted ground. In other cases, as with two pairs of dishes made for the Marquess of Londonderry in 1810 and 1817, the centre was embossed with a Tudor rose surrounded by sprays of flowers and foliage in straight or curved panels, the edges in all cases being scalloped. It is clear, then, that the dishes of William Pitts were not contemporary in design or feeling and tended to hark back to Caroline times (Pl. 46C). Such classical *motifs* as the Adam brothers had introduced obviously did not appeal to him, and he would have applauded the remark of George III recorded by Joseph Farington (*Diary*, 16 January 1800) to the effect that he considered that the Old School was not enough attended to and that the Adams had introduced too much of neatness and prettiness.

Moreover, it must be remembered that at the time there was very little Græco-Roman plate from which to copy, and the great classical hoards were yet to be discovered. Any delving undertaken was not into the hidden recesses of a cache, but rather into the pages of Ovid's *Metamorphoses*. In 1814 another sideboard circular dish appeared. It had a design by Thomas Stothard, R.A. In the centre is the 'Triumph of Bacchus and Ariadne', (Pl. 46D). The happy couple stand side by side in a chariot drawn by four prancing centaurs who are playing on musical instruments or wielding the cone-tipped *thyrsus*, which is also seen in the hands of both Bacchus and Ariadne. But it is the broad, flat rim that concerns us particularly, for here we see a strange assortment of Bacchic emblems of all kinds – the syrinx, *thyrsus*, *pedum*, tambourine, and over a dozen masks arranged both singly and in pairs. Some of them seem familiar, and are, in fact, taken from the famous Warwick Vase. Owing to persistent misconceptions regarding its age, history and facsimiles, a brief statement of facts concerning this vase may be of interest. It was found in 1770 with many other marbles, in a very bad state of repair, in the stagnant lake of Pantanello on that great site, fifteen miles east of Rome and two miles south-west of Tivoli (Tibur), known as the Villa Adriana, or Hadrian's Villa. The excavator was the Scottish painter Gavin Hamilton (1730–97), who with his partners, the unprincipled Thomas Jenkins, and Joseph Nollekens, an equally strange character, was buying and digging up statues, busts, vases, etc., to sell to British collectors after they had been restored by such men as Cavaceppi, Pacetti and Piranesi. Sir William Hamilton came from Naples to inspect the great vase and agreed to pay for its restoration, which was immediately put in hand. The work was done chiefly by Nollekens and Piranesi, and included the addition of several new heads – or masks, as they are usually called – and when completed Sir William tried in vain to sell it to the British Museum. He was, however, more successful with his nephew, George Greville, Earl of Warwick, and after a pedestal had been made for it with a pompous inscription explaining the large part Sir William had played in its restoration, it reached Warwick Castle in 1774 (Pl. 47A).

Four years later Piranesi published his important *Vasi, candelabri, cippi* ... , which included three excellent engravings of the Warwick Vase,[16] and in due course a copy of the large oblong folio found its way to Paul Storr's workshop, where it was discovered among his papers just prior to the last war, when it was destroyed with everything

[15] See E. Alfred Jones, *op. cit.*, p. 194 and Pl. XCVIII, and for other dishes by Pitts see p. 114, Pl. LVIII, and the two (unillustrated) pairs on p. 219.

[16] Among others it had two engravings of the Lante Vase, also found on the site of Hadrian's Villa, and having masks very similar to those on the Warwick Vase.

else. Storr at once realised how suitable was its shape for cups, soup-tureens and ice-pails, while the bearded heads, the lion's skin hanging from the projecting 'shelf', and the Bacchic emblems would provide classical *motifs* of which endless use could be made. The Prince Regent showed particular interest in the Warwick Vase and ordered a set of eight silver-gilt ice-pails of two sizes, the larger having basins for iced fruit. They were finished in 1812, and four concave fluted pedestals were added for the larger set in 1813 and 1816. In 1814 another four of smaller size were added, bringing the complete set up to the dozen.[17] Edward Lascelles, created Earl of Harewood in 1812, also ordered a pair with fruit dishes in that same year (see Pl. 47B).

Meanwhile in 1813 Lord Lonsdale (3rd Earl, 1787–1872) gave an order to Rundell, Bridge and Rundell to make a full-size facsimile of the vase in solid silver. The necessary set of wax models was duly made, but disagreement over the price caused the project to be abandoned. Some seven years later the firm decided to use these models in making a facsimile of the vase in bronze. Accordingly, they searched for an eminent bronze-founder and, failing to find one in England, entrusted the work to Charles Crozatier of Paris. Two copies were cast, and the work was excellently done. As soon as George IV saw them he purchased one for Windsor, where it is still to be seen on the steps leading from the Castle into the East Terrace garden. It is of interest to note that Crozatier also cast the large statue of *Hercules* for Windsor Castle which graces the same garden only a few yards from the Warwick Vase. The King seems to have had a particular liking for the vase, for in 1827 he had a reduced copy made which is now entered in the furniture inventory at the Palace as an 'indoor article'.

The other bronze facsimile found its way to the lawn outside the Senate House at Cambridge, to which university it was presented in 1842 by the Duke of Northumberland on his election as Chancellor. The only other facsimile of the Warwick Vase ever made was one cast in iron with a metallic 'finish' invented by its maker, Edward Thomason of Birmingham. Although many years were spent in perfecting the process, its success was only temporary, and after the 'bronze' had worn away it began to rust badly and is now in a sorry plight in the grounds of Aston Hall.

Copies of the Warwick Vase in varying sizes were made by firms other than Rundell's.

In some cases while the original shape was retained the heads were replaced by other ornamentation. Thus on the cup belonging to the Goldsmiths' Company oak foliage has been substituted. In other cases the central body has been left plain, sometimes to receive a crest or coat of arms. When used as a racing cup, horses' heads replace the Bacchic masks, as in the example at the Art Insitute of Chicago.

As to the date of the original marble vase, evidence, into which we cannot enter here, proves conclusively that those portions of the vase that are genuine are of Hadrianic age and must be assigned to the second century A.D. It should be realized that in concept and decoration the vase is Greek, not Roman, and was very possibly made by Greeks employed by Hadrian in Rome. His object was to demonstrate the importance of Greek idealism in art as a valuable possession for the Roman world. It was, in fact, an example of classical revival in Roman times. How strange that it was destined to play a similar role again – but this time in the nineteenth century.

As already mentioned, Philip Rundell had employed John Flaxman (1755–1826) as a designer for much of his neo-classical plate. In 1794 he had returned from his seven years' residence in Italy a famous man. He had not only made reductions and adaptations from the antique and executed numerous commissions for classical and emblematic groups, but had achieved an enormous success with his outline illustrations to the poems of Homer, Aeschylus and Dante, based on drawings on Greek vases.

One of the first commissions Flaxman received from Rundell was to design the Trafalgar Vases, of which sixty-six were made between 1804 and

[17] For further details see E. Alfred Jones, *op. cit.*, p. 208, and the 1914 Royal Inventory, pp. 22–3, where the dates differ in some details.

A

B

C

D

(A) and (B) PAUL STORR, 1812–13. The silver-gilt Theocritus Cup, designed by John Flaxman, R.A. Side showing two youths contending for the favour of a maiden. Height $9\frac{1}{2}$ in. Weight 90 oz. 15 dwt. *From the Royal Collection at Windsor Castle, by gracious permission of H.M. the Queen.* (C) and (D) PAUL STORR, 1817–18. Memorial two-handled cup depicting scenes from the Fields of Elysium, designed by John Flaxman, R.A. Height $9\frac{5}{16}$ in. Width $9\frac{7}{8}$ in. Weight 82 oz. 9 dwt. *Courtesy the Duke of Wellington, K.G.*

PLATE 49

(A) Peter Rundell, 1821–2. The Achilles Shield, designed by John Flaxman. *From the Royal Collection at Windsor Castle, by gracious permission of H.M. the Queen.*

(B) Peter Rundell, 1822–3. Silver-gilt Salver designed by Benedetto Pistrucci, with a central plaque of St George and the Dragon, and a border adapted from the procession of cavalry on the frieze of the Parthenon. Diam. 28 in. *Victoria and Albert Museum.*

(A) and (B) WILLIAM ELEY, 1798–9. Toasted-cheese dish. The hinged and removable cover is surmounted by a finial in the form of a viscount's coronet and cap. The interior is fitted with six small square dishes. The edge of the dish is gadrooned, and the reeded handles project horizontally. Engraved with the arms and crest of Lord Stewart. Width 12½ in. *Courtesy the Marquess of Londonderry.*

RICHARD COOKE, 1809–10. Tea-urn, with the lower part of the body and the lid gadrooned. Ovolo mouldings to the rims and circular base, reeded handles springing from lion-masks. Reeded spigot with ivory tap. On a square pedestal with scroll feet. Height 17 in. *Courtesy the Marquess of Londonderry.*

PLATE 52

PAUL STORR, 1814–15. Hot-water jug, with gadroon, leaf and shell ornament, vertical reeding on the base. The ivory handle springs from two serpents and rises to a single winged head. Engraved with the royal arms and those of Lord Stewart. Height 10 in. *Courtesy the Marquess of Londonderry.*

(A) Tea and coffee service in silver-gilt. Chased with an all-over floral pattern. The knops surmounting the larger covered pieces are in the form of the bust of a Chinaman. Mark: SH in an incurved oblong. London 1818–19. *Courtesy the Marquess of Londonderry.*

(B) PAUL STORR and PHILIP RUNDELL, 1818–19 and 1819–20. The Congress of Vienna gold inkstand, made from snuff-boxes presented by the various European countries to Lord Castlereagh. Length 17 in. Width $9\frac{5}{8}$ in. Weight 145 oz. *Courtesy the Marquess of Londonderry.*

PLATE 54

(A) PAUL STORR, 1821–22. A selection of the silver-gilt altar plate presented by H.R.H. Frederick, Duke of York, to St Pancras Church, London.

(B) HANNAH NORTHCOTE, 1805–06. Inkstand of 'Treasury' pattern, with borders of reed-and-tie design. The top hinged, with a central handle, and the interior divided, one half fitted with two cut-glass containers for ink and sand. Engraved with the arms of Lord Stewart. Length 12 in. *Courtesy the Marquess of Londonderry.*

(A) The Galvanic Goblet. This shows the first electro-gilding in England. *From the Royal Collection at Windsor Castle, by gracious permission of H.M. the Queen.*

(B) HANNAH NORTHCOTE, 1805–06. Two-handled Vase and cover; reed-and-tie ornamentation on the handle, rim, base and edge of the cover which is surmounted by a Viscount's coronet and cap. Engraved with the royal arms and those of Lord Stewart. *Courtesy the Marquess of Londonderry.*

PLATE 56

1809. He also executed several important orders for George IV, as Prince of Wales, Prince Regent and King. In 1809 he designed the pair of massive candelabra, five feet in height, one representing the Three Graces gathering the apples of the Hesperides (Pl. 48A), the other Mercury presenting Bacchus to the Nymphs. Each candelabrum has three double and six single branches for candles, and it is between these two tiers that the classical subjects are modelled. Below the lower tier three piping fauns sit on the projecting base of a truncated column which forms part of the central support. According to the royal copy of the 1914 inventory a total sum of £4,003 15*s*. was paid for the pair in 1811. An interesting item, formerly in the possession of the Prince Regent and now in the collection of Charles Oman, is a pair of jugs, said to have been designed by Flaxman from Roman vases, to which spouts, handles and lids were added. They are quite plain, except for bearded heads affixed beneath the spouts and handles. They were made by Paul Storr in 1810–11 (Pl. 48B). One of the most notable Flaxman pieces, made in 1812, is the so-called Theocritus Cup, the subjects on which are taken from his first Idyll. One side shows two youths contending for the favour of a maiden (Pl. 49B); the other depicts an aged fisherman dragging his net, while above a boy squats on a rock intent on making a cricket-cage [?] to the advantage of a fox who sniffs at his wallet placed onthe rock behind him (Pl. 49A). Both subjects are framed above and laterally by vine-branches and grapes. Although the cup is formed in the shape of a Greek Krater, Theocritus' original description clearly refers to a rustic bowl of Kylix shape. Another two-handled Krater, based by Flaxman on the Theocritus cup, was commissioned in 1817 by Mrs Saltren, sister of Lady Manvers, as a memorial of Charles, 1st Earl Manvers[18] who had left her a legacy in his will. Its chief interest lies in the fact that the scenes are not taken direct from Greek mythology, but were apparently designed by Flaxman to represent in Homeric idiom the Fields of Elysium to which favoured heroes are translated by the Gods (see Pls. 46C and D).

Of interest in the history of goldsmiths' work is the little gilt cup on a slender stem made in 1814 and decorated from designs by Flaxman with three floating figures of the hours, linked by a floral garland, with a chaste ivy scroll on the foot. It bears the badge of the Prince of Wales, and underneath are the words 'Galvanic Goblet' (Pl. 56A). Thus we have here a very early example of electro-gilding, for the introduction of electro-plating is usually attributed to Arthut Smee in 1840, when it was immediately taken up by Elkington & Co. It is not known if the experiment was suggested by Storr, who made the cup, but this appears to be the only article produced by the process. Of considerable beauty is a Krater-shaped two-handled vase at Windsor made by John Bridge in 1826–7 from a design by Flaxman[19] based on Hesiod's description of the Gold and Silver Ages in his *Works and Days* (lines 110–39). One side is in white silver, the other in gilt. The subjects of the two Ages are in rectangular panels, slightly tapering with the lines of the vase. The lower portion is engraved with a Greek running scroll pattern, while at the base, and also on each side below the handles, is a shell ornament. It is engraved with the Garter and motto. Height, $5\frac{1}{2}$ in.; 7 in. at mouth and $3\frac{3}{4}$ in. at base. Perhaps the most famous creation of Flaxman was the Shield of Achilles designed in 1818 to the order of Rundell, Bridge and Rundell. The subject was taken from the XVIIIth book of the *Iliad*, where from line 478 to the end is a detailed description of the great shield made for Achilles by Hephaestus. After the general design had been modelled it was then cast in plaster, and finished by cutting away. The silver-gilt shields were made from this model, the first of which was purchased

[18] Major-General Lord Charles Wellesley, second son of the Great Duke, married the only daughter of the third son of Earl Manvers, and so the cup has become the property of the present Duke of Wellington.

[19] See E. Alfred Jones, *op. cit.*, p. 108 and Pl. LV. Plaques of the two designs are in the John Soane Museum. They were given by Flaxman's sister-in-law Maria Denman in 1836–7. There is also a plaque, with the figures reversed, at University College, London. See *A New Description of Sir John Soane's Museum*, 1955, p. 11.

by the Prince Regent and displayed at the Coronation banquet in 1821. Other copies went to the Duke of York, Lord Lonsdale and the Duke of Northumberland. Bronze versions were also cast, and Rundell presented one to each university. In 1834 the firm gave the cast to Sir John Soane. The diameter of the shield is 37 in. and the weight 660 oz. It bears the maker's mark of Philip Rundell and the date-letter for 1821–2. In his work on Flaxman, W. G. Constable describes the shield as undoubtedly a most skilful piece of work, exhibiting all Flaxman's powers of combining many figures into a harmonious, smoothly flowing design which served Wedgwood so well. But, he adds, like the illustrations to the *Iliad* and *Odyssey*, it expresses nothing of the full-bodied, heroic quality of the Homeric warriors (Pl. 50A).

With it we can compare the 28-in. silver-gilt salver designed by Benedetto Pistrucci, the famous gem-engraver and medallist, also for Philip Rundell. In 1820–1 he had engraved the coronation medal for George IV, as well as the coins of the early part of his reign. In the centre of the salver is a fine relief of St George and the dragon, such as had appeared on the sovereigns. The border is adapted from the frieze of the Parthenon – the famous Elgin marbles. The rim is a design of anthemions and ovolos. It bears the date-letter for 1822–3, and is in the Victoria and Albert Museum (Pl. 50B).

Fig. 2. Wine label, modelled with a design of grapes and vine leaves and a lion's mask. Paul Storr, 1811–12. *Victoria and Albert Museum.*

Each year a Regency Exhibition is held at the Royal Pavilion, Brighton. One of the chief attractions is always the wonderful display of Regency plate in the Banqueting Room, where the table is laid for twenty-four guests, reproducing the well-known painting in Nash's *The Royal Pavilion*, 1826. In past years H.R.H. the Princess Royal and the Earl of Harewood have lent a large portion of plate, with loans from many other famous collections, including that of the Marquess of Londonderry. The 1957 Exhibition, however, displayed all the Londonderry plate of the Regency period, which includes many magnificent pieces, as well as the famous gold inkstand with its great historical associations – to be described in detail shortly.

Much of the silver was purchased by Charles, 3rd Marquis of Londonderry (1778–1854), who, as General Sir Charles Stewart, served with the Duke of Wellington in the Peninsular campaign. In 1814, as Ambassador to the Emperor of Austria, he was in Vienna during the Congresses. Britain was represented by Lord Stewart's half-brother, the famous Viscount Castlereagh. Several pieces of his plate are shown here. Of the non-Ambassadorial plate, many fine examples were purchased by the second wife of Lord Stewart, Francis Anne (1800–65), daughter of Sir Henry Vane-Tempest, Bart.

One of the earliest pieces to fall within our period is the toasted-cheese dish made by William Eley in 1798–9 (Pl. 51). Its beauty lies chiefly in its plainness, the only decoration being the gadrooned edge to the dish and the horizontal reeded handles. The cushioned cover, hinged to the body, but removable, is surmounted by a baron's coronet and cap upon a cushion, and is engraved with the arms and crest of Lord Stewart. It is 12½ in. wide. The interior is fitted with six small square dishes. With this type we can compare that at Brasenose College, Oxford, made by Storr in 1815–16, which has a small reeded handle on the cover and a pear-wood handle fitting into a protruding socket at the back. In this case there are twelve cheese containers. The humble wine-label is well represented in a fine set of nine in silver-gilt made by Benjamin and James

Smith in 1809–10, with a design of grapes and vine-leaves (cf. also Fig. 2). The same design was also made by Digby Scott and Benjamin Smith. There is an example of 1806–7 in the Cropper collection in the Victoria and Albert Museum, and another in a private collection.[20] We pass on now to a typical example of a Regency tea-urn (Pl. 52). It stands on a plain-square plinth, the lower part of the body being gadrooned, as is also the domed cover surmounted by a floral and reeded finial of acorn shape. Reeded handles each side spring from pairs of lions' heads. The reeded spigot has an ivory tap. It is 17 in. high, and was made by Richard Cooke in 1809–10.[21] Of light and graceful appearance is the pair of silver-gilt fruit-baskets and stands made by J. W. Story and W. Elliott in 1811–12. Both body and stand are of wire-work through which vine tendrils meander, bunches of grapes and vine-leaves completing the decoration. The edge is in the form of twisted rope-work, showing plain and striated sections alternately. The solid central bases are engraved with a marquis's coronet and Londonderry monogram. The base of the stand is formed of rococo volutes (Fig. 3).

We turn now to a fine pair of silver-gilt tureens, covers and stands made by Storr in 1813–14. They are decorated with the anthemion and lotus design, a great favourite of the period. The plain domed covers are surmounted by a winged dragon *statant*, the Stewart crest, while applied plaques each side bear the royal and Stewart arms respectively. The stands have small handles and lion-pad feet with water-leaves above (Fig. 4). A pair of matching ice-pails were made at the same time, with the anthemion and lotus design round the upper part of the bodies. Reeded handles spring from lions' masks. The rim and bases are gadrooned. Another typical Storr piece, made in 1814–15, is a hot-water jug, 10 in. high, with gadrooning on

Fig. 3. Silver-gilt fruit basket with stand. Of wire work decorated with grapes and vines, twisted rim showing plain and twisted sections alternately. The solid central base is engraved with the Londonderry coronet and monogram. Diameter 7½ ins. J. W. Story and W. Elliott, 1811–12. *From the collection of the Marquis of Londonderry.*

Fig. 4. Silver-gilt tureen with cover and stand. Enriched with palmettes and lotus ornament and gadrooning. Applied plaques bear the royal arms one side and those of Stewart on the other. The covers are surmounted by handles in the form of the Stewart crest, *a winged dragon statant.* Height of tureen 13 ins. Width of dishes 19½ ins. Paul Storr, 1813–14. *From the collection of the Marquis of Londonderry.*

[20] See *Journal Wine-Label Circle*, No. 3, December 1952, pp. 27 and 28.

[21] The earlier type of tea-urn, which had succeeded the tea-kettle about 1760, was pear-shaped, followed by the classical vase-shape of the Adam period. The type shown here was greatly favoured in the Regency period, many examples being made by Paul Storr.

the lower part of the body and a guilloche band round the neck (Pl. 53). An ivory handle, twisted near the middle, springs from the bodies of two serpents rising to a single winged head which rests against the neck. The broad spout is enriched with an anthemion on the under side. Of interest is the silver-gilt tea, coffee and breakfast service made in 1818–19 by an unidentified goldsmith whose initials are SH in an incurved oblong (Pl. 54A). The set is chased with an all-over floral pattern. The knobs surmounting the larger covered pieces are in the form of the bust of a Chinaman. The set comprises a kettle with stand and spirit lamp, a coffee-pot, two sizes of teapots, a sugar basin, milk jug, egg-stand, toast-rack and two small salts.

Quite apart from its value and rarity, the solid gold inkstand made out of twenty-two gold diamond-studded portrait snuff-boxes is of historical significance. It was presented to Lord Castlereagh after the signing of the various treaties both before and after the Congress of Vienna. As can be seen from the illustration (Pl. 54B), the inkstand is oblong in shape with rounded corners, and supported on four acanthus scrolled legs with lateral volutes to which bunches of grapes and a central shell ornament have been added. The rim is enriched with a shell and foliage design, while the handles at either end are formed of acanthus leaves in two sections, the voluted terminals of which meet in the middle. Below, the plain sides are covered with arms which will be noted further when we discuss the engraving. From the centre of the stand, and of the same oblong form with rounded corners, rises a plain platform with slightly concave sides, while each side is a round-ended channel for writing accessories. On the platform is the quill-cleaner in the centre, with the ink-pot one side and the sand caster[22] the other. The quill cleaner, filled with small lead shot, and also used as a pen-holder, is in the form of a bunch of lanceolate leaves, interspersed here and there with some campanulate plant like the Canterbury Bell. This bunch of foliage, which spreads out and hangs down at the top, is secured below by a calyx of acanthus leaves, while others are spread out on the platform as a base, the ends curling upwards. The two containers, which match exactly, have plain lobed surfaces and rest on four scroll feet surmounted by sprays of oak-leaves which spread out over most of the lower part of the bodies. The plain domed covers are edged with a shell and foliage design similar to that round the rim of the main body of the stand. A Viscount's coronet and cap acts as a finial, below which is engraved Lord Castlereagh's crest within the Garter motto – he had been invested on 28 June 1814. Along the front concave side of the central platform is an inscription which reads as follows:

*This Inkstand is Composed of the Gold taken*
*from the Portrait Snuff Boxes which were*
*presented by the SOVEREIGNS whose Arms*
*are engraven hereon.*
*To Viscount Castlereagh*
*upon the Signature of the Several Treaties concluded*
*in the Years 1813, 1814 & 1815.*

On the plain surface near each handle are engraved within laurel wreaths the arms of Russia, France, Austria and Prussia. Round the sides are twelve

[22] This is a more correct expression than *pounce-box*, for the use of pounce, powered gum sandarac (*callitris quadrivalvis*), or shells of cuttle-fish, was succeeded by that of sand, as being more easily obtainable. *Pounce*, derived from *pūmex*, pumice-stone, was originally used to prepare the surface of parchment for writing. Its absorbent nature also prevented the spreading of ink over an erasure or on unsized paper. Thus *pounce*, first applied to powdered pumice-stone, was also used for any absorbent powder, and even for powder used on a lady's hair. Several writers on silver say that the pounce-box or sand-caster were used prior to the introduction of blotting-paper. This is certainly not true. Blotting-paper was invented at least as early as the fifteenth century and has actually been found in account books of that date. We may well ask, then, why the sand-caster has persisted to quite modern times, and no use appears to have been made of blotting-paper. One can only guess the reason, but it may be because large pieces of coarse grey unsized paper appeared more suitable to the pages of a ledger, than to the sophisticated elegance of a silver inkstand, or standish – a word the etymology of which has never been satisfactorily explained. Whether the pouncet-box of *Henry IV*, *Part I*, Act 1, Sc. iii, 38 means a box for pounce or a pierced (i.e. pounced) box is still undecided.

other coats of arms, also within laurel wreaths. Those in front, reading from left to right, are Papal States, Bavaria, Portugal, Saxony, Sardinia and Hanover. Those at the back are Sweden, Wurtemberg, Naples, Spain, Denmark and Netherlands. At each end between the two sets are, respectively, the royal arms and the Castlereagh arms. Applied Tudor roses decorate the rounded corners. The inkstand was made by Rundell, Bridge and Rundell, but, as its various parts contain two sets of makers' mark, some explanation is needed. On unscrewing the wooden base which is fitted underneath, we find Rundell's Latin inscription with a full set of marks, including that of Philip Rundell and the date-letter for 1819–20. His mark also appears on the top of the stand without date, and on the inner lids of both inkpot and sand-caster with the date-letter for 1818–19. But the quill-cleaner, ink-pot and sand-caster, with the outer lids of the two latter objects are all stamped with Paul Storr's mark for 1818–19. The explanation of this seems to be as follows. We may take it that the whole inkstand was made by Storr, and it was perhaps the last thing made for Rundell, as he left the firm in 1819. This fact led Rundell to take out a mark for himself, which he did on 4 March 1819. There was just time for him to use it on the inkstand, a thing he must have made up his mind to do, because the goldsmiths' year starts on 29 May and as the 'c' for 1818–19 did not end until 28 May 1819, he was able to stamp those parts already done with his own new mark and the 1818–19 date-letter. The rest of the inkstand was finished the following year and naturally was stamped with the 'd' for 1819–20 – again with Rundell's mark. It should be realized that Rundell was not a working goldsmith at all, but a diamond merchant and jeweller. Storr never worked for the firm again until after Rundell's death in 1827.

In the MS. account of the firm by George Fox, one of their employees, there is an interesting and amusing section (cols. 85–8) about the inkstand. He tells us that when the snuff-boxes were broken up the diamonds 'were employed partly for Her Ladyship's jewels and partly for His Lordship's Star Badge, etc. etc.' The average value of the boxes was put at £1,000, and some of the gold therefrom was used on his sword, the rest went to the inkstand. He relates that the breaking up of gold presentation snuff-boxes became such a regular practice that Joseph Hume raised the whole question in the House. Fox then explains that when a snuff-box, supplied by their firm, was presented to a Foreign Ambassador it was immediately sold back to them, and was thus ready to be sold to Downing Street again. In some cases the same box was sold six times over. 'This was no bad means of making money!' concludes the sly Fox!

Another inkstand worth noting, if only to demonstrate the persistence of a type familiar from the days of Queen Anne, is one of the so-called 'Treasury' pattern, the characteristic feature of which is its division into two equal rectangular sections, each with a flat lid operating from a central joint. One of these divisions held the inkpot and sand-caster, often with additional partitions for wafers, etc. The other division was to hold quills, lead pens (pencils), sealing-wax, knives and so forth. In the offices of the Privy Council there are eight inkstands of this type, three being by Charles Shelley, 1685, one by 'M' of the same date, and four of 1702 by Philip Rollos. They have central hinged handles and four solid cast feet of foliage. In the Treasury are three more of 1685, one by Shelley and the other two by Francis Garthorne.[23] Reference should also be made to the beautiful one by de Lamerie originally belonging to Sir Robert Walpole,[24] and a very handsome plain one formerly the property of Lord Chesterfield of *Letters* fame.[25] The type is also known as the 'ambassador' inkstand, owing to the convenience with which such a flat object could be carried about. The Londonderry example (Pl. 55B) was made by Hannah Northcote in 1805–6. It is quite plain except for reed-and-tie borders, which also appear on the four feet. There is a

[23] See the pamphlet by E. Alfred Jones, *Catalogue of the Silver Plate in the Offices of the Privy Council and H.M. Treasury*, 1932.

[24] E. Alfred Jones, *Connoisseur*, September 1936, pp. 140–1.

[25] Helen Comstock, *Connoisseur*, April 1940, p. 165.

hinged central handle. One of the divisions contains a cut-glass inkpot and sand-caster. One lid is engraved with the royal arms, and the other with those of Lord Stewart. The breadth is 12 in.

Although a very large proportion of the plate which we have been discussing comes from royal or noble collections, much of it being gilt and of a ceremonial and official massiveness and grandeur, we must not forget that the amount of 'ordinary' plate being bought by the prosperous landed and mercantile classes – both in London and the provinces – was enormous.

The outstanding name in the history of factory-made plate, for either completed articles or component parts, is undoubtedly that of Matthew Boulton of Birmingham. After his success in the manufacturing of Sheffield plate, and adopting the use of the stirling 'silver thread' edge, he decided to turn his attention to silver plate. It was merely a change of material; the same machines, designs and workmen could be used as with Sheffield plate. The screw- or fly-press was capable of cutting out thin metal with great rapidity and forcing it into any required shape. Repetitive patterns in the flat could assume a circular or oval form when bent to the required shape and soldered, thus providing the carcasses for salts, mustard-pots, coasters, the lids of casters and many other objects. At first Boulton was faced with the trouble and risk of sending all his silver articles to Chester, York or London to be hall-marked. With Sheffield the distances were not quite so far, but both Sheffield and Manchester applied for separate Assay offices, which, owing largely to the tireless efforts of Boulton, they obtained in 1773. After this the industry increased immensely, as the lists of goldsmiths entered at both Assay offices testify.

Apart from salts, peppers, mustard-pots and casters, the types of plate most in demand included tureens, vegetable dishes, entrée dishes, coasters, sauce-boats, cruets, toast-racks, wine funnels, cake-baskets, tea and coffee services, salvers, waiters, candelabra, candlesticks, inkstands and all kinds of flat plate, including fish-slices, marrow scoops, etc. To a lesser extent can be added large centre-pieces, épergnes, complete dinner services, punch-bowls, wine-coolers, argyles, tea-urns and lamps. Of small articles we may mention skewers, caddy-spoons, wine-labels, strainers, vinaigrettes, snuff-boxes, table-bells, tobacco-stoppers, etc. Many of these display the most exquisite workmanship. Take, for instance, that charming trifle – the vinaigrette,[26] the very symbol of the Age of Elegance. A later development of the pomander, the dry-spice container, the vinaigrette, as the name clearly indicates, is a container for aromatic vinegar 'to correct the bad Quality of the Air'. The specially fine compact little sponge, which soaked up the aromatic liquid, was covered by a pierced grill on which the goldsmith lavished all his skill, producing charming designs of birds, flowers, musical instruments and even noble country houses.

As a separate entity, the vinaigrette dates from sometime between 1775 and 1790, and we find earlier specimens chased with typical classic *motifs*, such as the floral swag, the urn, etc. But every technique of the craftsmen was employed on these little objects – different colours of gold, sometimes severely plain and solid, at other times inlaid with precious stones, or fashioned from agate, bloodstone, cornelian or topaz. The designs tended to persist with little change, but if it were necessary to say which typified the Regency, one would indicate the plain engine-turned specimens. As to the makers, we find that the great majority are Birmingham craftsmen, thus indicating that after the Assay office had been established there in 1773, the vinaigrette was one of those miniature pieces which especially appealed to them. Such names as John Bettridge, Francis Clark, John Lawrence and Co., Matthew Linwood, Samuel Pemberton, John Shaw and John Turner may be mentioned. Several London goldsmiths, such as William Abdy, Robert Burton, Samuel Massey, T. Phipps and E. Robinson, are known as makers of both vinaigrettes and wine-labels. As so many of the articles mentioned above are of a type in constant use at the time, we must not expect their designs to conform to a single contemporary style, but to reflect

[26] See L. G. G. Ramsey, *Connoisseur*, October 1956, pp. 95–9, and Eileen Ellenbogen, *English Vinaigrettes*, Cambridge, 1956.

rather the personal taste of the owner. We have seen how both rococo and neo-classic designs were popular in Regency times, and it is no easy matter to recognize a typical Regency piece – whatever that is – among ordinary family plate.

There are cases, however, when the 'latest fashion' in silverware declares itself clearly, as for instance when an order is given for an 'up-to-date' set of spoons and forks, or, on the other hand, for something rather unusual in, say, tea-urns or lamps. Just as the age of the lovely Queen Anne tea-pot had long since passed, so, too, the beautiful Old English pattern[27] of spoons and forks had given place to what Jackson calls 'that type of nineteenth-century florid vulgarity known as the King's Pattern'. Its chief characteristic was, of course, the shouldered stem, which had first appeared somewhat unnoticed on double-drop and bright-cut spoons in the middle of the eighteenth century, to which the name of 'fiddle-pattern' was given. If quite plain, the type was simply called 'fiddle-pattern'; if it had reeded borders it was known as the 'Queen's pattern'; but with the additional ornamentation of shells and anthemions it became the 'King's pattern'. Occasionally, as in the two great sets by Paul Storr at Windsor, further embossing was added down the stems. The first of these sets, consisting of over 1,300 pieces, was made between 1811 and 1814, and is known as the 'Boar Hunt and Mask' pattern, while the second set, of slightly earlier date, runs to nearly 2,500 pieces and is known as the 'Honeysuckle' pattern. The line drawings in Fig. 5, taken from a photograph in the special royal inventory at Windsor, shows some of this latter pattern.

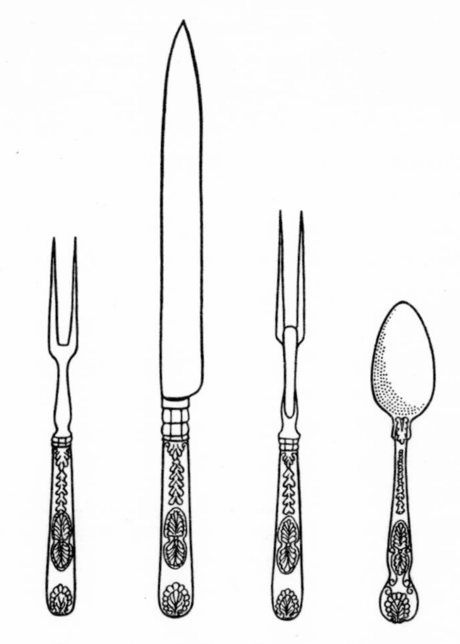

Fig. 5. Examples of the 'Honeysuckle' type of flat plate made by Paul Storr between 1808 and 1812 for the future George IV. *From the Royal Collection at Windsor Castle. Reproduced by gracious permission of Her Majesty the Queen.*

The only remaining piece of plate we need mention is the lamp. As we should expect, the neo-classical lamp was based on the Roman lamps such as we find reproduced in the works of Piranesi, Tatham and Hope. There is, however, a most original pair at Windsor made by Storr in 1817. They represent a phœnix rising from the ashes, on rocky plinths, and were intended to burn naphtha,

Fig. 6. One of a pair of phoenix lamps intended to burn naphtha. Paul Storr, 1817. *From the Royal Collection at Windsor Castle. Reproduced by gracious permission of Her Majesty the Queen.*

[27] Oman describes this pattern as more attractive and more usable than any other type produced since 1660.

which at the time was an early example of the use of such fuel for domestic lighting (Fig. 6).

In conclusion, it will have been noticed that we have confined ourselves entirely to secular plate. Ecclesiastical plate undergoes few changes, but in the case of St Pancras Church, London, which was built by the Inwoods on Athenian models, it was necessary to have plate to match. This was made possible through the generosity of H.R.H. Frederick, Duke of York, who commissioned Paul Storr, the greatest figure in Regency goldsmithing, to make a set of fifteen pieces, which he executed with his usual artistry, as our Pl. 55A testifies.

Typographical borders from the 1821 Specimen Book of Vincent Figgins. The top one shows an acanthus, the bottom a lotus flower design.

*Right*. Vinaigrettes dated between 1810 and 1830 from the Ellenbogen Collection, London.

# *Earthenware, China and Glass*

# Earthenware, China and Glass

G. BERNARD HUGHES

The Countess of Granville in the autumn of 1810 wrote: 'Dinner [for the earl and herself] consisted of soup, fish, fricassée of chicken, cutlets, veal, hare, vegetables of all kinds, tart, melon, pineapple, grapes, peaches, nectarines with wine in proportion. Six servants wait upon us, a gentleman-in-waiting and a fat old housekeeper hovering round the door. Four hours later the door opens and in is pushed a supper of the same proportion.'

Silver, plate, china and cut-glass for such a meal was equally profuse: when guests were present the amount tabled was prodigious. Butlers now stored their silver in strong rooms, although in old-fashioned establishments the plate was returned to chests deposited in the trunk room adjoining the master's bedroom.

China and glass not in daily use was stored in the china closet. Tiers of shelves to the ceiling displayed gleaming surfaces of glaze painted with rich, lustrous enamels. Many of these treasures were, of course, inherited: soft paste porcelains potted at Bow, Chelsea, Derby and Worcester, and fine earthenwares from Wedgwood and Spode. By 1810 these had been joined by bone china and the so-called semi-porcelains such as stone china (Pl. 57B) and felspar porcelain (Pl. 57A). These were fashionably enamelled with the family coat-of-arms in full colours, or might display fantastic birds with long tails and crested top-knots, among flowers of impossible colour and form; fierce dragons with knobbly claws and rolling eyes; rivers thickly sprinkled with tiny, fairy boats; English scenes and mansions among homely meadows and heavy trees. Every room in the house, too, was garnished with china, ranging from vestibule vases, capacious fish globes, and pastille burners to toilet sets in the dressing rooms.

It has become customary to decry English ceramics of the early nineteenth century. Those who do so fail to appreciate their technical excellence. Improved methods produced stronger and more colourful ware capable of giving enduring service yet within purse reach of the general public. The pottery industry was revolutionized and Britain dominated world markets for the next hundred years.

Bone china (Pls. 58A, B, and 59B) was the most important of the new ceramics, replacing as it did the soft porcelains. It was brought to perfection by Josiah Spode in the early 1790's, and ledgers still in existence prove it to have been on sale in 1794 under the name of British Cornish china. The term china was eventually deemed unsatisfactory, as for almost half a century it had been associated in the public mind with the more fragile soft porcelains. Josiah Spode II, then, in 1810, under pressure from his partner William Copeland, renamed their British Cornish china, calling it Stoke porcelain. When in 1814 Spode (Pls. 57B; 59A, B; 60A, C) was appointed potter to the Prince of Wales he was cited as 'Potter and Manufacturer of Stoke Porcelain'. Bone china is a late Victorian trade name.

Domestic ware in bone china gave enduring service, and its glaze was such that overglaze colours sank into it permanently and did not flake. Enamelling became a less hazardous process and the intense fusion produced a less painted-looking finish.

Greater brilliance in the hue of the enamel was possible after 1812 when Samuel Walker's high temperature enamelling kiln replaced the small box muffle in which ware had been baked without exposing it to direct contact with the flames. Hitherto it had been customary for purchasers to select their patterns from the china-seller's sheets of hand-painted designs. The dealer then commissioned an independent enameller to decorate the service, which had been bought from the potter in the white. The introduction of the enamelling kiln now meant that much more domestic ware was painted in the factory than formerly.

Oriental designs adapted to the English taste were ornamenting bone china table services by 1805 and had become the height of fashion by 1810. If analysed such patterns may appear more essentially Chinese than Japanese, although a superficial resemblance to Imari porcelain has led to their classification as Japanese. Less numerous on table services were decorations of the Kakiemon type. The Shanghai pattern by Spode was of Chinese inspiration and copied by other Staffordshire potters using the old muffle enamelling process on bone china badly flawed with specks. Although the Chinese influence on table services declined during the 1820's there was a distinct vogue for patterns in the Imari style, with flowers and shrubbery in vivid colours surrounded by gilt tracery.

Hard, translucent felspar porcelain, again a Spode invention, enriched many a nobleman's table in the form of magnificent dinner services in which the centre of each piece expansively displayed in full colours the owner's coat of arms (Pl. 57A) and the rims were radiant with heavily gilded ornament. Sometimes an old gold colour replaced gilding, its effect being considered more in harmony with the enamelled armorial design. Dessert services in felspar porcelain might bear painted landscapes with titles, and borders of conventional flowers. Stone china (Pl. 57B), a felspathic earthenware of delicate grey-blue body which emitted a clear ring when lightly tapped, was ornamented with old Chinese designs. Extensive table services in this ware were in great demand.

Families at this time were large and entertainment lavish. Dinner services were standardized to twelve covers, but frequently extended to thirty-six, with thirty serving dishes for game and meat. Plates for the three main courses were of the same size and the service also included soup plates. Dinner and dessert services combined became fashionable, the pieces matching. These ranged from soup and vegetable tureens to shell-shaped dessert dishes and dessert plates. The old practice of serving dessert on ware of a different type and pattern continued, however. A typical family service contained a pair of tazze, four dishes and twelve plates.

Special services were evolved for supper and from about 1815 were made up of about 130 separate pieces: four fan-shaped dishes and covers, four square dishes and covers, one octagonal dish, liner and cover, two sauce tureens and stands, with ladles, two oval egg-stands each with twelve egg cups, six octagonal meat dishes, four oval dishes, a salad bowl, twenty-four each of soup, dinner and dessert plates. The combined tea and coffee set with but a single set of saucers now gave way to one with a full complement of saucers.

The late Georgian period was the heyday of blue-and-white transfer-printed domestic ware (Pls. 57C and 59A), from table services to toilet accessories, in bone china and in earthenware. The majority were made in Staffordshire, many at Leeds and on Tyneside. Fine tone gradations were achieved by 1810 by combining line and stipple engraving on a single copper-plate. Skilful use of light and shade resulted for the first time in well-balanced pictures, clear in detail, yet covering every part of the ware, thus concealing surface flaws in the fabric which in consequence was of a cheaper quality than that needed for enamel painted decoration.

Blues became more brilliant from about 1816 when the close of the Napoleonic wars made it possible once more to import fine Saxon cobalt. Shades of blue were now given such trade names as Canton, zaffres, glowing blue, willow blue, mazarine, and flower-blue. The war-time English cobalt blues and synthetic blues continued in use but only on the cheapest earthenwares. In 1828 it was discovered that certain crushed enamel colours mixed with barbados tar would, like cobalt, print direct to the fired but unglazed ware known as the biscuit, without distorting during glazing. These were various tints of green, red and yellow, but although they had a few years of popularity they failed to oust Staffordshire blue.

Transferred subjects had been derived formerly from Chinese blue and white. These gave way from about 1810 in favour of purely English subjects. Dinner and tea services presented the English scene with imaginative enthusiasm – the beauty spots, cathedrals, cities and resorts then considered to qualify as picturesque views. Staffordshire blue was not intended for use on formal occasions, but for daily service in the home, its pattern being protected by the glaze.

Each flat piece in a Staffordshire blue table service, every dish, plate, sauce-boat and gravy-tray displayed a picture. Each piece of hollow-ware, whether jug, vegetable dish or sugar-bowl, carried three or four differing scenes on its inner and outer surfaces. At least twelve pictures belonging to a series would decorate a table service, but as many as seventy-two have been noted on a dinner service illustrating the travels of Dr Syntax. Between 1816 and 1830 the list of potters specializing in blue-printed ware exceeded fifty, in addition to the transfer-print departments operated by several of the great potters.

A glimpse of the large amount of miscellaneous ware that might be stored in the china closet was extracted from the Spode ledgers of this period by Arthur Hayden. Included were artichoke cups, asparagus trays, broth bowls, butter tubs and stands, card racks, chamber candlesticks with extinguishers, cheese dishes, cheese toasters, chestnut vases, chicken tureens, custard cups, cylinder pin-cases to screw, ice-pails, inkstands and pen-trays, match-pots, mugs, radish trays, roll-trays, root-dishes, rouge-pots, salad bowls, sandwich sets, scent-jars, snuff-boxes, snuffer trays, steak-dishes with compartments, strawberry baskets, sugar boxes, supper plates, syrup pots, toast-racks, turtle pans, violet baskets and wafer boxes. Punch and toddy bowls ranging from two gallon to quart capacity were bought in matching sets. It was customary for these drinks to be served hot, hence the tall foot rim for protecting the table surface from heat.

Ironstone china, patented by Charles James Mason in 1813, was a hard earthenware capable of development far beyond the range of table-ware, for which it was eminently suitable. Sets of bedposts, enormous vases for drawing-rooms and vestibules, huge wine cooling cisterns and goldfish globes were made as well as fireplaces in full- and half-size. Fireplaces, typically, were finished with a white-glazed ground enriched with trailing leaf-patterns in gold and panels of flower and foliage sprays in pink, puce, pale green, apple green, vermilion, blue. Panel ornament differed in each; flowers included peonies, full blown roses, hawthorn sprigs and daisies, all with their foliage, as well as dragonflies, butterflies and other flying creatures. It was Mason who evolved the celebrated jugs which bear his name and appear to have been in unceasing production since. These octagonal jugs with snake handles and colours of sparkling brilliance were issued in sets of a dozen sizes. Their low price precluded high quality in decoration and finish.

The Napoleonic style in ornamental ceramics is recorded in pattern books of 1810, with such features as the plinth base with lion-paw feet. Details were sumptuously gilded, often with scroll-work in low relief, as evolved in 1802 by Henry Daniel. Solid grounds in burnished or matt gold, and grounds of gold scale on blue and of stippled gold were fashionable. Increased domestic illumination from oil-lamp and gas-chandelier made the most of this brilliance. The revived Rococo style of the silversmiths was adopted by Coalport and Rockingham and within five years every leading potter had followed their example.

Pictorial reserves (Pls. 58A and B; 59A and B), from about 1815, tended towards the English rural style with such border *motifs* as birds, landscapes, flowers, fruit, shells and feathers. These were usually painted on the white against such ground colours as dark and scale blues, apple green, yellowish green, deep yellow, canary yellow, greyish turquoise, marbled brown, marbled blue, crimson, salmon, lavender and cane colour. Designs favoured half a century earlier by Chelsea and Worcester were revived, and much of this bone china now masquerades as soft porcelain in the cabinets of collectors. The claret ground with bird decoration in gold, a Chelsea style, was widely copied, the finest coming from Spode, but even his ground colour failed to reach Chelsea's full splendour until the 1830's. Spode did succeed, however, in reproducing the *gros bleu* of Dr Wall's Worcester, although in the salmon-scale ground his blue was livelier than the original.

George IV as Regent and as King was an extravagant collector of pre-Revolution Sèvres porcelain. He established a vogue that made the French ware so scarce that by 1815 it was almost unobtainable. The trade in Sèvres for decorating the home became so profitable that any expedient was used for acquiring supplies. These was a demand, long in vain, for an English potter capable of reproducing old-style Sèvres complete with the famous double-L monogram. In 1825 Thomas Randall established a pottery for this purpose at Madeley in Shropshire, but refused to forge the Sèvres mark. His productions were virtually indistinguishable from Sèvres, and many china cabinets of the period and today preserve old Madeley instead of Sèvres. Consignments of Madeley porcelain are known to have been sent to Dover and from there despatched to London as fresh arrivals from Parisian dealers.

The finely modelled figures in soft porcelain that had formerly decorated pier tables and wall brackets and had been grouped at the centre of dining and dessert tables, were now superseded by ostentatious vases, singly, in pairs or in garnitures of three or five. Three tall urns flanked by a pair of pot-pourri vases decorated in a matching design constituted a drawing-room vogue of the period and in the late 1820's these might be centred by a clock set in a flamboyant flower-encrusted case of bone china.

For drawing-rooms, entrance halls and passages there were massive covered vases in bone china, sometimes exceeding a yard in height, supported on separate pedestals rimmed with pierced galleries of ormolu. Oval *jardinières* might have a dark blue ground with rims encircled in non-repeating flower patterns and mounted with elaborate ormolu work. Some vases early in the period displayed Moorish characteristics in their richly gilt arabesque patterns. Later vases with a *bleu de roi* ground were enriched with reserves containing meticulously painted pictorial scenes or copies of French paintings.

Ceramic figures (Pls. 61 D and E) were made in vast quantities, but these were mainly in earthenware and found no place in the fashionable home unless in kitchen or servants' quarters. The Derby factory continued making the figures that had brought wealth to Duesbury in the eighteenth century, but now in bone china. These were more lively and of greater charm than any competing figures until the 1830's. There was little enough to recommend them, however, beyond a general gaudy splendour.

The general public, nevertheless, clamoured for the crudely formed, garishly coloured earthenware figures issued in many tens of thousands each year and sold in the streets from a tray of twenty or thirty specimens balanced upon the hawker's head. A prolific maker of these was John Walton of Burslem, using a cheap, brittle earthenware capable of high-speed moulding. Almost every small home in the country possessed a few of these colourful trifles costing only a few pence each. Ralph Salt of Hanley specialized in the rather more costly *bocage* pieces, sporting dogs, and sheep with hand-raised wool: these had a country-wide sale. Among the twenty other potters producing figures at this time was Obadiah Sherratt of Hot Lane, who made some popular large chimney-piece ornaments; his 'Politos Menagerie' of about 1816 was considered a triumph of casting and firing.

Any home of pretension, no matter what its size, ensured that every room was sweet-smelling in those days of perfunctory sanitation by using pastille burners. Such a burner from about 1820 might be in the form of a bone-china or earthenware cottage containing a slowly smouldering perfumed cone composed of powdered willow-wood charcoal, benzoin, perfumed oils and gum arabic. These cottages represented old-world dwellings surrounded by gay flower-beds, minute coloured flowers encrusting the walls and edging the roof, with gilt chimneys from which curled the pastille's scented fumes. There were also turreted castle gateways, circular toll houses with conical roofs, clock towers, thatched farmhouses with flowery arbours, and many another rustic building.

Night-light shelters in the form of cottages immediately followed the invention of the self-consuming candle-wick in 1825. Faint, unflickering light from a short, thick mortar candle that did not require periodic snuffing glowed from the cut-out windows. The tiny flame was well-protected against draughts, too, and was a source of flame in those days of laborious flint-striking.

Lithophane night-light shelters date from 1828. These pictorial transparencies were made from a thin, glassy hard porcelain and gave the effect of detailed mezzotints by precise variations in the thickness and consequent opacity of the material. Lithophanes were also used as firescreens and panels for hall lanterns. Even teacups with enamelled decoration on their sides might surprise the visiting users with lithophanes in their bases, the pictures becoming visible as the cups were tilted against the light.

Food warmers, catalogued as pap-warmers, performed the duties of night-light shelter as well as keeping hot liquids warm enough to drink during the night. These vessels were in three parts: pedestal, loose cup and cover. The pedestal was an open-sided cylinder fitted with a mortar which acted as a source of heat and a night-light. Fitting loosely into its open top was a round-based covered cup. The pedestal top from about 1825 might be made in a piece with a deep inner bowl for containing boiling water. Into this fitted the covered drinking cup. This was still heated by a mortar. At about the same time appeared tea warmers in bone china and porcelain (Pl. 59D). The fully enclosed pedestal held a teapot, the whole being enamelled to match the tea service.

The scintillating glints of lustre ware began to enliven the living-rooms and kitchens of lesser homes during this period and even tea services were decorated with films of lustrous metal. Silver lustre, obtained from platinum oxide, was introduced by the Wedgwood firm in 1805, but the all-over form which made earthenware resemble sterling silver plate or plated ware began its astonishing vogue in 1823.

Stencilled effects were evolved by John Davenport in 1806, but little was made until 1810, when it met with the competition of silver resist lustre. In the same years Peter Warburton of New Hall patented a method of transfer-printing in gold and silver lustre. Moonlight effects, now known as marbling, were introduced in the same year. Later came the mottled pink lustre of Sunderland (Pl. 59C).

Mocha ware, so named because of its resemblance to the quartz mocha stone, was in demand for kitchen jugs and mugs and large cups and saucers after its invention about 1780. Its base was of cream-coloured earthenware. The shaped clay was covered with chestnut brown, green or yellow slip: over this was applied a slip in contrasting colour – usually brown, but green, blue and black might be used – mixed with tobacco and hops. This spread into patterns suggestive of trees, feathers and moss. From about 1830 a stronger base was used, either white earthenware or cane-coloured stoneware.

Dipped ware was also a favoured decoration for inexpensive but colourful kitchen earthenware. This consisted of hollow-ware in which slips of three colours – blue, brown and yellow – were applied to the biscuit. Skilful workers could produce attractive bands, stripes, spots, curves and spirals at great speed. The ware was fitted into a lathe and, when revolving, slips were poured into a three-sectioned funnel, emerging from adjoining openings and held in such a way that a fine stream of tri-coloured slip flowed upon it.

A list of major potters is given on page 103.

### *Glass*

Flint-glass was never more splendid than in the days of the Regency and George IV. Lavish cutting gave it a spectacular prismatic fire, as innumerable diamond shapes were cut deeply and expertly over the entire surface of table ware or ornament. But equally notable in its way was this period's accomplishment in providing a reasonably effective substitute for this craftsman-created glitter, so that middle-class homes could enjoy less costly decorative glassware shaped by blowing in open-and-shut moulds and only finished by hand. Glass-cutters from about 1810 were installing steam-driven cutting wheels, the speed of production enabling more complex patterns to be cut at no extra cost. The high excise duty, however, ensured that finely cut flint-glass remained in the luxury class of domestic refinements. The size of the diamonds was gradually lessened, the tendency being to reduce cross-cut diamonds to small plain diamonds and the latter to even smaller dimensions from about 1820, when prismatic- or step-cutting was also used with scintillating effect.

Armorial table services were a source of pride to those who could afford them at this period. A combined wine and dessert service would consist of more than five hundred matching pieces, blown from the finest piling pot glass and each engraved with an expansive coat of arms cut on a shield against a plain ground reserved in the cutting design. Some of these coats of arms were superb examples of the glass engraver's craft, the Lambton arms, for instance, possessing a shield with twenty-five quarterings. The Marquess of Londonderry's service made by the Wear Flint Glass Company in 1824 cost two thousand guineas. This was designed for twenty-four covers and consisted of more than five hundred pieces, including wine-glasses in four sizes, ship's decanters and other quart-size decanters (Pl. 62B), claret jugs, water jugs (Pl. 62A), finger bowls (Pl. 62D), wine-glass coolers (Pl. 62D), tumblers, dry sweetmeat jars (Pl. 62C), dessert dishes and plates.

The shapes of table ware during the period were based on geometric forms (Pl. 62B). Decanters, for instance, were cylindrical, at first with deep relief cutting on the shoulders and from 1820 with prismatic cutting, and by the mid-1820's with horizontal shoulders. These vessels were of thick section and much heavier to lift than formerly. The body was fashionably encircled with two or three bands of contrasting cut motifs separated by flat polished rings. These were produced in endless variations. Some of the most complex designs in diamond-cutting are to be found on cylindrical decanters from about 1820. Mushroom stoppers continued in use until about 1820 when heavy pinnacles became the fashionable stopper finials. Mouths flared widely and gracefully outward from immediately above the neck rings. At the coronation of William IV in 1831 Apsley Pellat introduced the 'royal shape' nearly cylindrical decanter with sides slanting outward from the shoulder to base and these cut with twelve or fourteen bold vertical flutes. Fancy decanters date from the same year.

The fashion for drinking hot toddy increased during the late Regency years, and many a home possessed a pair of giant rummers in which the toddy was prepared. A bucket or ovoid (Pl. 63B) bowl was usual on such a rummer, and this might be lavishly engraved with personal emblems or cut in a stock pattern with a cartouche left for engraving crest or cypher. Such a rummer was accompanied by a toddy lifter (Pl. 63C) – a pipette with a long slender tubular neck terminating in a bulbous container, drilled with a hole in its flat base. Among other glassware that now found a place in the home were such pieces as beehives and covers for honey, butter boats with handles, and egg-cups.

Table glass might be blown within a two-piece open-and-shut mould which had come into general use by 1810. By this means the form of the vessel and elaborate all-over designs in relief could be made in a few simple hand operations. By 1820 three-piece moulds were in use. This process brought flint-glass to the everyday tables of the middle-classes and into general use on formal occasions among the not-so-rich.

Almost every vessel made by free-blowing and hand-cutting was reproduced in the open-and-shut mould, such as celery vases, sugar basins, *compote* bowls, salt cellars, hats for tooth-picks, jugs, casters. Some hollow-ware vessels, such as cordial decanters, salad bowls, rummers and so on, were given pinched square feet, made separately and welded into position. Until the early 1820's the patterns on blown-moulded glass were geometrical; then baroque ornament was made possible by the three-piece mould and designs included fanciful curves in high relief with the addition of honeysuckle flowers, hearts, shells, fans, trefoils and the guilloche motif specifically designed to suit the new method.

Heavy tumblers were made in both fine quality

A porcelain sugar-bowl, with cover and stand, painted by Thomas Pardoe. Mark (on stand) "NANT-GARW" above "C W", impressed. Nantgarw; about 1817-20. Ht. $5\frac{3}{4}''$.
Vase, probably painted by Lavinia Billingsley. Nantgarw or Swansea; about 1815. Ht. $9\frac{1}{2}''$.
*Victoria and Albert Museum.*

(A) Blue and white transfer-printed earthenware: 'The Bridge of Lucano' set in a border of corn, vine and olive motifs. Spode. *c.* 1820. *Spode-Copeland Museum, Stoke-on-Trent.*

(B) Bone china plate painted with a country scene. The buff-coloured rim is ornamented with gold spots and brown bell-shaped drops. Marked SPODE impressed. From 1819. *Spode-Copeland Museum, Stoke-on-Trent.*

(C) Sunderland pottery ewer and basin in mottled pink lustre with transfers of the Wearmouth Bridge and the sailing ship 'Northumberland'. Marked DIXON & CO. 1813–19. *Lent by Dr J. Dixon Johnson to the Sunderland Museum.*

(D) Swansea porcelain tea warmer heated by spirit lamp or scented mortar candle. 1814–17. *Victoria and Albert Museum.*

(A) Ice cream pail with cover and lining. The body and cover are painted with flower groups in natural colours and the crimson ground is ornamented with arabesque embossments in gold. Marked SPODE *967* in red. *c.* 1825. *Spode-Copeland Museum, Stoke-on-Trent.*

(B) Earthenware jug painted with 'The Prince of Wales' stage coach which operated between London and Swansea. Inscribed 'Jacob Goodwin 1810.' Rim and base decorations are in silver lustre. *Brighton Art Gallery and Museum.*

(C) Bone china teapot decorated in the Imari style in deep blues, bold patches of brick red, and green enamels, with gilding. Marked SPODE *967*. *c.* 1820. *Spode-Copeland Museum, Stoke-on-Trent*

(D) Loving cup in cream coloured earthenware, inscribed 'George Barlow, Ecclesfield, 1822'. *Courtesy Clifford Chubb, Esq.*

PLATE 60

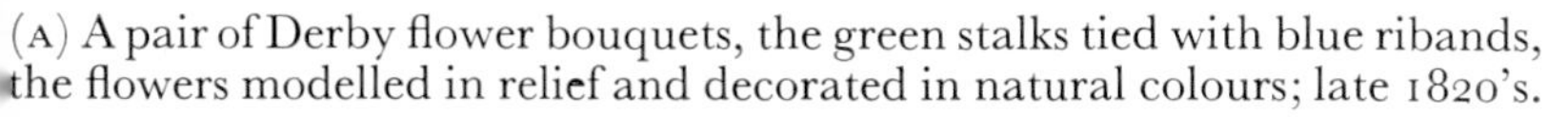

(A) A pair of Derby flower bouquets, the green stalks tied with blue ribands, the flowers modelled in relief and decorated in natural colours; late 1820's.

(B) Rockingham toby jug in bone china; early 1820's. Formerly in the Penrose collection. *Trust Houses Ltd.*

c) Rockingham china figure ornaments in the form of a dog with puppies and a cat with kittens in baskets. Early 1820's. *Wernher Collection, Luton Hoo.*

D) Staffordshire earthenware figures: a baker's errand boy and pair of deer with trees, all in painted enamels. *c.* 1825. *Wernher Collection, Luton Hoo*

(E) Pearlware figures: Mars in the centre $10\frac{1}{4}$ in. high, flanked by symbolic figures of Spring and Autumn and two figures of musicians. All marked LEEDS POTTERY. Before 1820. *Leeds City Art Gallery.*

PLATE 61

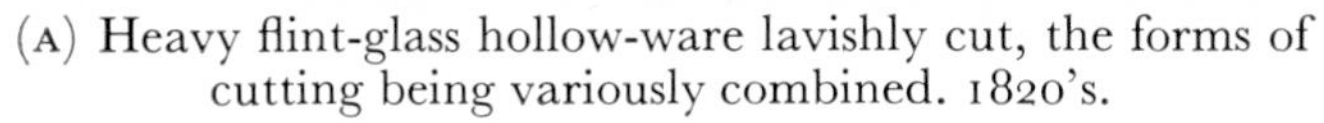

(A) Heavy flint-glass hollow-ware lavishly cut, the forms of cutting being variously combined. 1820's.

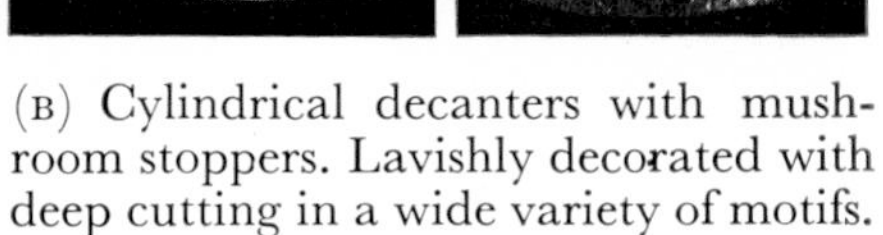

(B) Cylindrical decanters with mushroom stoppers. Lavishly decorated with deep cutting in a wide variety of motifs.

(C) Jug, honey-pot and toilet table bottle decorated with large relief diamonds and prismatic cutting.

(D) Finger bowls cut with bands of plain sharp diamonds and fluted bases, and, *below*, wine glass coolers star-cut beneath and with bands of plain sharp diamonds. 1820's. *Courtesy R. Holland, Esq.*

(A) *Crystallo ceramie* cup with portraits of George III and the Prince Regent between panels of fine diamond-cutting: made by Apsley Pellat. Early 1820's.
*By gracious permission of Her Majesty the Queen.*

(B) Rummer for serving toddy engraved with scenes in the life of a butcher. This view shows him on his way to deliver meat to a country house. *c.* 1810.
*Courtesy O. N. Norris, Esq.*

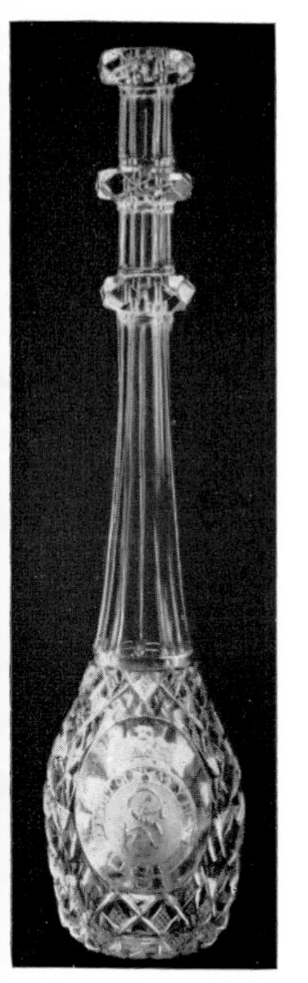

(C) Flint-glass toddy lifter made for the Duke of Sussex. *c.*1820.
*Victoria and Albert Museum.*

(D) Pair of girandole candlesticks in flint-glass with revolving canopies, gilded metal stem units, and round feet radially cut beneath. Late 1820's. *Corning Museum of Glass, U.S.A.*

PLATE 63

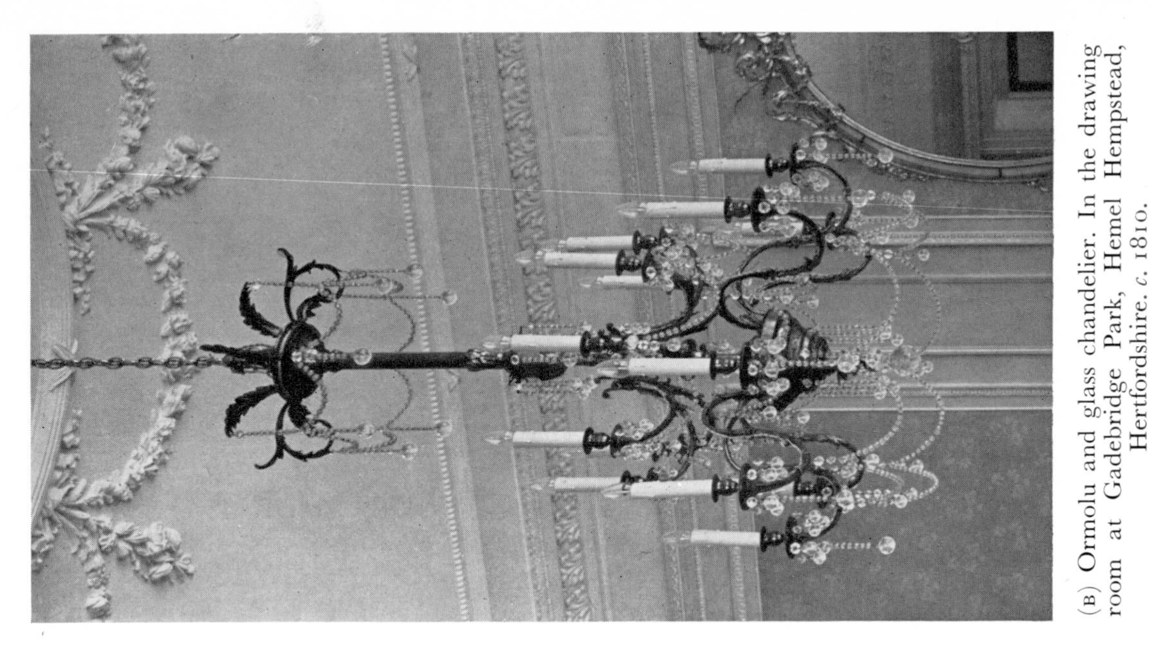

(B) Ormolu and glass chandelier. In the drawing room at Gadebridge Park, Hemel Hempstead, Hertfordshire. *c.* 1810.

(A) Glass walking sticks: the majority are solid with coloured twist decoration, others are hollow and filled with 'hundreds and thousands' in bands of alternating colours. 1810–30. *Courtesy the Rt. Hon. Alan Lennox-Boyd, M.P.*

PLATE 64

and tale flint-glass by this method. Tumblers in tale glass, a second quality glass taken from the top and bottom of the melting pot, now toughly annealed, replaced pewter mugs in taverns and other places of public resort. Tumblers at this time were short, broad and heavy-based. In best flint-glass the sharpness and fine detail of the cutting gave to the metal in certain lights a brilliance akin to that of silver. Serving jugs in great variety were moulded for pattern and body shape in open-and-shut decanter moulds and finished by hand manipulation.

Wax candles, faintly perfumed, burning in cut-glass fixtures were considered the ultimate in Regency illumination. The crystal arms to such fixtures were festooned with ropes of carefully faceted lustres and often the candles rose from flower-calyx sockets. The chandelier of the mansion stateroom now became a vast canopy of pendant lustres closely spaced and entirely enclosing the central shaft, now of metal; from concentric rings fixed to the base sprang several short branches fitted with sockets. These were entirely of glass, except for the rings. Less lavishly there was a central ornamental shaft of glass constructed from blown units, with six, eight, or twelve branches extending from an urn-shaped member near the base. Canopies and base were hung with lustres. Sets of wall lights were entirely of glass, except for the back-plates of gilded brass: there might be as many as a dozen matching lights on the walls of a drawing-room in addition to a single magnificent chandelier. These were festooned with strings of lustres. In the 1820's joints in the shaft and the socket holders might also be in gilded brass.

By 1810 candelabra for pier table and mantel-shelf had lost their attractive light reflecting finials: instead, every part of the glass surface was diamond-cut, and by 1820 foot, pillar and canopy might be step-cut, the prisms cut at angles best suited for reflecting the light. Lustre drops were now elongated into a drooping slenderness: these were used in association with festoons of smaller lustres. They were succeeded by flat-surfaced hanging prisms more adequately reflecting the greater illumination provided.

The girandole-candlestick was now made with an inverted saucer foot of the same diameter as the canopy, its edges either plain or encircled with short, narrow flutes. Then, in about 1815, came the umbrella canopy and from a heavy, facet-cut knop rose an expansive saucer-shaped socket with a spreading horizontal rim. The entire surface was diamond-cut in relief. This was followed by the double-cascade girandole-candlestick. In the early 1820's the flat, disc foot was preferred and long lustres resembling thin, pear-shaped icicles, each extending almost the length of the body (Pl. 63D).

Desks, dressing-tables and dining-tables during the 1820's might be enriched with glass accessories containing profile portraits, coats of arms and other ornaments emitting a silvery brilliance within the glass. These were invented in 1819 by Apsley Pellat and marketed as *crystallo ceramie* (Pl. 63C). Late Georgians were fascinated by the wide range of glass in which these trifles were embedded: decanters and stoppers, goblets, tumblers, mugs, sugar-basins in tea-caddy sets, ice plates, knife-rests, scent and aromatic vinegar bottles, and wall plaques of celebrities.

Coloured glass in quantity began to enrich the English home from about 1815, its cost being one penny per pound more than clear flint-glass. Bristol blue had been harshly purple in hue because of war-time withdrawal of supplies of Saxon zaffre and smalt, synthetic ultramarine being used as an alternative from about 1805. By about 1820 the use of Saxon smalt was producing a royal-purple tinge. This became known as king's blue when George IV expressed his admiration of a coronation gift of a gilded blue glass spirit set – three labelled decanters, a dozen glasses and a large oval tray of blue glass. It thereupon became a fashionable conceit to make finger-bowls and wine-glass coolers in this metal, the remainder of the table equipage being in fine-quality cut flint-glass. King's blue was costly and found only in blown ware. Pot metal coloured with zaffre was used for cheaper glass. Pale green hock glasses with wide hollow stems were also fashionable, a style revived from the late seventeenth century. They were catalogued as 'Hock Glasses, threaded and prunted, 1/- per pound more than wines'.

Christmas lights – they were of course used for other occasions – were blown in open and shut moulds from transparent pot metals of blue, purple, green, ruby red and amber, the surface decorated with a close diamond-quilted pattern. The little oil-burning bowl, without stem or foot, was rimmed to take a wire for hanging.

The colourful trifles in glass associated with the name of Nailsea, but made also at other glass centres such as Tyneside and Stourbridge, gave a touch of luxury to many otherwise austere homes. A pale-green bottle glass blown into flasks and decorated with loops, mottles and flecks in white had been evolved to avoid the high tax payable on flint-glass. By 1815 this low-taxed glass was coloured with metallic oxides to give shades of blue, green, amber and red. These flasks in flattened baluster forms were produced in large numbers: for the most part they were sold as containers of toilet waters. For toilet water too was the gimmel flask – a twin flask with two containers and spouts. Some were given a crimped or petal foot for standing upright on the toilet table.

Flasks in the form of hand-bellows were made in flint-glass enriched with notches, loops and trailed work, and in coloured glass such as blue or red with loops and trailed work in white enamel. Giant bellows flasks, a foot or more in height, for mantelshelf or dressing-table, were made, their nozzles expanded into deep saucer shapes and crimped. These were filled with perfumed water, which pleasantly scented the room.

Coloured glass bells with clappers in clear flint-glass had a delightful resonant tone and were used on the table to summon a servant or in the hall to summon the family at meal-times. These were made in pot-metals, handle and bell in contrasting colours.

Among the larger ornaments intended to hang on parlour walls during the 1820's were slender poignards and dress swords; coaching horns, measuring forty to forty-five inches in length and often containing three loops; giant tobacco pipes; riding-crops. There were walking sticks (Pl. 64A), too, and canes and shepherds' crooks, red, white and blue spirals being particularly popular. These were tapered at the ends and might be enriched with spiral threads in red, blue, green, amber or white opaque glass. Hollow canes of clear flint-glass were filled with comfits and the ferrules plugged with cork.

Rolling-pins in bottle-glass continued their traditional use as salt containers until about 1820, hanging in the kitchen fireplace to keep dry the expensive salt then burdened with a tax of thirty times its cost of manufacture. Some were sold filled with tea or sugar. By 1815, made in clear flint-glass, rolling-pins might be filled with colourful comfits, and became attractive gifts for sweethearts. Soon they were being gilded, painted and engraved with mottoes and good wishes. Such rolling-pins were regarded as lucky charms and were not removed from the wall until pastry was being prepared ceremoniously for a wedding breakfast. They were also advertised as 'sailors' charms'.

Glass spheres, known as watch-balls, in which a whole room was mirrored in miniature, continued to be made, but with some distortion in the reflections. Nailsea also made balls in coloured glass intended as jug-covers to prevent the entry of insects and dust. From 1820 these might be spotted, looped or spiralled in opaque white.

*The principal products of the leading Regency potters*

| NAME OF POTTERY | DATE OF ESTAB. | CERAMICS POTTED 1810–1830 |
| --- | --- | --- |
| Adams (Stoke-upon-Trent) | 1790's | cream-coloured earthenware; basalt; stoneware; bone china from 1816 |
| Coalport | 1795 | bone china; felspar porcelain from 1822 |
| Davenport | 1795 | earthenware; cream-coloured earthenware; bone china; stone china; lustre ware from *c.* 1820 |
| Derby (Bloor from 1815) | 1749 | bone china |
| Herculaneum (Liverpool) | 1800 | bone china; earthenware |
| Madeley | 1825 | soft paste porcelain |
| Mason | 1797 | earthenware; bone china; stone china; ironstone china from 1813 |
| Minton | 1793 | earthenware; bone china |
| Nantgarw & Swansea | 1813 | soft paste porcelain and soapstone porcelain until 1823 |
| New Hall | 1781 | hard paste porcelain to about 1810; bone china from 1810 |
| Ridgway | 1802 | fine earthenware; stone china; bone china |
| Rockingham (Brameld) | 1807 | cream-coloured earthenware; stone ware; bone china from 1820 |
| Spode | 1776 | earthenware; bone china; felspar porcelain; stone china; new stone china from 1810 |
| Swansea (Cambrian Pottery) | 1769 | earthenware; cream-coloured earthenware; stone china; lustre ware from early 1820's (see Nantgarw) |
| Wedgwood | 1759 | earthenware; cream-coloured earthenware; basalt; unglazed earthenware; bone china 1812–1822 |
| Worcester | 1751 | bone china |

With the exception of Madeley and Nantgarw, all the above issued blue and white transfer printed ware. There were also twenty other makers of bone china in Staffordshire listed in 1818. Earthenware potters in 1820 numbered at least a hundred, established in Staffordshire, Yorkshire, Sunderland, London, Derbyshire and elsewhere. Some of the more important of these were Joseph Stubbs, Enoch Wood, Clews, Rogers, of Staffordshire; Joseph Bourne of Denby; Doulton at Lambeth.

Spode's 'Grasshopper' pattern: the transfer for a six-inch tea plate taken from the original engraved copper plates. *Spode-Copeland Museum.*

# *Architectural and Domestic Metalwork*

# Architectural and Domestic Metalwork

BRIAN READE

*Cast iron*

By 1810 the Industrial Revolution had transformed the character of the metal industries to a point where differences between metropolitan and regional craftsmanship scarcely existed. For all but the very rich, who could still afford to commission anything, it was the beginning of a ready-made age. An industrial hierarchy similar to the one we know had emerged, from manager to workman; and the products of the iron industry originated not from blacksmiths' fancies, out of tradition, but in the heads of designers, materializing at the hands of skilled, but largely dependent, artisans.

The art of casting from moulds goes back a long way. It was the scale that was new. And the scale of a cast-iron factory had to be fairly large to work economically. In other words, multiple production paid only when a large enough market was foreseen to justify the expense of equipment. Since moulds were not scrapped until they wore out, consumers had to accustom themselves to a degree of inflexibility in designs that was altogether novel. Some of the iron moulds made in 1810 are known to have been in use in 1830, and grates and railings designed in 1830 were still to be had new, without any modification of form or detail, in 1850. Moreover, while it was possible for someone in the depths of the country to order a stove of the best quality in the latest fashion, it was equally possible for someone in London to order a new stove in the style of many years back – and such things often took place. So that the age and generation of the consumer became more significant than his locality, and his tastes could be restricted within limits by the iron trade just as long as those limits were profitable. In this context, therefore, conservatism became the new provincialism, and the time factor became more important than the geographical one.

The English metal industries had taken a considerable lead in these developments during the late eighteenth century, and at the end of the Napoleonic War there were even better opportunities for cast iron. Household and architectural fittings were produced in it more and more, leaving the blacksmith with little else than his horse-shoes and pothooks. An anonymous writer in Ackermann's *Repository* number of 1st December 1816, reflects some of the optimism that the iron-founders must have felt then.

> 'The manufacture of iron [he reports] has been greatly benefited by improvements in the art of casting it, by which the embossed parts are relieved from the moulds with so much purity, that little labour is afterwards required to complete the richest ornamental work in this metal, which is therefore performed at a small expense compared with the execution of such work a short time since, and as iron itself is now at a very reduced price, it may be expected that richly embossed works will come into frequent use.'

He adds that cast iron was by that date 'so generally substituted for several other materials, that the century may not improperly be called another *iron* age' ... and even less improperly perhaps a cast-iron age.

Although some of the great foundries were situated in London, many more were in Birmingham and Sheffield, and in other towns near to the coalfields: indeed, one of the biggest of them was the Carron Company, in the village of Carron in Stirlingshire. These foundries sometimes issued pattern-books of their products for the use of retailers; and what was probably the most ambitious book of cast-iron patterns issued during the Regency, with designs for grates, railings and other constructions, was published in 1811 by M. and G. Skidmore, founders, of High Holborn and Clerkenwell. 'The great Utility of this Work', says the preface, 'will appear ... to those whose Premises or Capital will not permit them to keep a Stock in Hand, and who are not willing to risk the Fluctuations of Patterns.' By and large, the patterns may be said to show the pervading influence of Soane. The motifs are mainly neo-classical, with reeding and lattice decoration to the fore; but Egyptian details abound, and there are quite a number of neo-Gothic designs. It was possible, as the preface explains, to vary the cast-iron members: frets, grate fronts and fire-pieces, for instance, could be transposed. But there is evidence too of the way in which these patterns survived the 'fluctuations' of twenty years in the fact that J. S. Morris, a stove manufacturer of Devonport, reproduced one for a Gothic grate in an advertisement in the Plymouth directory of 1830 (Fig. 1).

The Skidmore engravings show the hob grate, with cheeks and back in one piece; the vase grate in the new shape of a sarcophagus; the open grate in the late eighteenth-century style; and, most typical of the period, the register grate inspired by Count von Rumford's heating improvements of 1796. This type of grate was closed at the back, with a little hinged lid opening into the chimney, which arrangement not only concentrated the draught, but reduced gusts of smoke. In later designs, such as those issued in the 1820's by Longden, Walker & Company, of the Phœnix Foundry, Sheffield, the ornaments have become – as the Ackermann writer foretold – more richly embossed (Pl. 65B). They have acquired a stolid kind of elegance to match the architecture of Basevi and furniture in the style of the Nicholsons. Apart from the older anthemion, waterleaf and acanthus ornaments of the Grecian taste (treated more naturalistically, however), the Longden patterns show a good many spiral

Fig. 1. Engraved advertisement from Robert Brindley's *Plymouth, Devonport and Stonehouse Directory*, 1830.

(A) Marble chimney-piece and cast-iron grate with fender and fire-irons of brass, in Sir John Soane's house, Lincoln's Inn Fields, *c.* 1812. *Sir John Soane's Museum.*

(B) Design for a cast-iron grate published by Longden, Walker & Co., of the Phoenix Foundry, Sheffield. *c.* 1820–30. *Victoria and Albert Museum.*

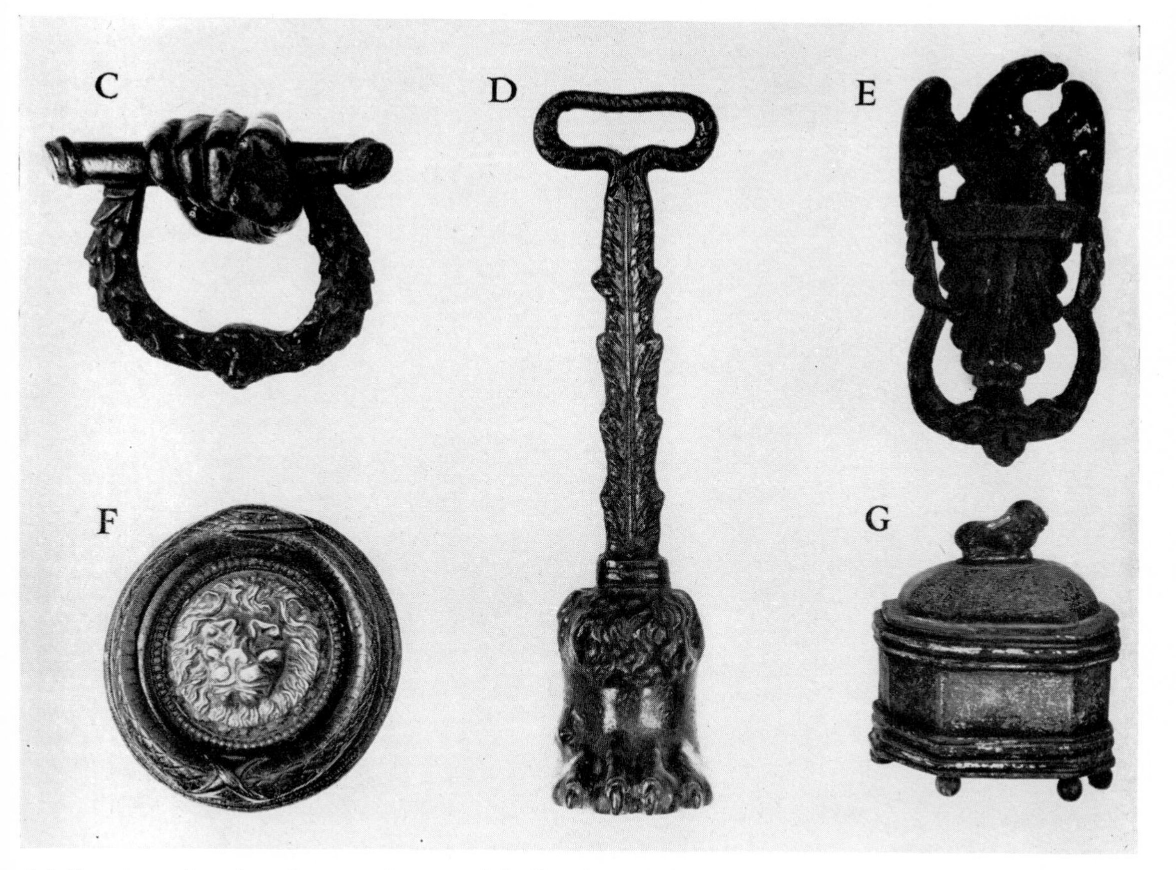


(C) Cast-iron door-knocker, *c.* 1820–30. (D) Cast-iron door-porter, *c.* 1820–30. (E) Cast-iron door-knocker, *c.* 1820–30. (F) Door-knocker of cast-iron with brass centre, *c.* 1810–20. (G) Lead Tobacco-box, *c.* 1820. *Edmund Ware, Esq., Messrs Pratt & Sons Ltd., and author.*

PLATE 65

A

B

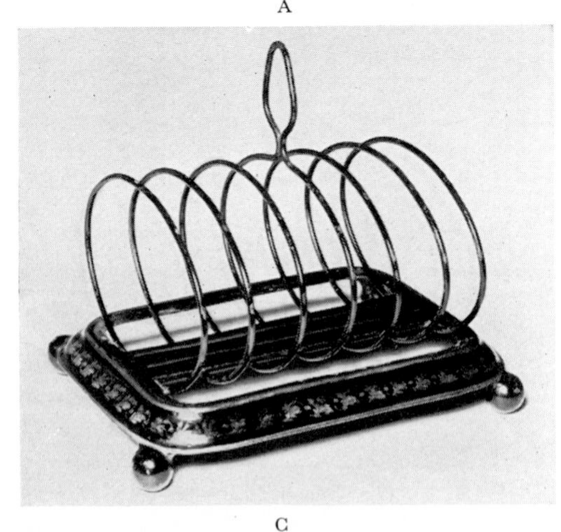

C

D

(A) Usk tea-pot of japanned iron: chocolate ground with decoration in gold; *c.* 1810–20. *National Museum of Wales.*

(B) Table with bronze base and shaft (in the style of a Herculaneum lamp-stand) and rosewood top inlaid with brass. *c.* 1820. *Woburn Abbey.*

(C) Toast-rack of japanned iron: black ground with decoration in gold. Probably by Shoolbred, Loveridge & Shoolbred, Wolverhampton, *c.* 1830. *National Museum of Wales.*

(D) Garden chairs of wrought iron, *c.* 1810–1820. *Courtesy John Fowler, Esq.*

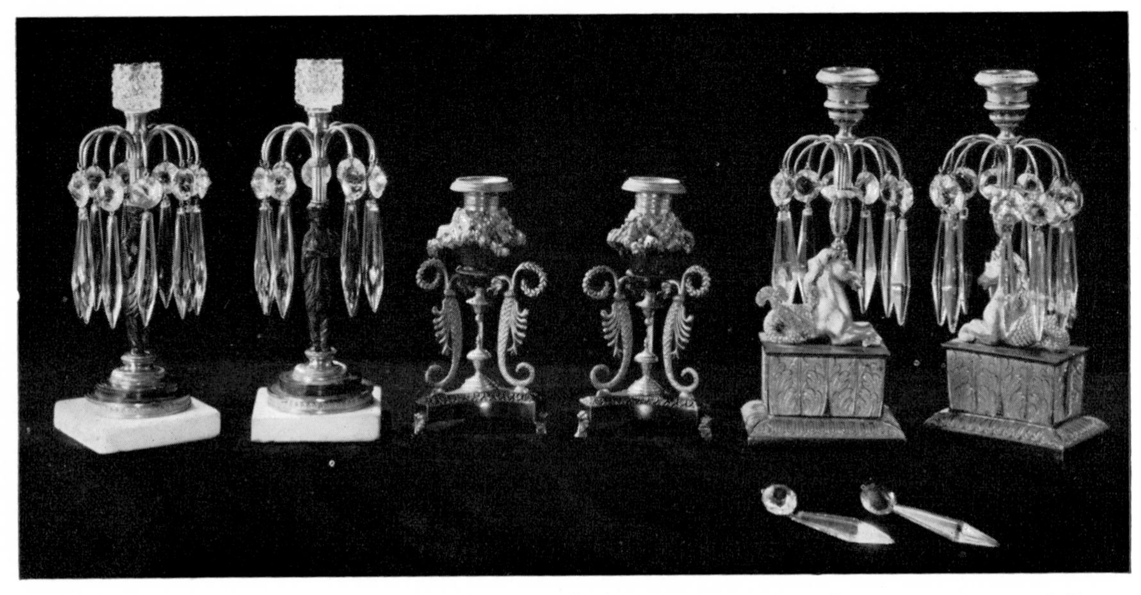

(E) Three pairs of candlesticks, the middle pair lettered: 'PUBLISHED DEC 1 1809 CHENEY LONDON'. Brass, partly bronzed and partly gilt; *c.* 1810. *Courtesy W. G. T. Burne, Esq.*

A

B

(A) Sinumbra lamp of brass partly bronzed, with glass shade ground on the inside. Labelled: 'BRIGHT & CO. LATE ARGAND & CO. BRUTON ST'; *c.* 1830. *Woburn Abbey.*

(B) Candelabrum of bronze, partly gilt (one of a pair), *c.* 1820.
*Victoria and Albert Museum.*

C D E

(C) Pot-pourri vase of marble and ormolu, *c.* 1810–20. Showing Nysa receiving Dionysus from Hermes, etc. Similar vase-designs appear in the Tatham letters of 1795 (V. & A. M.), T. Hope's *Household Furniture*, 1807, and H. Moses's *Antique Vases*, 1814. Cf. also krater by Salpion in Naples Museum. (D) and (E) Candlesticks with painted ground-glass shades: brass, gilt and partly bronzed, *c.* 1810–20.
*Courtesy Raymond Barnett, Esq.*

(A) Brass reading-lamp with green japanned - iron shade. Labelled 'BRIGHT & CO. LATE ARGAND & CO. BRUTON ST'; *c.* 1830–40. (B) Brass candlestick, *c.* 1820. (C) Brass Argand lamp for table or sideboard, *c.* 1820. (D) Drawer-handles of stamped brass, gilt; *c.* 1820–30. *Courtesy Raymond Barnett, Esq., Edmund Ware, Esq. and author.*

Articles of bronzed brass, (J) excepted. (E) Bust of Sir Walter Scott, *c.* 1830. (F) Egg-timer, *c.* 1830–40. (G) Table-lamp with lid, partly gilt, *c.* 1810–20. (H) Wax-Taper holder, mainly stamped and partly gilt. *c.* 1830–40. (I) Watch-holder, *c.* 1830–40. (J) Pastille-burner of bronze, partly gilt, *c.* 1820. (K) Box in the shape of a lavacrum, *c.* 1820. (L) Pastille-burner, *c.* 1820–30. *Courtesy Raymond Barnett, Esq., and author.*

PLATE 68

colonettes and beadings, a few wreaths and roses, and motifs of an indigenous character based on ivy- and oak-leaves. Some of the fire-bars are turned in baluster fashion, with large knops: some of the pedestals are decorated with acanthus leaves on consoles. Cast brass details are indicated more plentifully than in the Skidmore designs, making it clear that whereas in the eighteenth century the contrast of brass and steel or iron in a grate was a contrast of parts, by 1820 it had become a contrast of background and applied ornaments.

Closed stoves in the Continental style were also used, but mainly in public rooms. They were generally of the urn-and-pedestal shape, like the Empyreal Stove made by Izons, Whitehurst & Izon of Birmingham. At the end of our period the London firm of Rippon and Burton, established in 1820, patented the Chunk Stove, which was doorless, in the shape of a fluted half-column, with a pipe-flue to run under the floor.

It was the age, too, of the kitchen range (Fig. 1). Like the register stove and grate, this contrivance appeared on the market at the end of the eighteenth century, in the wake of Count von Rumford's researches. Describing a range in 1807 in his *Letters from England by Don Manuel Espriella*, Robert Southey tells us that 'the top of the fire is covered with an iron plate, so that the flame and smoke, instead of ascending, pass through bars on the one side, and there heat an iron front, against which food may be roasted as well as by the fire itself; it passes on heating stoves and boilers as it goes, and the smoke is not suffered to pass up the chimney till it can no longer be of any use. On the other side is an oven heated by the same fire, and vessels for boiling may be placed on the plate over the fire. The smoke finally sets a kind of wheel in motion in the chimney, which turns the spit.' With little modification, and not much improvement, this type of kitchen range survived until the middle of the nineteenth century.

In 1811 the Skidmores gave designs for six ranges, the most interesting of which is one with what they called a 'Rumfordized Inside', wind-up cheeks, caps on the cheeks that wind under the hobs, fall-down top-bar, swing trivet, sliding spit racks, and a fret underneath that drew out to form a dripping pan, stand or footman. One of the other designs shows a range with a stewing and ironing stove on one side, and a copper boiler on the other.

The factories which made stoves sometimes made fenders and fire-irons as well. Twenty-seven of these are listed in the Sheffield directory of 1828, including those that specialized in fenders. But there were only eight fender and fire-iron specialists in London in 1823, or, anyhow, eight who were important enough to be recorded. Of the ten fender-makers recorded in Birmingham in 1818, Nicklin & Son were in business throughout the Regency, and were evidently leading manuturers of wire fenders, together with bird-cages and other things in brass and iron wire. At its simplest this kind of fender consisted of wire lattices, or intersecting hoops (giving it a neo-Gothic air) between brass top-rails and bases. Other types incorporating bands of fret-cut brass or steel, with brass top-rails and bases and lion-paw feet, continued the forms evolved during the Adam period, without the apparent fragility of late eighteenth-century examples. The most conspicuous changes were changes of outlines. Serpentine fronts, which had been common until 1800, went out of fashion, to be superseded by straight, or slightly convex, fronts with rounded corners. Some fenders of the finest quality were embellished with cast brass figures of lions or sphinxes on pedestals at the corners: simple ones in solid cast iron were sometimes decorated with reeding or wavy flutes. Soon after 1820 a style of fender came into fashion which was made up of two tiers of openwork friezes between convex and reeded bands of metal, generally brass or steel.

The pierced designs decorating fire-shovels remained very formal. Though fire-iron handles were still being made with urn-shaped finials in the 1820's, many followed the baluster fashion in being emphatically knopped. In 1827 Ackermann's *Repository* published an engraving with some designs for neo-Gothic fire-irons by Augustus Charles (the Elder) Pugin (Fig. 2), and the influence of English on French taste at this time, when the *Style Cathédrale* was being fostered by the Duchesse de Berry, is suggested by the appearance of a copy of Pugin's designs in Mésangère's *Meubles et Objets de Gout*, issued, it seems, a year or so later.

With the development of landscape gardening came the need for iron seats and benches to rest on, during what the writers of the period called 'rambles'. In the first half of the nineteenth century much of this garden furniture was made of rods and strips of iron wrought into the skeleton forms of ordinary chairs and sofas (Pl. 66D). *Jardinières*, for example, were made usually on the principle of a dumb waiter with circular shelves diminishing in size upwards, but carried out in bent rods and strips; and here of course the blacksmith, as a unit in a factory, came into his own again. If we are to judge by Thomas Upfill & Son of Birmingham, a firm with a great reputation for garden furniture, the industry was a conservative one. Some of the designs in the Upfill advertisements of the 1850's are exactly similar to those of the 1830's.

Fig. 2. Designs for fire-irons by Augustus Charles Pugin. From Ackermann's *Repository of Arts*, 1st September, 1827.

Cast-iron embellishments were probably not common in this field until well into the Victorian age, when seats composed of fern and other leaf forms came into vogue. In the issue of the *Repository* dated 1st September 1816, however, there is an article on garden furniture with two illustrations of recent inventions. The ironwork of these would have been mainly cast. One consisted of a garden seat protected by an umbrella structure with a roof of copper sheeting, inspired, so the author remarks, by 'those buildings in India that were frequently erected for monumental or devotional purposes'. The other seat is shown in the form of a bench with console-shaped feet involving the anthemion motif. A marquee covering of cloth painted with neo-classical motifs protected the bench, and this covering was supported on an iron trunk, or shaft, and roped and pegged to the ground.

As for the railings and balconies of cast iron manufactured during the Regency, many of these are still in use, or at least in place, as evidence of the outburst of activity in each grade of building at that period (Fig. 4). Before 1810 nearly all the neo-classic features in architectural iron were traceable directly to the Adelphi and other designs of Robert Adam, who was keen to take advantage of improvements in casting as a means to revive the ornamental use of this material. The firm of J. Collinge, in the Lambeth Road, came forward soon afterwards with the greater use of lead as a substitute for wood in ornaments and dripping-eaves. Certain motifs began to appear more prolifically among the older palmettes and Greek keys, such as the fleur-de-lys and the spear-head, which by the 1820's had become a pike with a tassel (Fig. 3), as in the gates to John Nash's house in Waterloo Place put up in 1822, and in much of the exterior ironwork in the Regent's Park neighbourhood. In the advertisement of a gatemaker, William Neville of Great Brooke Street, Birmingham, published in 1818, lyre-shaped finials are shown on the tops of a pair of gate piers, and another pair is shown with thin trellises of intersecting arcs in marked contrast to the heavier ironwork at the tops and bottoms. At Brighton, Cheltenham, Clifton and Plymouth, where building proceeded apace after the Napoleonic War, many of the stock motifs of the French Empire period were adopted in architectural iron. The outlines of these Hellenistic attributes, of which the commonest were perhaps arrows (Fig. 4D), wings, thyrsi and wreaths, were somewhat relaxed in English hands. At the same time crowded designs and fullness of forms were qualities typical of all the important outside cast ironwork of the 1820's: together they produced the sumptuousness seen in L. N. Cottingham's *Smith and Founder's Director* of 1823–4 (Figs. 3, 4) – or, better still, in the gates at Constitution Hill, cast by Bramah from the designs of Decimus Burton. By 1820 Chinese lattice patterns were no longer much favoured for railings and balconies, and the English taste for the Romantic was gratified more than ever by neo-Gothic designs. After 1830 the shells and scrolls of the neo-Rococo style began to appear in window guards, following a fashion which had declared itself in English silver twenty years previously.

### *Japanned iron*

The town of Pontypool in Monmouthshire had great renown in the eighteenth century for its productions of japanned iron: so much so that the word 'Pontypool' was used generically at one time in Europe for all wares of this kind. But in 1813 the Cambrian Travellers' Guide noticed that the Pontypool works, founded by a member of the Allgood family nearly one hundred years before, had 'declined exceedingly'. This was shortly after the business had passed into the hands of Mary Allgood; and at her death in 1822 it became extinct.

Meanwhile the art of japanning metal had been carried on also at Usk in the same county, where a workshop had been founded by another of the Allgoods in 1763. The last owner of this name at Usk was Edward Allgood, who died at the end of the eighteenth century, the works then passing to John Hughes, and from him in 1814 to John Pyrke, and in 1826 to Evan Jones. By 1835 the business had dwindled to a point at which it could be described by the Commissioners of Corporations as 'a small manufacture'. It succumbed finally in 1860 to

Fig. 3. Design for lamp, pier and railings of cast iron. From *The Smith and Founder's Director* by L. N. Cottingham, London, 1823–4.

the cheaper japanned iron produced in great quantities by long-established and much larger organizations in the Midlands.

Although, therefore, the amount of true Pontypool japanned iron dating from 1810 to 1830 is negligible, the output of the Usk works during these years remained steady, and of high quality. What is more, a sufficient number of authenticated pieces survive to give some idea of its general characteristics.

The black-iron and tin-plated-iron sheets on which the japanning was done at Usk were bought from the iron mills at Caerleon six miles away, and later from Pontypool itself, where there was a famous mill; and doubtless at times from other nearby mills, such as those at Lydbrook and Monmouth. Trays and large articles were made usually from black-iron plate, and the smaller articles from tinplate, the sheets being manipulated into the required forms by the japanners. Such details as lead bases, brass handles and silver borders were frequently added. All objects thus fashioned were enamelled on the clean surfaces with ground colours and decorations in colours and gold, undergoing repeated 'stovings' during these processes, and a long, slow stoving for the top varnish. The media that gave the brilliant hard effect peculiar to japanning were composed slightly differently according to the colours intended, but nearly all of them after 1750 contained as basic ingredients high proportions of linseed oil and metallic oxides. Both at Pontypool and at Usk the owners kept up the legend that there was something unique and secret about their recipes for japanning, yet in the later phase at Usk the varnishes are known to have been bought ready-made from Wilkinson, Heywood & Clark, Ltd, of London, and from various paint-manufacturers in Birmingham.

In the eighteenth century, black, tortoiseshell, red and dark blue grounds had been the favourites at Pontypool, and apparently at Usk; but by 1810 the grounds used at Usk were chiefly black, crimson and chocolate-brown. During the Regency the most notable features of Usk decoration were floral sprays treated in a delicate linear style, reminiscent of certain contemporary chintzes: in these star-shaped flowers occurred repeatedly (Pl. 66A). Formal patterns included spaced stars, circuits of intersecting arcs, and the kind of vermicular ornament seen on Worcester porcelain of the same date, and known as the Stormont pattern. A letter of 1807 in the National Library of Wales describes a visit to the Usk japan works in that year, and records that 'any person wishing for a particular pattern – to have his Arms emblazoned – or a view of his house or grounds painted and japanned upon a tray or other article, upon sending a drawing, may have it executed to his wishes'. Examples of private commissions of this sort still exist.

On the whole, however, pictorial decoration, such as the landscape vignettes on French and Dutch *tôle peinte*, was not a common feature of Usk, or of English, japanning, although many oblong and oval trays were made with decorations copied from prints of hunting scenes and battles in the Napoleonic War. Most of the smaller metal articles japanned at Usk were either made there, or sent there from London and other towns for japanning. Brass and pewter as well as iron objects are known to have received this treatment. But chestnut-urns and knife-boxes, like those for which Pontypool had once been celebrated, had gone out of fashion by 1810 and were no longer manufactured at Usk during the Regency period.

Perfunctory stoving, less durable varnishes, less resistance to heat, less careful workmanship all round, and a greater range of colours were characteristics brought to the japanned-iron trade by the japanners of Birmingham, Bilston and Wolverhampton. The earliest factories of note in Birmingham were those of John Taylor (who had a reputation for snuff-boxes), and his rival John Baskerville, better known as a type-founder. Then, at the close of the eighteenth century, came Henry Clay, who moved to London in 1802, having for some time concentrated more on *papier-mâché* than on japanned iron. The Clay business passed in 1816 to Jennens & Bettridge, and these partners continued to produce articles in iron, although the bulk of their trade was in *papier-mâché*. One of the staple industries of the city remained in the production of japanned-iron snuff-boxes and other small objects, for which there was still a large export

Fig. 4. (A) and (B), patterns for balcony panels, from *Designs of Stoves, Ranges, Virandas, Railings, Belconets, etc.* by M. and G. Skidmore, London 1811. (C) and (D), designs for window-guards executed in London, (E) and (F), patterns for balcony panels, all from *The Smith and Founder's Director*, by L. N. Cottingham, London 1823–4.

market in the first half of the nineteenth century. Oddly enough, there was also a countervailing trade in the importation of similar objects from the japanned-iron factories of Holland, France and Germany, which makes for confusion.

At Bilston fifteen japanners were recorded in 1818. The export of tea-caddies, cash-boxes and useful articles like coal-scuttles and trays from there to North and South America was evidently considerable, but it is no longer a simple matter to distinguish its products from those of other Midland towns. The oldest Wolverhampton japanners were Ryton & Sons, founded in 1775; equally famous was the factory of Benjamin Mander, later known under the name of his son Charles Mander, and later still under that of William Shoolbred, to become then Shoolbred, Loveridge & Shoolbred, and from the 1840's until 1918, the well-remembered firm of Henry Loveridge & Company. Wolverhampton trays were produced in enormous quantities (50,000 in 1850), and were as a rule more interestingly pictorial than the ones made at Usk. The favourite early-nineteenth-century decorations were tigers, Chinoiseries, and landscapes in North Wales; but to identify the makers is seldom possible. Green and Naples yellow seem to have come into regular use as ground colours by the cheaper japanners slightly before 1830: indeed, the fashion for Naples yellow ran parallel with the use of the same shade in simulated bamboo woodwork, which was itself imitated in japanned iron. Black, however, was the commonest ground shade (Pl. 66c). Dark blue had been used at Pontypool in its heyday, but a lot of the blue, green and yellow grounds in existence are, in fact, on *tôle* of continental origin.

### *Pewter and Britannia Metal*

From the middle of the eighteenth century the history of pewter is the history of a trade in decline. Two factors contributed to this state of things: the complacency of the Pewterers' Company in London, and the growth of the trade in fine pottery, such as that of Wedgwood and his imitators. The invention of bone-china in Staffordshire and the rise of the tax-free glass industries in Ireland reduced the market for pewter even more. By comparison with such materials as these pewter had three disadvantages: it was dearer; it was more sombre; it gave off a slightly metallic scent which affected the taste of food and drink. None the less it was still in regular use until well into the nineteenth century for the tankards, cutlery and cruets of taverns, and for the ink-wells of counting-houses and offices. At the end of the reign of George IV the Pewterers' Company, with its Hall in Lime Street, was still a circumstantial body, governed by a master, two wardens and twenty-eight assistants; but its statutory powers of interfering in the trade to maintain high standards were no longer put to the test, and in 1863 the Pewterers' Bill was repealed. Originally the Company had been empowered to make regulations whereby each pewterer had to put his name on large articles and his registered mark on small ones. This practice of marking with 'touches' died out in the nineteenth century. The last touch recorded on the plates at Pewterers' Hall is dated 1824.

Writing in 1823 the anonymous author of a tale called 'The Rookery', published in *La Belle Assemblée*, describes a farmhouse kitchen of the period in which the servants took their meals. And for this purpose, he says, 'there was a large white dresser, surmounted by a variety of pewter dishes and plates ... whose chief merit consisted in the brightness of their polish'. The passage gives a hint of the surroundings with which pewter was associated, and had been associated for quite a long time. From a factor's list in the Victoria and Albert Museum (E.I.D. Dept: M63a) we know that the prices of pewter dishes fluctuated very much at that date, suggesting the weakness of the market because of uncertainty in the trade.

Meanwhile the pewter relics from this last phase in the history of an alloy once treated with great respect imply that the profitable lines of production, apart from those already indicated, were on a small scale: salts, hot-water dishes, scale-plates, measures, jugs, pot-lids, bleeding-basins, ladles and kitchen spoons, candlesticks and snuff-boxes. Not many of these articles were made in the highest grade of pewter known to the seventeenth century. Indeed, the proportion of lead in them was often decidedly more than it ought to have been. For some reason the majority of tobacco-boxes were made in lead, not of pewter (Pl. 65G). With the exception of these leaden boxes, which had styles of their own, objects of pewter took shape from the current forms in Sheffield plate and silver, in which threads and gadroons were the routine enrichments. Even the better lathes that had been invented in the eighteenth century cannot be said to have affected the standard of turning in Regency pewter, which on the whole was rather rough.

Yet another, though minor, set-back in the pewter trade appeared when a new alloy was invented in 1770, composed of tin, antimony and copper, in the proportions of 50:3:1. This material was called White Metal from 1769 until 1797, and was first sold under that name by the earliest large-scale producers of it, Messrs Hancock & Jessop, of Sheffield. From 1797 it was generally referred to as Britannia Metal, and among the leading Regency manufacturers advertising it under that name were James Dixon & Sons, of Cornish Place, Sheffield (still making it today), and John Vickers, of Britannia Place, Sheffield, who was succeeded in the business before the beginning of Victoria's reign by Rutherford, Stacey, West & Company. Both firms stamped their wares plainly with their names. In Birmingham the most prominent Britannia Metal smiths seem to have been Brown & Hardman of Paradise Street, and William Thompson & Company of Ashted. Soap-boxes and ink-stands were specialities of James Whitworth of Aston Road, Birmingham, and Dixon of Sheffield was noted for teapots on pedestals, though these were made by other firms too. It is interesting to recall that Sir Walter Scott possessed a set of Britannia tea equipment, which was reproduced in Hudson Moore's *Old Pewter* (New York, 1905). Otherwise the range of Britannia Metal production was rather similar to that of Sheffield plate. The commonest application of the alloy, it appears, was in the manufacture of cheap spoons. These were cast from iron or brass moulds in the popular fiddle-pattern style, and were distinguishable by long ridges along the backs of the stems, which helped to strengthen them.

Spoons were also made in a white metal alloy called Tutania, patented by William Tutin in 1770. This consisted of brass, antimony and tin in proportions of 8 : 32 : 7. For a time in the late eighteenth century, before they went out of fashion, buckles as well as spoons were produced in Tutania by the firm of Tutin & Haycraft of Coleshill Street, Birmingham.

### *Brass, bronze and small iron articles*

When the first directory of Birmingham was published in 1777 it gave the names of thirty brass-founders in the city. Forty years afterwards the number had risen to seventy-nine, which gives some idea of the rate of expansion in the hardware industries, out of all proportion to the growth of population in Britain at that time. The products of this expansion were absorbed by a greatly increased middle class, whose mounting prosperity brought even more prosperity to the rich. Even so, that class alone cannot be held entirely responsible for such a huge trade, this being due in part to an export drive that was one of the remarkable features of the period 1770–1870. After the battle of Waterloo, the chief markets of the Birmingham brass-founders seem to have been in North America, Portugal, Spain, the Low Countries and Central Europe; also in the colonies, and for a time in Latin America. Surviving pattern-books sent by the founders to retailers during the first quarter of the nineteenth century show such things as wafer- and waffle-irons, intended clearly for North American customers. In the designs of these books, portraits of Washington and of the Polish patriot Thadeus Kosciusko appear alongside representations of Louis XVI's tomb, for Royalists, or later, of Napoleon in a pensive attitude, for Buonapartists: all of which indicates how far the tastes and feelings of foreign patrons were considered.

Brass articles were both cast from moulds and stamped from dies, most foundries using both processes. While in the technique of stamping metal the English led the way, it seems that finishing with a chaser was not carried out to any marked degree, except in ormolu. Brass was often lacquered and sometimes bronzed, but the standard of finish in ormolu was generally lower than in France:

on the other hand, French ormolu of the *Empire* and *Restauration* periods had a hard, finical quality that was never present in English metalwork. It is quite likely that in some cases the furniture fittings exported to France were chased by French cabinet-makers before being attached. There was, however, at this time an increase in the English use of rose engines with elliptical chucks for turned decoration. Henry Maudsley in the 1800's, and Holtzapffel in the second decade of the century, both invented improvements in the ornamental turning lathe, so that the mechanistic look of the formal enrichments on highly decorated brass and bronze objects of the period can be seen as the natural outcome of the desire to exploit these developments.

In cast or stamped brass the notable products were door-fittings, door-knockers, door-stops (or door-porters), curtain-bands, bell-handles, furniture-fittings (including castors, feet, mounts (see p. 52) and beadings), fender-footmen and candle-sticks. After 1825 the repertory began to be extended more to pastille-burners, paper-weights, letter-racks, watch-holders, spill-vases and other small articles, often made of bronzed brass (Pls. 68E–L). The increase in the number of motifs with Romantic rather than Classical associations, such as representations of ivy- and clover-leaves, roses and even fuchsias, was very marked from 1820 to 1840, and went hand in hand with the revival of rococo ornament. Some factories concentrated on purely functional products, like hinges, bolts and stair-rods. Birmingham screws were world-famous, Maudsley's improved screw-cutting lathe invented in 1800 having facilitated the production of screws of better quality than were made anywhere else. Other factories specialized in the higher ranges of craftsmanship, in lamp- or fender-making, for instance. Tall objects in bronze, like the *guéridons* and lamp-stands fashionable on the Continent since the *Directoire*, seem to have been made very little in England at first, although it is known that things of this kind were produced in Italy to the specifications of English designers. It is true that in 1807 Thomas Hope published designs for Grecian-looking candle-stands of gilded bronze, and possibly some actual examples of these stands existed at Deepdene, his house in Surrey; but it is doubtful if more than a very few were ever made of bronze in the 1800's outside his circle. In 1823–4 appeared the third edition of Lewis Nockalls Cottingham's *Smith and Founder's Director*, with designs for large- and small-scale bronze objects modelled on Classical and French prototypes (Fig. 5); and by that time the larger sort of bronze furniture was evidently made in England (Pl. 66B). Brass too was being used more in furniture. A history of Birmingham published by Jabet and Moore about 1817 records that B. Cook & Company of Broad Street in that city were already making bedsteads of hollow brass pieces. Rods of brass had been used since the eighteenth century for sideboard railings, and by 1810 similar, if stouter, rods were incorporated in music-stands and other slender types of furniture (Fig. 6).

Fig. 5. Design for a vase in brass or bronze in the form of a Rhyton. From *The Smith and Founder's Director* by L. N. Cottingham, London 1823–4.

The evolution of the candlestick after 1805 was somewhat influenced by the introduction of the tall glass open globe or shade (often painted or wheelcut), which kept the flame from flickering, but which required the candlestick itself to be slightly shorter in proportion and heavier at the bottom, otherwise it would have overbalanced (Pl.

67D, E). From about 1805 to 1835 the vogue for short candlesticks, cast in brass and partly bronzed, was strongly maintained. The earlier ones were enriched with all the current neo-classical motifs that were appropriate, from Greek frets on the plinth bases to acanthus leaves on the shafts. Sometimes there would be a corona of leaves below the nozzle, or a circle of branches or 'showers', as they were called, for holding cut-glass 'icicles' (Pl. 66E). This kind of candlestick went on the chimney-piece. Eagles, putti, sphinxes and women in Hellenistic garments were used frequently for supports, either on columnar pedestals, or on triangular plinths with concave sides. About 1815 less classical forms came into fashion for the supporting figures, such as elephants bearing castles, and reclining hounds at the tail-ends of which stems, or sometimes the tails themselves, curled upwards to hold the nozzles off-centre. In large candelabra, figures of Atlas (Pl. 67B) and of Egyptian slaves were favoured; in fact the popularity of this type of supporter began to decline only when neo-rococo scrolls became the rage in the 1830's.

All this time the manufacture of plain brass candlesticks went on, some being short, like the fashionable ones, others being as tall as they had ever been. Probably the most characteristic base was oblong in plan (Pl. 68B): by 1830 the bases were usually oblong with chamfered corners, and the shafts had bold knops, often decorated with facets or with turned reeding. But the candlestick industry was without question reduced in scope by the new oil-lamps and finally by the arrival of gas.

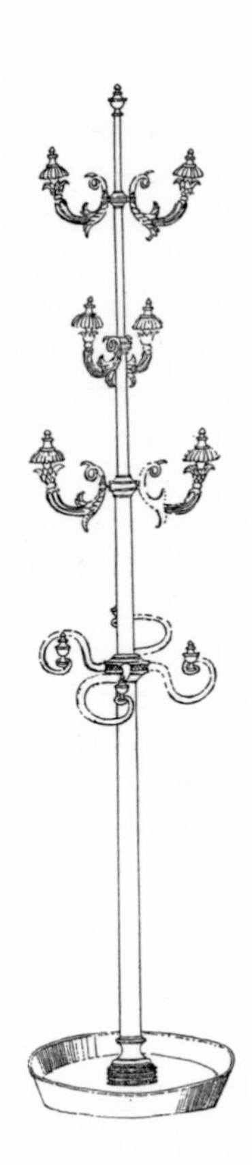

Fig. 6. Umbrella and hat-stand. From a brass-founder's pattern-book, *c.* 1820. *Victoria and Albert Museum.*

Much of the best workmanship of the period went into the making of these lamps in either brass or bronze, which was chiefly undertaken by specialists. In comparison with candlelight, there was something very romantic about the moon-like glow of a lamp through a 'French-roughed', or ground-glass, globe. Such globes were occasionally referred to as 'moons'. There was, no doubt, another reason why so much attention was given to lamps in the Regency, and that was the presence in England of Aimé Argand, the Swiss physicist, who died here in 1803, having given his name to a business at 37 Bruton Street, for the production of the kind of lamp he had patented, with an air-burner and a cylindrical wick. In the early years of the century the Bruton Street business went under the names of Argand and Elgar, but at the end of our period the family of Bright, who were Sheffield-platers established at the same address, took over the business, and it became known in the 1830's as 'Bright, late Argand & Company'. Another famous lamp-maker of the time was J. Smethurst of 138, New Bond Street, a patentee of the lamp with a spiral burner. In Birmingham the two leading lamp manufacturers seem to have been W. Blakeway & Son of

Edgbaston Street, and Joseph Shelton of Bradford Street.

Open-wick lamps were still made, from the crusie type for Scottish farmhouses and the American backwoods, to ornamental types in the forms of ancient Roman lamps. But those with air-burners on the Argand principle were the most characteristic of the period. This contrivance was used in chandeliers with as many as six burners, and in table and sideboard lamps, either with one burner, or with two burners at the ends of arms set slightly forward from the shaft (Pl. 68C). The oil was poured into an urn-shaped reservoir or tank at the top of the lamp, running from there along the arm and into the cylindrical wick in the burner. Until 1840 it would have been spermaceti oil (from the sperm whale) or colza oil (from the colza seed), both of which were so heavy that they worked best when draining downwards to the wick.

In the course of George IV's reign, apparently, two new kinds of lamp were devised: the reading lamp with an adjustable Argand burner and a japanned-iron shade (Pl. 68A); and the Sinumbra lamp, wherein the burner was set below a hollow ring which acted both as a tank for the oil and as a rest for the large hemispherical, or sometimes flask-shaped, shade (Pl. 67A). The poisoner, Thomas Griffiths Wainewright, in one of his essays, describes the apartment of a London dandy, that is to say his own apartment in 1821, as being illuminated by what he calls a 'new elegantly gilt French lamp, having a ground glass globe painted with gay flowers and gaudy butterflies'. It is probable that the term 'French lamp' was generic; but in the advertisement of C. F. Younge in the Sheffield directory of 1828 it was clearly applied to the Sinumbra lamp, and this type of lamp, though doubtless invented in France, became very popular in England. As the name tells us, it cast no shadows. Quantities of Sinumbras, probably of English origin and dating from the 1830's, survive, rather green from disuse, in the palace of Mafra in Portugal.

The principle of the Argand burner was retained well into the Victorian age for gas-lighting. In this form of illumination the English had been pioneers since the day in 1798, when it was first used experimentally at Boulton & Watt's foundry in Birmingham. Although relatively few have lasted to the present time, brass chandeliers and wall-brackets for gas, with prominent anthemion and acanthus features, were in production well before 1830. Cottingham, too, in his *Director*, gives some designs for gaslight stands which follow the conventions of oil-lamp stands and candelabra in the same book.

One of the accomplishments of Bucks and Corinthians under George IV was that of tearing off knockers from doors. They must have found out there was a kind of knocker in which the larger part consisted of the rapper secured to the door by a single pin, the other part being a mere bolt for the rapper to strike upon. Such was the wreath-and-hand knocker, very popular in the 1820's (Pl. 65C). Other knockers of the period seem to have been designed mainly on the following lines: those with ring-shaped rappers of bronzed iron on shields with brass centres (Pl. 65F); lyre-shaped rappers suspended from heads; semicircular or elliptical rappers suspended from urn forms. But the variations of detail were countless. Ring rappers in lions' mouths continued to be made as in the eighteenth century, but with small differences. More characteristic were the eagle-and-palmette knocker (Pl. 65E), and the kind with an acanthus leaf pointing downwards and a loop-shaped rapper.

The firms that made door-knockers were mostly in Birmingham, and the same firms generally made door-stops as well. These objects, then known as door-porters, were to be had in iron or brass, like the knockers, or with iron bases and brass handles. A conservative design going back to the late eighteenth century consisted of a base shaped like a bell cut in half longitudinally, with perhaps ball or lion-paw feet and a long, thin shaft topped by a lifting ring. Around 1820 the designs of door-porters became more fanciful, involving shell, acanthus, anthemion and lotus forms; and a favourite under George IV was that of a big lion's paw from which grew a long leaf ending in a handle simulating rope (Pl. 65D).

It is surprising how some of the patterns conceived in the first thirty years of the nineteenth century for functional articles survived as proto-

Fig. 7. Design for a bell-pull by Augustus Charles Pugin. From Ackermann's *Repository of Arts*, 1st September, 1827.

types. The old kind of coffee-mill, for instance (Fig. 8), still to be seen in Edwardian kitchens, with its bowl and pedestal outlines, is essentially a Regency invention, and was clearly thought out at the time when sloping Egyptian jambs began to fascinate designers and architects. Izons, Whitehurst & Izon of Birmingham showed one of these mills in an advertisement of 1818. A pattern-book of about 1820 shows a four-ale beer-pump with brass fittings, not very different from the ones we know. The Gillott steel pen, patented around 1820 by Joseph Gillott of Birmingham, is still with us, almost unchanged; and so, too, is corrugated-iron sheeting, which (in spite of the Oxford Dictionary) dates back certainly to the early 1830's, and probably before then. Regency designs were taken for granted only a generation ago. There is about them a curious mixture of the classical, the romantic and the whimsical. Whether ornate or severe, whether in coffee-mills or in lamps, the styles thus evolved passed with the political and commercial influence of England into the material culture of almost the entire civilized world of the nineteenth century.

SHORT BIBLIOGRAPHY

On most of the subjects discussed above no monographs exist, and little is to be gained by referring to general works on the history of brass and iron manufactures. In this connexion the Victoria and Albert Museum catalogue of *Old English Pattern Books of the Metal Trades* (1913), by W. A. Young, is of interest.

I am, however, much indebted to *Pontypool and Usk Japanned Wares* by W. D. John, Newport (Mon.), 1953; to *Tutenag and Paktong* by Alfred Bonnin, O.U.P. 1924 (for white metal alloys); and to *The Story of Cutlery* by J. B. Himsworth, London, 1953. *Old Pewter, its Makers and Marks* by H. H. Cotterell, London, 1929, is a standard book on the subject of pewter generally, to which may be added *Chats on Old Pewter* by H. J. L. J. Massé, London, 2nd edition, 1949. See also J. Seymour Lindsay's *Iron and Brass Implements of the English House*, London, 1927.

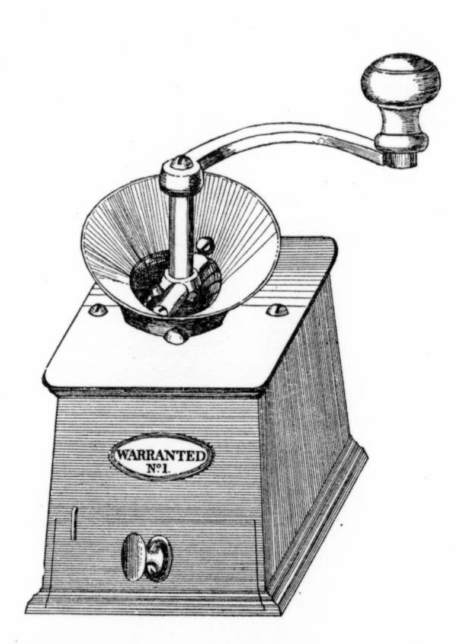


Fig. 8. Coffee-mill of iron and brass. From a brassfounder's pattern-book, *c.* 1820. *Victoria and Albert Museum.*

## *Textiles*

# Textiles

BARBARA MORRIS

## *General introduction*

Nothing could be further from the truth than the general assumption of the chaste and elegant *Regency-stripe* as the dominant style in textiles throughout the period 1810–30. Stripes do appear, in printed fabrics, but not until 1824, when the Regency proper had already ended, and their introduction is an anticipation of styles which became increasingly popular in the 1830's and 1840's. In the field of printed textiles the patterns had never been more exuberant or the colours more brilliant than during the Regency. In woven fabrics, however, the English manufacturers do not appear to have imitated the elaborate Empire designs of the Lyons silk weavers; and where such designs have been found on English upholstered furniture, the silk is almost certainly of French manufacture, for in spite of parliamentary legislation forbidding the import of French fabrics, a certain amount undoubtedly reached this country. Modified eighteenth-century floral damask patterns, or plain coloured silks and worsteds were most favoured, but the restraint in pattern was more than compensated by the lavish use of fringes and braids, and by the elaboration and complexity of the draperies.

Silk, wool or cotton damasks, or plain woven fabrics, including velvet and horsehair, were used for the furnishing of dining-rooms and libraries. Silk was also used extensively in drawing-rooms, bedrooms and boudoirs, but in these rooms chintz was a close competitor. At the beginning of the Regency, chintz was in high fashion among Royal circles and the nobility. In 1811 the Prince of Wales commissioned a 'rich furniture chintz' from Abraham Allen, a leading linen-draper in Pall Mall, for his bedroom at Carlton House. Allen was also patronized by H.R.H. Princess Elizabeth, and in 1813 the Duchess of Bedford selected 'an olive chintz for furniture' (with a small design of roses) for her new 'cottage' in Devonshire. At the end of the period, however, chintz was not in such high fashion, and in 1826 George Smith in his *Cabinet Maker's and Upholsterer's Guide* decrees that 'printed calicos may answer extremely well for secondary apartments, or for those in houses of persons of small fortune; but they are not at all suitable for those of persons of rank and splendid income'. These furniture chintzes were used for window and bed draperies, usually with a plain-coloured contrasting lining, and edged with variegated fringes. Chintz, particularly when patterned in imitation of damask, was also used extensively for upholstery. The Gillow account books at Lancaster for the years 1812–14 give considerable details of the use of chintz for furniture. Couches and sofas and the head- and foot-boards of French beds were covered with chintz as well as the loose cushions for both sofas and curricle chairs. Hassocks and footstools also had chintz covers. Chintz was also used extensively for 'throw-overs', that is dust-covers for the protection of furniture.

It is worth noting that the furnishings of the period were produced not so much for the great houses as for the terraces and squares of Brighton, Cheltenham and Regent's Park, and for the villas and '*cottages ornés*' scattered throughout the country. Few Regency interiors have remained intact, and since very few actual textiles appear to have survived, our information has therefore to be gathered almost exclusively from contemporary illustrations or written sources.

### *Drapery*

Throughout the period the elaborate draperies, for both windows and bed-hangings, tended to be copied from the French and were often acknowledged as such in being described as 'French window curtains'. The Greek or classic style continued in favour throughout the period, but from 1825 onwards draperies in the Gothic taste were the recognized alternative to harmonize with the Gothic furniture popularized by the elder Pugin and others.

Whatever the individual modifications, the general scheme, whether symmetrical or asymetrical, consisted of an upper drapery or pelmet at the top of the window, behind which were floor-length curtains of the same or contrasting colour, and against the window itself sub-curtains of muslin or other transparent materials which served 'to break the strength of the light, without entirely secluding [sic] the cheering effect produced from the solar rays' (Geo. Smith, *Cabinet Maker's and Upholsterer's Guide*, 1826).

Until about 1818 fairly heavy styles were most favoured. The upper drapery was usually fringed and looped up at intervals, and from these points tassels were often suspended. Laurel wreaths, or other classical devices, were often embroidered on the upper drapery (Fig. 1). The main curtains were generally edged with a bullion or ball fringe, and the borders embroidered (or painted if of a heavy woollen material) with Greek designs of anthemion or similar motifs. Heavy wool or damask curtains were unlined, but chintz or light-weight silk curtains were usually lined with a contrasting colour. The muslin sub-curtains were often embroidered at the edge with a running floral or classical design, and edged with a vandyked or scalloped border, or with chenille fringe (Pl. 69A).

For single windows the simplest type of drapery consisted of a single curtain which was slung over a pole so that the shorter part in front formed the upper drapery or valance, and the longer part behind the main curtain. The curtain was then looped to one side by means of a curtain-pin attached to the wall, revealing the muslin sub-curtain beneath. Circular-topped windows were often filled in at the top with drapery pleated fan-wise to a central ornament. When there were several windows in one wall, it was usual to unite them by a continuous upper-drapery.

In 1819 a more fanciful type of drapery came into fashion which, although if anything more elaborate than the preceding styles, was of a lighter appearance, and had been fashionable in France some years earlier. In the description of a suite of draperies for drawing-room windows, published in March, 1820, Ackermann remarks on the 'playful external swags' which are formed by a continuous drapery looped over and under the curtain pole on either side of a central ornament to form a series of festoons. The central ornament often took the form of a bird, usually an eagle or a peacock (Pl. 69B), and the festoons were suspended from elaborate devices of carved and gilded wood in the form of clusters of grapes and leaves, pineapples or scrolling acanthus foliage, which were attached to the cornice pole at intervals by strong wire. The naturalism of the ornaments, although still basically classical in form, gave a more fanciful appearance to the whole scheme, and the curtains in this type of drapery were usually of light-coloured silks rather than of heavy velvet or wool (Fig. 2).

'Curtain cornices', a kind of rigid pelmet of carved and gilded wood, first introduced by Chippendale about 1775, appear again in 1819, and by 1820 Ackermann remarks that they 'are now adopted in a great variety and will probably very soon supersede the late fashion of suspending draperies by poles and detached ornaments'. These cornices were particularly suited to 'Gothic' styles of decoration and became increasingly popular after 1825, often being carved in imitation of architectural crocketting (Pl. 69C). With this style of drapery, the upper festoons were replaced by a more rigid valance made of buckram covered with velvet and cut into fancy shapes at the lower edge. Fleur-de-lys or other Gothic devices were applied in a contrasting colour, and the edge might be further embellished with tassels. Another type

(A) *left:* Drawing room window curtain from Ackermann's *Repository*, March, 1815. The drapery is of azure blue silk edged with bullion fringe, the curtains held back by silk cords. The muslin sub-curtain has an embroidered border. *Victoria and Albert Museum.*

(B) *right:* Roller-printed cotton (in the possession of Messrs. G. P. & J. Baker) showing a draped window of about 1820.

(C) Curtains for a Gothic room from George Smith's *Cabinet Maker's and Upholsterer's Guide*, 1826. 'The cornice is supposed to be of oak, in which case, it will require to be wholly carved; but . . . it may be made of deal, and the ornamental parts made of composition . . . the arrangement would answer equally well for the drawing room, dining room, or library'. *Victoria and Albert Museum.*

PLATE 69

(A) Damask table-cloth signed and dated 'F. & C. Smith 1828'. *Victoria and Albert Museum.*

(B) Chair seat of silk brocade probably woven at Spitalfields for the Saloon of the Royal Pavilion, Brighton, about 1817.
*By gracious permission of H. M. The Queen.*

(A) Polychrome wood-block chintz, printed by Peel & Co., Church, near Accrington, in 1812. Another piece of the same design is stamped with Peel's mark and the excise stamp for 1812. *Victoria and Albert Museum.*

(B) Panel for a patchwork quilt, wood-block printed in polychrome, about 1815. Property of the Musée de l'Impression of the Société Industrielle de Mulhouse, Alsace.

(A) Cotton, roller-printed in blue and green. This is one of the earliest roller-printed furnishing fabrics known to have survived and was printed in 1818, probably by Samuel Matley of Hodge, Cheshire. *Victoria and Albert Museum.*

(B) Pillar print, roller-printed in sepia with yellow added by surface roller. Printed by Samuel Matley & Son at Hodge, Cheshire in 1826. Collection of Messrs. G. P. & J. Baker.

(A) The British Isles. Cotton, roller-printed in red, probably by John Marshall & Sons, Manchester, between 1818 and 1824. *Victoria and Albert Museum.*

(B) Striped chintz, printed from wood-blocks with 'tea-ground', *c.* 1824. Property of Miss Josephine Howell, New York.

Axminster hand-knotted carpet re-assembled from fragments of the carpet made for the Saloon of the Royal Pavilion, Brighton, in 1817.
*Reproduced by gracious permission of H.M. the Queen.*

PLATE 74

(A) Two designs for carpets from George Smith's *Collection of Ornamental Designs after the Manner of the Antique*, London, 1812. *Victoria and Albert Museum.*

(B) Part of the skirt of a muslin dress (not made up) embroidered with cotton thread and further decorated with cut-work filled in with needlepoint stitches. Worked by Lady Mary Finch, daughter of the 4th Earl of Aylesford, probably shortly before her death in 1823. *Victoria and Albert Museum.*

(A) Sampler. Silk on linen; cross-stitch, tent, satin and encroaching stitches. Signed and dated 'Mary Ann Cook 1813'. *Victoria and Albert Museum.*

(B) 'The Setting Sun', after Gaspard Pousin. Fabric collage of tailors' cuttings worked by Mrs Dickson about 1825–30 and exhibited in Brighton and London about 1831. *Victoria and Albert Museum.*

PLATE 76

Fig. 1. Drawing-room window curtain first published by Ackermann, 1st February 1813. The cabinet was designed by George Bullock.

of upper-drapery used with the cornice was termed 'hammercloth' or 'petticoat' drapery, in which the material was gathered into simple flutes from each of which a tassel was suspended.

An example of yet another type of pelmet, used mainly for libraries or dining-rooms, is illustrated by Ackermann in September 1819. The material, either moreen (a coarse fabric of woollen and worsted mixture) or velvet, was pleated into vertical pipes, stuffed with wool and mounted on to a stiff canvas, giving the appearance of much-enlarged corrugated cardboard. The centre portion of the pelmet was usually left flat and ornamented with a painted or embroidered figure.

Bed-drapery falls into three main types. The first type, the heavily-curtained four-poster bed, remained in favour throughout the period. The curtains and valances were made of chintz, silk or merino damask, ornamented with fringes and tassels. The draperies round the top of the bed sometimes reached an amazing degree of complexity, but the lower valance was kept fairly simple.

The lighter 'tent' or 'field' bed was found more suitable for small rooms or for the fashionable 'cottages' and villas. The posts, which were lower than those on the four posters, were masked by draped curtains and were united by curved rods, covered by drapery to form a tent or canopy.

The third type, the 'French bed', was in fact a kind of couch, which was placed against the wall, the drapery being suspended from a pole at right-angles to the wall about ten feet from the floor, or, alternatively, from a small canopy at the head.

*Woven fabrics*

In the field of woven fabrics, the introduction of new types of materials assumes more importance than superficial changes of pattern. In the manufacture of printed fabrics it was necessary to produce new and novel designs in rapid succession, for what was fashionable in one season was already out of favour in the next. With woven fabrics, however, because of the complexities of manufacture and the fact that the fabrics were intended to last for a longer period, the same considerations did not apply, and there are no very marked stylistic changes in design throughout the period. Towards the end of the period, however, the gradual introduction of the Jacquard loom made possible the production of more elaborately figured textiles at lower cost and paved the way to the more complex patterns of the Victorian era.

In contrast to the eighteenth century, when the costly hand-woven figured silks dominated the scene, during the Regency period plain fabrics in silk and wool, Manchester or cotton velvets, worsted and cotton damask, merinos and moreens, came to the fore as a result of the increasing mechanization of the textile industry. The evidence given to the Select Committee on Arts and Manufacture in 1835 makes it clear that the Spitalfields silk industry was not in a very flourishing condition throughout the period. There were no outstanding designers employed in the drawing of patterns and the weavers were engaged in producing plain silks or velvets or small figured patterns which showed very little originality, and the chair seat shown on Plate 70B must be regarded as something of a rarity. In spite of the fact that the import of French silks was forbidden, most of the designs seem to have been copied from the French, and the lifting of the ban in 1826 seems to have effected an improvement in inspiring the Spitalfields manufacturers to meet increasing competition by raising the standard of both design and colouring. In this year we read that 'our fair countrywomen have resolved to make silk of the Spitalfields manufactory a considerable portion of their dress (to relieve a distressed industry). His Majesty has given orders that the rooms of his palace at Windsor shall be hung round with silk of Spitalfields manufacture.' Presumably this latter was part of the extensive alterations and redecorations which were begun at Windsor in 1825, and the Windsor archives contain a detailed invoice for nearly £15,000 worth of silk from a Wm. Edward King, Silk Mercer.

While the Spitalfields industry was obviously in a state of decline, it is clear that other centres of weaving in the Manchester area, in Yorkshire and in Norwich, were rapidly advancing. In Ackermann's *Repository* for February 1821, it is stated that the 'loom of our country is now in that state of advanced perfection that damasks of the most magnificent kind in point of intensity of colour and richness of pattern are manufactured at prices that permit their free use in well-furnished apartments'. The introduction of power, and of the Jacquard apparatus, which did not necessarily go hand in hand, enabled woven fabrics to be produced in far greater quantities and at considerably lower cost. Power-weaving, which had developed particularly in Lancashire, was nearly always confined to the production of plain fabrics other than silks, such as calico and twills, and was wholly and necessarily conducted on the factory system. The Jacquard machinery, however, could be applied to almost any loom and was at first introduced in Yorkshire in places where the weaving industry was still on a cottage basis. The evidence of M. Claude Guillotte, a manufacturer of Jacquard machinery, given before the 1835 Select Committee on Design, affords details of its introduction into England. The first Jacquard looms were installed in Halifax, Huddersfield and the surrounding country in 1824. The earliest looms seem to have been used for producing small patterns, principally for waistcoats, but their use soon spread to the production of merinos and woollen damasks and by 1835 there were about 8,000 Jacquard looms in operation. The merinos (a thin woollen twilled cloth, sometimes a mixture of silk and wool) and woollen damasks, which were made in Norwich as well as in Yorkshire, were much in demand for curtains and bed hangings, for as George Smith put it in his *Cabinet Maker's and Upholsterer's Guide* they 'make up very beautifully, not requiring a lining'. The *Repository* includes in its 'Pattern of British Manufacture' for November 1812 'an entirely new article (a white cotton damask with a traditional pattern of formalized leaves and flowers) for white beds and other furniture. It has a beautiful effect in the piece and produces a rich appearance when made up. This handsome manufacture will be found desirable to persons who have large establishments to furnish, for it wants no lining.' It is not surprising that this last consideration was an important one, for an enormous yardage must

Fig. 2. Draperies for circular windows, designed by Stafford of Bath, and first published by Ackermann, 1st February 1820.

have been taken up by the complexities of the festoons and draperies then in fashion.

Similarly, on grounds of economy, the 'Manchester velvets', of cotton instead of silk, found a ready market. The Report of the Select Committee on the Duties Payable on Printed Cotton Goods, 1818, quotes the evidence of Thomas Hargreaves, a leading calico-printer, on woven cotton goods. He mentions that 'there is a good deal of dyed cottons which are embossed with machine, which are used as furniture'. These fabrics, which were stamped with small diaper patterns, seem to have been used mainly for upholstery and were presumably cheaper than the woven figured stuffs.

Considerable advances were made during this period in the production of linen damasks in the Yorkshire area, particularly in Barnsley. The linen and flax industry had been established at Barnsley about 1790, but until 1810 production had been confined to heavy linens such as sheetings, ducks and dowlas (a coarse, half-unbleached linen cloth). In 1810, however, production was extended to 'finer goods embracing huckabacks, diapers, damasks, fine broad sheetings ... rivalling in beauty the handsomest productions of Scotland and Ireland, and possessing great superiority in the quality of the material' (William White, *History, Gazeteer and Directory of the West-Riding of Yorkshire*, 1837). Although power was introduced for the weaving of some of the plain cloths, the production of damasks was organized on a cottage basis, the flax-yarn being purchased by the 'manufacturers' from the spinners and given out to handloom weavers who wove it in their own homes returning the finished goods to the 'manufacturer'. The Victoria and Albert Museum has several

English damask tablecloths of this period, including one with an all-over check and herringbone pattern dated 1818, the one illustrated (Pl. 70A) and an elaborate pictorial design dated 1830.

*Printed textiles*

The high standard which printed furnishing fabrics reached during this period has not generally been realized. Attention has been almost exclusively directed to the pictorial *toiles* printed from copper-plates, and since the few Regency examples that have survived are manifestly inferior to both eighteenth-century English examples and the contemporary French 'classical' *toiles*, English printed textiles after 1800 have been dismissed as of little interest. It has not been appreciated that by the turn of the century, the earlier copper-plate designs had been replaced in public favour by polychrome floral chintzes printed from wood-blocks. Recently discovered records have shown that these, far from declining in merit or interest after 1800, were immensely popular during the first decades of the century, and showed no deterioration of standards. Similarly, the high standard which roller prints achieved during the 1820's has also been ignored. Many of the finely-engraved designs were printed in fugitive colours, and since those pieces which have survived tend to be badly faded, it is only an examination of unexposed pieces in pattern-books that enables a true assessment of their merits to be made.

Although Thomas Bell's initial invention of rotary printing by engraved metal-rollers was patented in 1783, it was not until about 1820 that furnishing fabrics began to be printed by machine and until then the polychrome wood-block printed chintzes dominated the scene. Whereas in the eighteenth century most of the important calico-printing factories were situated near London, by 1810 most of these had closed down, or turned over to silk-printing, and the centre of production had shifted to the Lancashire area. Hundreds of different patterns were brought out each year by the leading factories such as Bannister Hall, near Preston; Peel and Co., Church, near Accrington; Samuel Matley of Hodge, Cheshire; and Hargreaves and Dugdale of Broad Oak, Accrington. The Bannister Hall pattern-books (now in the possession of Stead, McAlpin Ltd) and others in the possession of the Calico Printers' Association provide a firm reference in plotting the various styles, month by month, throughout this period, and changes of style are so frequent and so marked that most of the surviving textiles can be pin-pointed to a particular year.

The various patterns were in the main 'engaged' to the leading London linen-drapers and reserved exclusively for their use, although the designs were frequently pirated by other firms. The Copyright Act of 1787 (27 Geo. III c. 38) gave two months' protection to a design, and this was extended to three months in 1789 (29 Geo. III c. 19). However, the period was too short for the protection to be effective, and it was not until 1842, when registration of a design with the Patent Office gave three years' protection, that the copyrighting had any real meaning. It was usually the linen-draper who commissioned the design and sent it to one of the Lancashire firms for printing. The anonymity of the designer was in the main preserved, but the names of a few of the leading designers are known through extant signed designs, among them Daniel Goddard, who was active during the first ten years of the nineteenth century, and Vaughan, who is known to have been working between 1806 and 1826. The Bannister Hall records contain a separate series of original designs carried out for Richard Ovey, of Tavistock Street, Covent Garden, who was one of the leading suppliers of 'furniture prints' from 1790 to 1831. The fact that Ovey, and other leading linen-drapers such as Abraham Allen of Pall Mall; E. B. Dudding of Bond Street; Liddiards of Friday Street, and Miles and Edwards of Oxford Street, all called themselves 'furniture printers' has led to some confusion, for none of these merchants were in any sense manufacturers but merely retailers who used the big Lancashire firms as commission printers.

For the first ten years of the century the most fashionable 'furniture prints' had been in the 'drab style', that is, printed in shades of dull brown with some yellow and green but no red. By 1810, however, this style had in the main given way to polychrome chintzes which exploited the full palette available with the madder dyes and enabled the floral designs to be realisitically treated in natural colours. Plain blotch grounds, of which the beige 'tea-ground' and a sky-blue ground were the commonest, were widely used throughout the period.

From 1812 to 1816 architectural motifs were introduced into the floral designs which were usually arranged in a half-drop repeat (Pl. 71A). Both the Classic and Gothic tastes were represented by the introduction of appropriate ruins, but there is rarely any sense of scale or pictorial reality, the architectural motifs being introduced extraneously into a conventional floral chintz. From 1814 to 1816, game birds, particularly partridges, grouse and pheasants, were a popular subject, usually depicted singly or in pairs under a blossoming tree or an exotic palm (Pl. 71B). From 1810 to 1815 specially printed panels with matching borders were made for the centres of patchwork quilts, which achieved great popularity during the Regency. These were similar to the panels printed earlier in the century for chair-backs and chair-seats. The patchwork quilt panels are all polychrome, and all the surviving panels have such close stylistic affinities that they may have been the speciality of one printer. Some of the designs are commemorative, such as that made on the occasion of the wedding of Princess Charlotte in 1816; others depict baskets or bunches of flowers, birds, deer and *chinoiserie* subjects.

Patterns imitating damask, usually printed in shades of one colour, are found throughout the period, particularly between the years 1812 and 1814. Some of the designs are traditional damask patterns of formalized flowers and leaves, others are elaborate patterns of coiling acanthus foliage, and some are simple diapers of stars or other classical motifs. Many of these chintzes have an elaborate border, modelled on a classical frieze, with a simple filling in the ground of the chintz. A number of the designs are similar to plates in George Smith's *Collection of Ornamental Designs after the Manner of the Antique* (1812), which was intended for the use of the calico-printer no less than other manufacturers. A curious feature of these 'damask' chintzes is that the whole ground is often covered by fine diagonal parallel lines, printed by machine after the main design had been printed by wood-blocks, usually in dark purple or blue. The purpose was, presumably, to imitate the effect of a twill weave, as the diagonal lines are rarely found except in those patterns which imitate a woven silk.

It was not until 1824 that any form of striped chintz, usually presumed to be characteristic of the Regency, appears in the pattern-books. The striped designs usually consisted of alternating vertical stripes and floral sprigs (Pl. 73B), but in some cases the vertical stripe was formed of overlapping lozenges placed one over the other in a continuous band. This latter variety remained in fashion for about two years and, as with the damask designs, there was often a broad border at each side of the chintz, and the pattern was so organized that it could be used vertically for curtains or horizontally for valances.

Chintz blinds, which were semi-transparent and intended to be hung flat without any folds, first appeared in 1825. Most of the designs were Gothic, with architectural tracery and imitation stained-glass panels of an heraldic character, but a number of chinoiserie designs have also been found. The fashion for Gothic chintz blinds lasted well into the 1850's, but by that time the designs had become extremely crude.

In 1829 there arose a fashion for large flowers, accurately drawn in the manner of a botanical plate. The pattern-books show that many of these designs were produced between 1829 and 1836, but very few of the actual fabrics appear to have survived. The same year, 1829, also saw the introduction of long-tailed birds and butterflies into the design. A favourite subject was the bird of paradise, and several chintzes, including one with the stamp of Miles and Edwards, have been found with life-size representations of the species.

The earliest furniture chintzes printed entirely by machine that have survived date from 1818 (Pl. 72A), and it is not until 1820 that they are found in any quantity. The majority of the designs are floral, but a number of pictorial designs, of the type printed from copper-plates in the eighteenth century, have also been found, including a group of rustic scenes from the printworks of John

Marshall of Manchester, which operated for six years from 1818–24 (Pl. 73A).

The styles found in the roller-prints do not exactly parallel those found in the wood-block printed chintzes, for much finer detail was possible with the engraved rollers. A number of what may for convenience be termed 'traditional' floral chintzes were produced with the red printed by engraved roller and the blue and yellow added by block, or surface-rollers, but more interesting are an entirely new range of furniture chintzes in which the whole basis of the design was finely engraved on a metal roller. The design was printed either in a monochrome version, or with additional colours added by block or surface roller (Pl. 72B). The standard of draughtsmanship of these early roller-designs was often extremely high, but the effect was often marred by the indiscriminate use of the new mineral and chemical dyes such as John Mercer's antimony orange (1817), Prussian blue and cochineal pink.

The fashions in the roller-prints were even more ephemeral than those in the wood-block field, and shipping-order books in the possession of the Calico Printers' Association show an almost unbelievable turnover of patterns. An account of the printworks of Hargreaves and Dugdale of Broad Oak, Accrington, reprinted in the 1850 *Journal of Design*, lists the different styles produced by that factory, which were also adopted by other Lancashire printworks. The standard of engraving at Broad Oak was high owing to their employment in 1822 of John Potts, a painter by profession, who was regarded as the 'foremost engraver of his generation', but the development of engraved rollers probably owes even more to Joseph Lockett, whose firm was famed throughout Europe as engravers of 'cover-rollers', from which were printed the fancy machine grounds popular in the late 1820's and 1830's.

Potts' first designs consisted of 'single columns of flowers in trails and stripes with stippled grounds'. A method of printing graduated stripes in 'rainbow' colours, was first introduced at Broad Oak in 1824, and this garish style was rapidly copied by other printers. The 'rainbow' ground was over-printed, or discharged, with various mossy patterns, and also with abstract designs of stars, concentric circles and 'Catherine-wheel' patterns giving the effect of bursting fireworks.

The year 1826 saw the revival of the pillar-print, popular in wood-block chintzes at the beginning of the century. Corinthian or Ionic columns, with elaborate capitals, entwined with finely engraved flowers, were printed on stippled grounds of graduated stripes or marbled effects (Pl. 72B). In the same years 'feather' patterns were introduced, and also designs of dancing cherubs.

Perhaps the most interesting of all the roller-prints, however, are a series of designs of birds and flowers, found in the Calico Printers' Association pattern-books, copied directly from Audubon's *Birds of America*, of which the first plates appeared in 1827. Six designs after Audubon were produced between 1830 and 1834, four of them in as many as twenty-five different colour-ways.

### *Carpets*

There are few extant carpets of the Regency period, and our knowledge of them derives mainly from written sources and contemporary illustrations. Although in this period the main bulk of production was of carpets in which the pattern was woven on the loom, it is the more expensive hand-knotted carpets that have in fact survived.

A few documented pieces, made at the Axminster factory founded by Thomas Whitty in 1755, are extant. Two of these are fragments of the large hand-knotted carpets made for the Royal Pavilion, Brighton, in 1817. The carpet illustrated (Pl. 74) has been reassembled from pieces of the Saloon carpet which originally measured thirty-six feet in diameter and cost £620. The design of this carpet shows a mixture of oriental and floral motifs, but the carpet for the Music Room, a portion of which also survives, was of purely Chinese inspiration with a pattern of pairs of confronting dragons and Chinese sacred symbols in shades of gold on a blue ground. A similar carpet was also made at Axminster for the Banqueting Room. The pattern consisted of 'a dragon, three serpents coiled around and involving it, form the central ornament; this is surrounded by circles diversely wrought, and increasing in diameter towards the border'. No portion of this carpet appears to have survived. All three carpets were designed by Robert Jones, and a fairly good estimate of the original appearance of them can be made from the plates of Brayley's *Illustrations of Her Majesty's Palace at Brighton* (1838).

Fragments of another Axminster carpet, woven in 1823, are in the Soane Museum, but the design is of less interest, being of an Oriental type based on Turkish *Ushak* carpets. The Victoria and Albert Museum has a hand-knotted carpet with a naturalistic floral design on a green ground which was probably made at Axminster during the last years of the factory which closed down in 1835. The Rev. Thomas Moore in his *History of Devonshire* (1829–31) regarded the factory as a flourishing concern and wrote that the 'carpets were never in higher repute than at present. His Majesty's Palaces at Brighton and Windsor are graced by the labours of the women of Axminster, as are also the mansions and country seats of the nobility.' At that time about a hundred people, mainly women, were employed in the manufacture, but since at least five women were employed on each loom, there must have been less than twenty looms in operation. The Axminster carpets were naturally luxury productions, for, as Moore says, 'the thickness of these fabrics being greater than any others of the kind, and the quantity of raw materials used in the manufacture of them being consequently large, – the labour, as the work is done by the fingers, being minute and tedious, – and considerable sums, occasionally thirty or forty pounds being spent on the pattern, the price of them is necessarily high'. Axminster was ultimately unable to compete with the increasing production of cheaper, woven carpets, and in 1835 the factory was closed down, and the equipment transferred to Wilton.

The carpets with the pattern woven on the loom were of the types known by their contemporary names of Brussels, Wilton, Kidderminster, Scotch and Venetian. In the Brussels type the worsted woollen warp was brought to the surface in raised loops to produce the pattern, the binding weft, of fine linen or hemp thread, being hidden by the pile. The Brussels loom was a draw-boy [1] loom which necessitated the weaver having an assistant. The Wilton type was a modification of Brussels in which the looped pile was cut after weaving to give a velvet effect. The Kidderminster and Scotch carpets were both of the ingrain variety. They were non-pile carpets, were usually reversible, with the warp and weft both contributing to the pattern. These carpets were normally of double-cloth or two-ply weaving, but in 1824 a stronger three-ply version was perfected at Kilmarnock and afterwards made elsewhere. The Venetian carpeting was an even cheaper variety, woven in a simple check pattern, with the weft covered by the heavy woollen warp.

A number of Brussels carpets were made for the Royal Pavilion, but no fragments appear to have survived, and their appearance can be judged only from contemporary illustrations. In the King's New Bedroom and the Library the same design was used, a geometric diaper of flattened hexagons arranged horizontally and vertically at right angles to each other. Patterns of this type are found in Ackermann's plates of *Fashionable Furniture* and the two carpet designs from George Smith's *Collection of Ornamental Designs after the Manner of the Antique* (1812), illustrated on Plate 75A are also similar. In the North and South Galleries of the Pavilion, Brussels carpeting in a trailing floral pattern on a cream ground was used, and in the Banqueting Room Gallery a Persian pattern in crimson and drab. The Brussels carpet was woven in strips and joined together and cost approximately £2 12*s*. a square yard.

Carpets were also made for Gothic interiors. Buckler's *Views of Eaton Hall* (1826) show both hand-knotted and woven carpets in Gothic patterns. William Porden embarked on the rebuilding of Eaton Hall in 1804, but the work was not completed until 1825. The drawing-room was equipped with a large hand-knotted carpet the central motif of which echoed the Gothic architectural detail of

[1] Draw-boy. The boy who pulls the cords of the harness in figure-weaving; hence, the piece of mechanism by which this is now done.—*Shorter Oxford English Dictionary*.

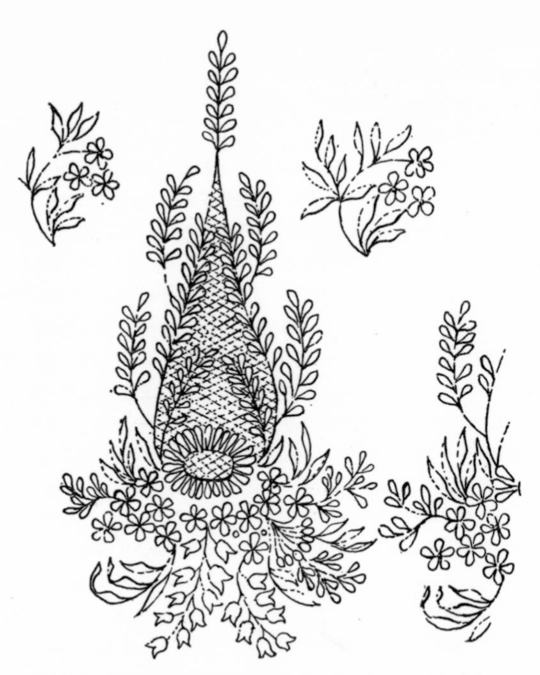

Fig. 3. Needlework pattern for muslin embroidery from Ackermann's *Repository* for August 1815.

Fig. 4. Muslin pattern from Ackermann's *Repository* for May 1828.

the elaborately vaulted ceiling. The dining-room carpet appears to have been of the Brussels or Wilton type, woven in strips, with a border imitating Gothic tracery and bosses, and the Library carpet had an all-over diaper of a quatrefoil design. The Gothic furniture in Ackermann's *Repository* is shown standing on carpets of similar design.

Brussels carpets were woven at Wilton, Kidderminster and in the West Riding of Yorkshire. The Wilton factory was established in about 1740 for the production of Brussels carpets, and the Wilton type, with the cut-pile, was first introduced there. Hand-knotted carpets were not made at Wilton until the Axminster equipment was transferred there in 1835.

Considerable advances were made at Kidderminster during the Regency period. In 1807, 1,000 carpet looms were in operation, and by 1838 there were 2,020, but in spite of the increase in the number of looms, the shuttle was still thrown by hand. Most of the carpets woven at Kidderminster appear to have been of the Brussels type, although the two-ply non-pile carpets, to which Kidderminster gave the name, were also woven there. The Jacquard apparatus was first introduced at Kidderminster in 1825, and was used for the weaving of the two-ply carpets. Among the leading Kidderminster firms were William Grosvenor and Co. (now Woodward, Grosvenor and Co. Ltd), and Brintons, established by Henry Brinton in 1819.

The English carpet-weaving industry also flourished in the West Riding of Yorkshire, particularly in the towns and villages of Leeds, Halifax, Dewsbury and Heckmondwike, and to some extent in Sheffield, where, in 1822, in addition to the weaving of carpets, some 100 looms were employed in the weaving of horsehair for upholstery. Although some of the larger establishments were organized on a factory basis, in many of the towns and villages the industry was still on a cottage basis, with the weaver producing the carpets on looms situated in their own homes. Edward Baines' *History, Directory and Gazeteer of the County of York* (1822) lists seven carpet manufacturers in the village of Heckmondwike. One of the largest concerns appears to be that of John Hanbury, whose family also wove carpets at Dewsbury. Another Heckmondwike factory was that of William Cooke, which was concerned mainly with the production of rugs. Cooke's son Samuel later established the firm of Cooke and Sons at Liversedge, a neighbouring village. Five carpet-weaving establishments, mainly producing Brussels carpets, are listed at Dewsbury, and four at Halifax. The factory of Crossley and Sons, now one of the largest in the country, was begun in a very small way in 1803 by John Crossley, a hand-loom weaver.

In addition to the hand-knotted and woven carpets, which were made on a commercial basis, a number of embroidered carpets made by individuals for their own use have been preserved. Some of these were purely floral, others copied the Empire designs of the French Savonerie carpets on a more modest scale, and a few the geometric designs of the Brussels and Wilton carpets. An interesting needlework carpet, now in the possession of Lady Leconfield, was worked by Mary Hutton Gooch, who died in 1836. The general scheme of the design, with the repeating pattern of hexagons and leaf border, is close to the designs of George Smith, but the floral sprays in the hexagons are of a type which seems to have been confined to needlework carpets. Each of the hexagons were worked separately and joined together to form the carpet which took fifteen years to complete.

### *Needlework and embroidery*

The Regency period was not outstanding for its embroidery, and most of it that has survived is in the form of white-work embroidery for costume. Although the earliest embroidery patterns issued month by month in Ackermann's *Repository of the Arts* were for embroidery in coloured silks, chenille and worsteds, as well as in white thread, from 1815 onwards they were exclusively *muslin patterns*, that is patterns for embroidery on fine cambric in white thread with needlepoint fillings, and insertions of net and cutwork with buttonholing at the edges. The Victoria and Albert Museum has five sketch-books (from different hands) of designs for muslin patterns. These sketch-books contain thousands of different designs dating from 1809 to the 1840's, and provide additional evidence of the immense popularity of this type of work during the Regency period.

This type of embroidery, or *Moravian work*, to give it its contemporary name, was extensively used on the fashionable 'jaconet muslin' round dresses and open robes (Pl. 75B), on petticoats, aprons, handkerchiefs, collars and on baby clothes. The earlier patterns, which were fine and delicate, were mainly floral in character (Fig. 3), although there were a number of running borders of formal decorative patterns. By 1825 the patterns were generally larger in scale, and somewhat coarser, with eyelet holes and stylized flowers and leaves in the manner of *broderie anglaise*. The borders normally had a regular vandyked or scalloped edge (Fig. 4), but in 1828 there was a fashion for asymmetrically scalloped edges.

The 'muslin patterns' were also used for embroidery on the new machine-made net, which had been patented by Heathcoat in 1809, and was made into veils and scarves in imitation of expensive, hand-made bobbin laces. The embroidery, which was worked in white thread mostly in running or tambour stitch, normally consisted of a border of sprays of flowers and leaves with a filling of tiny detached sprigs. Muslin or net curtains were also embroidered in white thread, sometimes with vandyked borders, or a running classical border, or with small detached sprigs scattered over the ground. Muslin bed-covers for daytime use were similarly embroidered.

Embroidery in satin stitch in coloured silks, or gold and silver thread, was used on upholstered furniture and on the borders of curtains and pelmets. The backs of sofas, and the loose cushions, were often covered with velvet, or plain silk, and embroidered with laurel wreaths, or other classical devices. These were probably made in imitation of the Lyons silks of the period, as woven silks of Empire design of English manufacture do not appear to have survived, and probably were not even made in this country. Appliqué embroidery in silk or velvet was used for curtain borders and pelmets, in designs appropriate to either the *Greek* or *Gothic* taste. Most of the embroidery for furnishings was in the classical style, but from 1825 onwards embroidery in coloured silks in designs of an architectural or heraldic character are found on upholstered furniture in the Gothic taste.

The beginning of the century saw a revival of tent-stitch embroidery on canvas. The year 1810 is that normally given for the introduction of 'Berlin wool-work', and although it is true that the Berlin patterns were not imported in any considerable quantity until about 1830, there is firm evidence that the designs, which were printed on squared paper so that they could be copied stitch by stitch on to square-meshed canvas, were in fact known in England as early as 1805. There are a number of original designs in the Bannister Hall pattern-books (see Section on Printed Textiles) and a corresponding textile in the Victoria and Albert Museum, which are called 'Needlework chintzes' and show a square mesh with vases of flowers and other floral motifs filled in by tiny squares of colour in exact imitation of the Berlin patterns. The 'Berlin wool-work' of the Regency period is more restrained than during the hey-day of the fashion in the 1850's and 1860's. The flowers, although drawn with a marked degree of naturalism, are not yet so elaborately shaded as to appear to stand out from the ground. The colouring is also more subdued, for the aniline dyes producing the characteristic magenta and vivid greens were as yet unknown. This tent- and cross-stitch embroidery was used for upholstery and for smaller household articles such as pole-screens. An impressive example of Regency needlework is a set of two sofas, six armchairs and a footstool, now at Buckingham Palace, worked by Frederica, Duchess of York, in 1815. The back and seat of the sofas have a design of a spreading basket of mixed flowers, drawn with the precision of a Dutch flower-piece, enclosed in a running border of curling leaves and flowers. The chairs, although worked at approximately the same time, show a design that has more in common with the later Berlin wool-work with a heavy wreath of elaborately shaded ivy-leaves on the back and oak-leaves on the seat. The bedroom chairs at Eaton Hall, Cheshire, had seats embroidered in tent-stitch in Gothic designs, but have not survived.

Samplers were as popular during the Regency period as in the preceding era, and show little change in either design or execution, being worked in either silk, or, less frequently, wool, in cross-stitch on fine canvas or 'tammy-cloth'. The sampler had firmly established itself as a child's exercise, and the general format was a squarish oblong with a running-floral border enclosing a variety of symmetrically arranged motifs, a religious or moral verse, and the child's name, age and date of working (Pl. 76A).

Embroidered pictures, in coloured silks and chenille on satin, known at the time as 'satin-sketches', continued in favour throughout the period, with subjects copied from popular engravings and the faces and other details painted in water-colours. Mary Linwood's (1755–1845) copies of oil-paintings in coloured worsteds, which she had first exhibited as early as 1776, received continued admiration, and her permanent exhibition in Leicester Square, opened in 1798, was still one of the sights of London in the 1830's. During this period, however, a type of embroidered picture, which may be regarded as the ancestor of the modern 'fabric-collage', came into being. Instead of laboriously imitating a painting with thousands of stitches in coloured worsteds, small pieces of fabric were cut out and roughly sewn to a fine canvas ground. As the pieces of fabric were overlaid one on the other, the surface of the picture was slightly uneven, and had the effect of a thick impasto. The foremost exponent, and apparently the originator, of this type of craft was a Mrs Dickson, who produced copies of oil-paintings using scraps of fabric from tailors' cuttings (Pl. 76B). Her work was exhibited at Brighton under Royal Patronage, and at Soho Square in London in 1831, shortly after her death. The London exhibition consisted of eleven copies of oil-paintings, after old masters such as Rembrandt and Titian and contemporary painters such as Angelica Kauffman. Five of Mrs Dickson's pictures are now in the Victoria and Albert Museum.

# *Costume*

# Costume

ANNE M. BUCK

## WOMEN'S COSTUME

### *The changing style*

In the battle of classical and Gothic taste at the beginning of the nineteenth century, women's dress was a field of minor skirmish. So when Thomas Hope published his *Costume of the Ancients* in 1809, this was welcomed not only for its historical interest but as a practical manual of dress for the discerning woman of fashion, 'To Mr Thomas Hope's recent publication on Ancient Costume is the latest change in dress principally to be attributed ... it is to be hoped that the publication ... will become the vade-mecum and toilet companion of every lady distinguished in circles of fashion.'[1] Henry Moses' volume of drawings of about the same time, *Modern Costume*, showed women's dress almost as antique in style and detail as that of Thomas Hope's book (Fig. 1). In turn some of the fashion journals 1807–10 gave plates and description which might be transcriptions of the designs in *Modern Costume*. And some women did turn to Thomas Hope for inspiration in their dress: 'Her dress was white satin trimmed with white velvet cut in a formal pattern then quite the rage, a copy from some of the Grecian borders in Mr Hope's book.'[2]

But the battle here was already lost. Judging from the dresses which have survived and from the portraits of Englishwomen painted at this time, this last wave of Grecian taste washed only lightly over English dress. In 1810 women's dress was basically the same as it had been for the past ten years, a plain brief bodice, a narrow skirt falling straight and close to the figure from the high waistline in flowing, clinging lines of white muslin. The draped lines of soft white fabrics gave this style of the early nineteenth century an affinity with the sculptured forms of Greece and Rome, but its inspiration was romantic. The change from the eighteenth-century style to the nineteenth-century style was a movement from the formal, the restrained – the real classical temper – to the natural, the free – the romantic temper. And this romantic temper turned dress consciously back to the past. The inconstancy of its inspiration by the classical movement shows even in the first unfolding of the style, when between 1800 and 1810 such unclassical details as vandyked ornament, an 'antique stomacher', and 'Elizabethan' ruff appear within the classical form. And in 1811, when there were new offerings for Grecian taste, and while the word 'Gothic' was still the most severe censure for erring taste in dress or detail, the real direction of fashion is revealing itself. 'I fear the monstrous forms, discordant colours and ostentatious display of ornament, which distinguishes the dresses of the fourteenth and fifteenth centuries, are really more admired by ladies in their hearts than the pure taste and modest elegance of the Grecian costume.'[3]

[1] Ackermann's *Repository*, June 1809.

[2] Grant, E. *Memoirs of a Highland Lady*, p. 36, 1950.

[3] Ackermann's *Repository* ... March 1811.

Romantic extravagance turned not only to the past, 'All nations are ransacked to equip a fine lady.'[4] New forms were gathered from all parts of the world, particularly the more remote and exotic, in Moorish turbans, Circassian sleeves and laced peasant bodices. The campaigns of the long war with France also brought their fashions, the 'Vittoria cloak' or Pyrenean mantle, the Cossack mantle, and the Prussian helmet cap, carried out in canary-coloured silk. All these become naturalised into the dress of the years before 1814. The war brought another influence, in the penetration of trimmings from military uniforms into women's dress. Frogs, epaulettes and braided and corded trimmings appear on spencers and pelisses: 'I walked out like a hussar in a dark cloth pelisse trimmed with fur, and braided like the coat of a staff officer.'[5]

At first the plainness of line and surface was still unbroken by ornament. The muslin, continuing the fashion of the previous years, was embroidered with small sprigs over the surface, or with outlining borders, and with 'lettings-in' of lace, ornament which was part of the surface of the fabric and did not disturb the line of the dress. Some of the embroidered borders of dresses, worked perhaps from the patterns for dress embroideries inserted in the fashion journals, are the chief witness of the Grecian influence of these years.

From 1810 the draped, clinging lines of the dress began to harden. In 1813, when the fashion writers were still speaking of dresses of real 'Grecian design',[6] the line itself began to change. Frills appeared at the hem: 'She had double flounces to her gown. You really must get some flounces.'[7] At first they were few, small and plain, but gradually they grew more elaborate, increasing in number and depth until, by 1816, they had spread half-way up the skirt, and the hem, widened by them, swung out gently from the body and lifted slightly from the ground. Embroidery was then concentrated on these flounces in 'a profusion of work', that is a profusion of white open-work embroidery, in vandykes and scallops, alternating with puffings, pipings, and tuckings of muslin and insertions of lace, which soften and break the line of the dress (Fig. 2). On silk, net and lace dresses the flounces are lace-trimmed and the hem made more elaborate by interlacing ornament and weighted by padded satin bands. Detail from the 'Gothic' past, military braiding, laced peasant bodices, met in the ornament which encrusted the bodice, although between 1815 and 1820 there was so little left of this part of the dress that it settled mainly on the sleeve, particularly on the full, short sleeve of evening dress. The dress of the early nineteenth century had moved into its decorated period.

This richness of ornament was changing its character, but to contemporary eyes the touchstone of classical or Gothic taste was the position of the waist. The English waistline had between 1808 and 1814 shown a Gothic tendency to lengthen, 'I can easily suppose that your six weeks here will be fully occupied, were it only in the lengthening the waist of your gowns.'[8] But in 1815, when English fashion was no longer cut off from France, it returned to a higher line. Ackermann's *Repository* was deceived into describing this as 'perfectly Grecian' in March 1817, but others were more aware of change: 'Waists are worn very short, but not in the foolish Grecian style we were once so pleased with, no, it is now a pretty little waist, very tight at the bottom, with the bust well marked out.'[9] The long flow of the skirt from its high waist-line kept up the illusion of a classical form until 1820. Then, as the waist at last began to move downwards, slowly but with certainty, the new character and form of dress began to appear clearly. As the waist line fell the skirt spread out more widely at the hem. And here the ornament, which had acted as a camouflage of change, became less lavish, gradually disappearing from the hem, until by 1830 the skirt was showing its new wide form in sharp, clear outline. Orna-

[4] *Mirror of the Graces*, 1811, p. 25.

[5] Grant, E., *Memoirs of a Highland Lady*, p. 214, 1950.

[6] *Lady's Magazine*, July 1813.

[7] Austen, J., *Letters*, Vol. 2, 14 October 1813.

[8] Austen, J., *Letters*, Vol. 1, 17 January 1809.

[9] *La Belle Assemblée*, July 1817.

Fig. 1. Drawings of costume, showing styles of dress with Grecian influence, which also appear in fashion plates 1807–10. From a drawing by Henry Moses in *Modern Costume*, 1823.

ment on the bodice was also smoothed out into flat, pleated bands, and on the sleeve was absorbed into a new spreading form. For from 1825 the sleeve became the dominant feature of the dress, and by 1830 was almost at its climax of fullness. Large balloon-like forms now billowed over the upper part of the body, where the longer bodice tightened to the figure. And below the falling, tightening line of the waist was the billowing spread of the skirt. This repetition of inflated forms gave to the whole dress its new character of exuberance and extravagance.

### *Fabric and colour*

White muslin had from the end of the eighteenth century been the main fabric used for women's dress. To this fabric the evolving style owed much of its form and character and also its evocation of the sculptured garments of classical antiquity. It was still the general and correct wear for dresses of all kinds in 1810. Jane Austen, who is revealed in her letters as a very fashion-conscious woman, gave, in Edmund Bertram's sober compliment to his diffident young cousin, the conservative, masculine approval of a long-accepted fashion: 'A woman can never be too fine while she is all in white.'[10] It was for the whole period pre-eminent for morning wear: 'Nothing but white can be worn in the morning', stated *La Belle Assemblée* in 1810, and ten years later it was still 'white dresses are universal, either for morning costume or half dress, in the former cambric, for the latter of India muslin'. Only in the months of mid-winter did the hardy Englishwoman abandon it for silk, poplin or wool: 'Late as it is in the season, morning dresses continue to be still made of

[10] *Mansfield Park*, 1811–13.

muslin.'[11] The number of surviving dress of this period and the proportion of white muslin ones among them give still visible support to the assertions of the fashion writers.

Although muslin was worn less for evening dress after 1810, it still continued to appear, especially for informal summer occasions: 'Muslin gowns are worn by many of an evening, chiefly with coloured borders', Jane Oglander told her niece Fanny, in 1820.[12] These coloured borders were embroidered or painted, and during the next few years they change from borders of one, to borders of many colours (Pl. 83). Satin was much worn for evening dress, but the most popular fabrics for evening wear, between 1815 and 1830, were the light, delicate textures of net, gauze or lace, transparent cream or white worn over a slip of white or coloured satin, pale pink, blue or yellow. The gauze was often woven or embroidered with sprays in bright colour, and the satin appliqué trimmings and bands matched the colour of the pattern. Or thin crape with pale colour revealed the lustre of a white satin slip beneath. The lace was often bobbin or needlepoint, but the development of a machine-made net, 1810-15, which was then embroidered with silk sprays, was a cheaper, but still fashionable substitute, with the interest of novelty (Pl. 80A). Blonde, a silk bobbin lace, was much worn for trimmings throughout the period.

The day-time silks were still light in texture. Sometimes they showed a small covering pattern in the weave or were striped, usually on a cream or white ground, or checked, particularly after 1815. Levantine, a soft, twilled silk, was a characteristic material of these years, used both for dresses and pelisses and spencers (Pl. 82).

In 1825 the fashion writer of *La Belle Assemblée* wrote: 'It is rather more than three years since our modish fair ones patronized even to excess the British chintzes, preferring them for the greater part of the year to the finest cambric for morning dress.' Later in the same year this writer described the chintzes: 'On the pale modest straw colour we behold in delicate mosaic the red fibrous seaweed ... or on a ground of yet deeper though not dark yellow or of green every flower that can be named.' Such designs appear on many surviving dresses – the fibrous seaweed and coral pattern, often as a background in pale colour for another printed design in deeper, brighter colour over it (Pl. 80B). Floral patterns, flowing in many colours over the surface of the fabric, were replacing the small formalised sprays – worked, woven or printed, in one or two colours on a white ground – of the beginning of the period. The flowers and other natural forms were delicately and gracefully drawn, with increasing realism. But the really elegant were always cautious about the flowering muslins: 'though many of them are really beautiful they never appear upon any female however dignified by nature, like the attire of a gentlewoman'.[13]

The colours of the beginning of the period, clear yellow, pale blue or pink, soft green, were worn always against a background of white, appearing in cloaks, mantles, spencers and pelisses over white dresses. Colour was used sparingly and always relieved by white. No other dress than a white one is ever shown with a coloured pelisse or spencer. Then, with the growing elaboration of dress, came a less controlled use of colour. The individual colour took deeper tones, and colour mingled with colour with less and less restraint; a change which added to the character of exuberance in the dress of 1825–30.

### *Forms and construction*

Three types of dress were in general use in 1810. In one the front of the skirt, open half-way down the side seams, was lifted to fasten round the waist like an apron, meeting a bodice, fastening down the centre front; in the second, a development of this, the front of the bodice was joined to the front of the skirt, and after the skirt had been lifted and fastened, the bodice front was lifted to fasten with pins or buttons on the shoulders; beneath it linen flaps, extending from the bodice lining, were pinned over each other to keep the back

[11] Ackermann's *Repository*, November 1816.

[12] Oglander, C. A., *Nunwell Symphony*, 1945.

[13] *La Belle Assemblée*, 1827.

Day dress of printed cotton, 1805–10. This dress is made with the bodice front fastening on the shoulders and shows the open neckline filled with white muslin. Chintzes with dark grounds, though much less common than white, are found amongst the plain morning dresses of these years. *Manchester City Art Galleries.*

PLATE 77

(A) Mrs Catherine Morey, 1817, by Michael Keeling. Her dress has the open bodice of 1815–20 and the portrait shows the skirt front meeting this at the waist. The muslin frill at the neck, the frilled cuffs and the cap, show an actual, personal expression of the growing elaboration of this date. *Walker Art Gallery, Liverpool.*

(B) Hat trimmed with ribbon and branches of 'Peruvian browallia': bonnet with arbutus and satin bands, with curtain veil of blond lace; a cap with a beret crown in white crape and blue satin; and a half-dress cap of gauze and lace. From Ackermann's *Repository*, 1826.

The Cloakroom, Clifton Assembly Rooms, Bristol, by ROLINDA SHARPLES, 1816–20. The short low bodices and the fuller skirts of ball dress, 1816–20, show vividly against the growing darkness of men's dress. The difference in headdress of the younger and older women also appears in this contemporary record of an evening festivity. *City Art Gallery, Bristol.*

(A) Ball dress of embroidered net over cream satin, 1821–23
*Manchester City Art Galleries.*

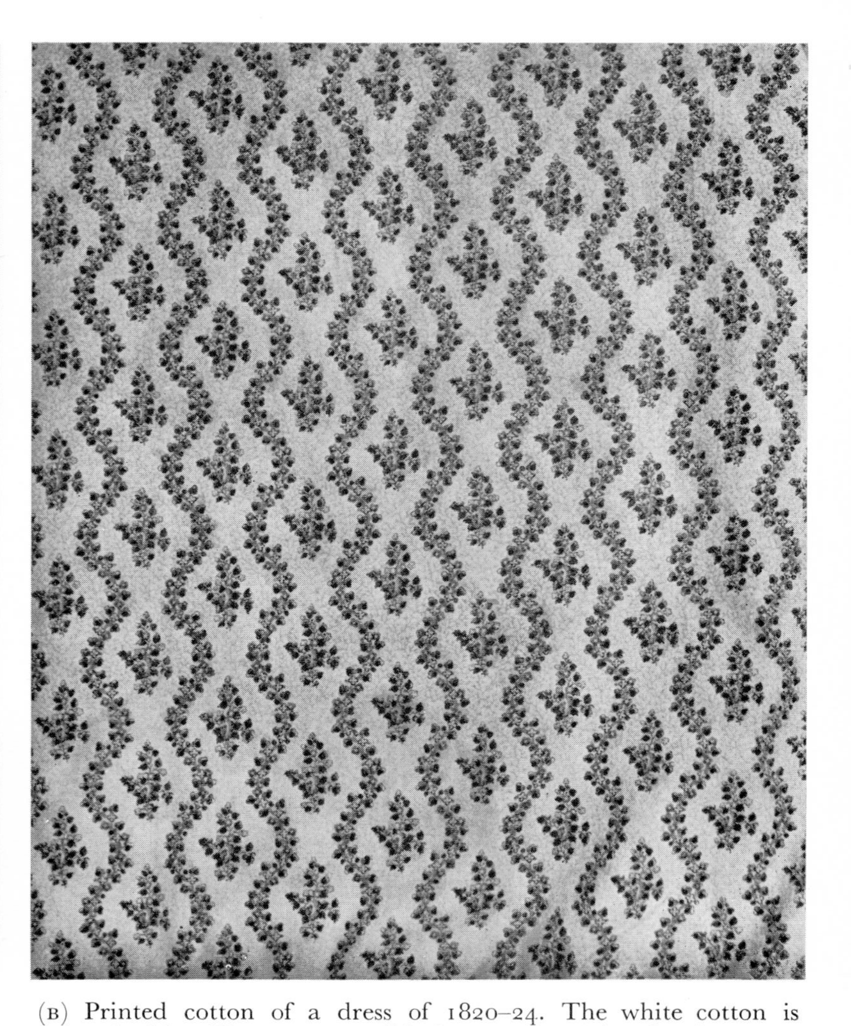

(B) Printed cotton of a dress of 1820–24. The white cotton is printed with a 'fibrous seawood' in fawn, and over it a floral pattern, still rather formalised, in red and blue. *Manchester City Art Galleries*

PLATE 80

(A) Lord Grantham, 1816, by J. A. D. Ingres. He is wearing pantaloons with hessians. His coat has the double-notched lapel which appears mainly 1800–25, though remaining later on evening coats, and is worn with the waistcoat just visible at the waistline. *Courtesy Major Edward Compton.*

(B) Coat of green cloth, of the type worn by Lord Grantham (*left*), double-breasted, with brass buttons; leather breeches; 1810–20. *The London Museum.*

Pelisse of green silk, figured, levantine with puffed over-sleeves; white satin bonnet, made on a framework of cane; cream silk scarf-shawl with ends and borders of woven pattern, 1818–20.
*Manchester City Art Galleries.*

Evening dress of white muslin, with trimmings of satin and embroidery in many-coloured chain stitch, 1827–28. The satin bands at the hem are wadded. The gathering of the bodice under satin bands gives a stomacher form, which is enclosed in the pointed lapels which make one of the bodice styles, 1826–29. The point, here extending below the waistline, foreshadows the later development of the bodice. *Victoria and Albert Museum.*

PLATE 83

Beriah Botfield, aged 21, 1828, by THOMAS PHILLIPS. The coat is dark brown; the waistcoat and cravat black, the cloak dark purple, with a deep, black velvet collar. The fawn trousers show a very long, loose cut of this garment at a time when it was worn with a great deal of variety of form. *Courtesy The Marquess of Bath.*

PLATE 84

Fig. 2. One of the patterns of 'the profusion of work' which was appearing at the hems of dresses. From the *Lady's Magazine*, 1815.

of the dress in position (Pl. 77); the third had a centre back fastening to just below the waist, with a drawstring across the back of the neck and waist. The first form is the oldest, a survival from the end of the eighteenth century, and was not much used after 1810. The second form was very common 1800–10 and was still very general until about 1820. The last form was used throughout the period, and became the normal after 1820. Other forms of dress were the pelisse robe with a fastening down the centre front, which appeared as a formal dress, 1820–30. There were also dresses of separate bodice and slip; and a coloured bodice over a white 'petticoat' was a popular fashion for many years; in 1813 it was 'so general that it can no longer be considered genteel',[14] but the fashion continued until 1820.

Between 1810 and 1825 a wrap-over form of bodice, and between 1815 and 1820 an open bodice, that is one with a deep V-neckline, meeting the high waist, were worn (Pl. 78A), but the normal and characteristic neckline was low and square, with a straight line across the bosom, meeting the narrow shoulder sections. After 1825 the new fullness of the sleeve drew the dress off the shoulder, the neckline and shoulder forming a single horizontal line across the top of the body.

Day dresses of 1810–25, as well as evening dresses, show this low neckline, but they were not so worn; the opening was filled with a tucker, habit shirt, or 'antique ruff' of white muslin: 'In the morning the arms and bosom must be completely covered to the throat and wrist'[15] (Pls. 77 and 78A). Many of the day dresses, particularly between 1820 and 1830, have a high, close neckline. As a contemporary writer pointed out, undress meant a closed neck and covered arms; half dress was rather more exposed and open; but full dress meant scarcely any covering for the upper part of the body at all[16] (Pl. 79).

Although day dresses usually had long sleeves and evening dresses short sleeves, there were years between 1810 and 1820 when long sleeves appeared with full evening dress. 'Mrs Tilson had long sleeves, she assured me they are worn in the evening by many.'[17] Transparent long sleeves depending from, or over, short sleeves, are very characteristic of evening dresses, 1820–30. At the beginning of the century sleeves were set far back into the back of the dress, making this very narrow across the shoulders, and giving a wide front to the bodice. This construction reveals the carriage of the body with the shoulders well back and the bosom prominent. It was changing by 1810, and the back of the dress became wider: 'backs are very broad and in slight materials usually full'.[18]

Trains had almost disappeared from day dresses by 1810, but they remained, though rather short, on evening but not on ball dresses, until about 1815. Widening gores at the sides of the skirt swept the new fullness to the back. Hems of silk dresses were padded, 1823–8, giving weight and swing as the skirt widened. The padding spread higher, but more thinly as ornament left the hem, 1829–30.

In 1810 cloaks and mantles, varying slightly in shape but bearing many different names, were worn folded loosely about the figure. But there were also the spencer and pelisse which fitted more closely, and these became the outer garments most characteristic of 1810–30. The early forms of spencer, before 1810, had extended below the waist, and the short form ending at the line of the waist was then referred to as the military spencer. After 1810 this form became general, although the high waist-line, 1816–19, meant it was then very short indeed. It remained fashionable until about 1827. The full-length companion to the spencer was the pelisse. This too was generally worn as an outdoor garment after 1810: 'Pelisses are higher than ever in estimation.'[19] Its waistline, sleeves and ornament followed the same changes as the dress. After 1827, when the large sleeves of dresses made a fitting form of outer gar-

[14] Ackermann's *Repository*, July 1813.
[15] *Mirror of the Graces*, 1811, p. 95.
[16] Ackermann's *Repository*, March 1812.
[17] Austen, J., *Letters*, Vol. 2, 9 March 1814.
[18] Ackermann's *Repository*, February 1816.
[19] Ackermann's *Repository*, April, May 1816.

ment impractical, cloaks, mantles and shawls replace the spencer and pelisse. Wadded, fur-lined and fur-trimmed cloaks and mantles were worn over a pelisse in carriages in the coldest weather. And a scarf or shawl was often worn over it. The scarfs and shawls were of all fabrics from gauze to cachemire, silk crape and silk twill with embroidered or woven borders being particularly popular (Pl. 82). In 1810 the usual form was a long scarf shawl, but by 1820 the square shawl, growing large and more enveloping, became a much used garment. Small squares folded, or a small triangle, were worn over the shoulders over a pelisse or spencer. Swansdown tippets, long ropes of swansdown, which had been a fashion in 1800–10, were worn again in 1829–30.

Nothing sets the dress of 1800–20 so much apart from the style before and the style which followed as the scarcity of the underwear beneath it. Although it was probably not usually so scarce as in the accusation that 'some of our fair dames appear summer and winter, with no other shelter from sun or frost, than one single garment of muslin or silk over their chemise – if they wear one, but that is often dubious',[20] it was scarce enough; a chemise of linen, long, reaching well below the knee; light flexible stays; a petticoat, cotton in warm weather, fine flannel in winter; and then the gown or slip. Many of the muslin gowns were worn over a silk slip. There is little evidence that the wearing of drawers was yet usual among Englishwomen. As the waist began to lower and tighten, the dominance of stays, which Englishwomen had felt only lightly for a quarter of a century, began to return. But as early as 1810 their wearing is beginning to influence the wearing of the dress: 'stiff stays have been creeping in upon us gradually and almost imperceptibly till at length concealment is no longer affected'.[21]

### *Hats and head-dresses*

In the different and changing styles of hats and head-dresses, 1810–30, one aspect is constant: their steadily increasing size. In 1810 hats were varied in shape, but all, except the flat-crowned 'gipsy' hat, which after a long life was just going out of fashion, were rather small. A soft crown with a stiff, turned-back brim was the basis of many styles; or a stiff, helmet-like crown with a small brim. Bonnets had a brim in line with the crown, jutting over the face. They were of silk and velvet or straw, and were trimmed with ribbon or feathers, but not a great deal with flowers.

By 1815 the tall-crowned French bonnet with its brim spreading round the face was being worn; the crown grew wider and the brim curved out round the face (1815–20): 'I do recollect when a lady did not think it necessary to wear a bushel measure on her head ... when a face was sufficiently pretty without the foil of a coal scuttle, or when a chimney pot with the sweep's brush sticking out at the top of it was not thought the most graceful of all models of a fashionable bonnet.' Such was a harsh, but fairly accurate, contemporary comment on the new bonnets of 1815.[22] Silk and velvet were often gathered over a framework of cane or wire.

Straw bonnets were worn during the summer months for walking, Leghorn or fine Dunstable straw, usually plainly trimmed. Fashionable for all the summers of 1815–30, they remained comparatively plain even in the years of excessive trimming: 'Leghorn and Dunstable bonnets in cottage form ... the plainer the more genteel.' In winter black velvet replaced them. Bonnet veils were worn with bonnets of all kinds.

By 1825 the crown was worn higher on the head, the wide brim was released, and the ribbons floated over the shoulders, giving a hat rather than a bonnet as the fashion of the next few years (Pl. 78B). Crowns and brims grew large, 1826–8: 'Hats and bonnets are monstrous.'[23] Then by 1830 the crown dropped to the back of the head, became smaller and less important, and the spreading brim met it at an acute angle with the crown.

As hats grew larger trimmings grew more profuse. Plumes of feathers appeared year after year, but after 1825 flowers appear as much as feathers:

[20] *Mirror of the Graces*, 1811, p. 77.
[21] Ackermann's *Repository*, February 1810.

[22] Ackermann's *Repository*, May 1815.
[23] *La Belle Assemblée*, August 1829.
ibid. August 1827.

'Branches of the tulip tree in blossom surmount the hat.' [24] For the next three or four years the fashionable hat was a tangle of loops and bows of ribbon. Lace and muslin caps were worn beneath the bonnets, 1830–20.

Indoors, caps of lace or muslin, usually fastening under the chin, were worn throughout the period; these, too, became more elaborate with bows and floating ribbons, when they were also, like the hat, worn on the top of the head, 1825–30. Caps were less worn at the beginning of the period, and young women did not generally wear them. Evening-dress caps and hats were also less worn about 1810 and seldom by the really young, whose head-dresses were flowers or bands of gauze. Turbans and berets, although 'confined to matronly ladies', were a characteristic fashion of these years, particularly 1825–30; and all head-dresses grew larger and more elaborate after 1820.

### *Boots and shoes*

For walking there were half-boots, just covering the ankle and laced down the front, of leather, cloth, cotton or silk, and shoes, usually of kid. The colour of spencer, pelisse or hat or the trimmings of the dress was often repeated in the shoes, though less after 1825, and shoes in neutral shades and of printed kid were also worn. For evening white satin slippers were the general wear. Both boots and shoes had small, very low heels or no heels at all. The toes curved to a point in 1810, but later became rounded and narrow, and then squared by 1830. The fashionable stockings were of silk.

### *Gloves, bags and fans*

For evening wear gloves were of white kid, to the elbow, or short of the elbow. For daytime wear they were of kid or suede, usually in yellow, buff or white. Small bags, called reticules or ridicules, were carried throughout the period, a necessity at the beginning with dresses which allowed no place for a pocket. They appeared in many shapes, and were made of fabric, often matching a part of the dress, or, less often, leather. They were drawn up with cords, or mounted on a frame. Fans which were used mainly for evening occasions were small. They had carved ivory sticks, or leaves of white crape, net or gauze often ornamented with spangles, and sometimes painted.

### *Jewellery*

Jewellery was worn sparingly at the beginning of the period, but after 1820, and particularly after 1825, in much greater quantity, 'Trinkets of all sorts too prevalent and redundant in every style of dress.' [25] The most characteristic use of jewellery in the period is the wearing, 1826–30, of three or four bracelets over the long full sleeve like a cuff.

## MEN'S COSTUME

The years 1810–30 are a period of particular significance in the history of men's dress, a period in which a change which had begun in the last quarter of the eighteenth century was, with lasting effect, completed.

In 1810 this dress was a coat, with high collar, double-breasted, the front cut away in a horizontal line at a high waist-level, leaving the thighs free (Pl. 81B). Its material was cloth, olive-green, claret colour, dark blue or black. Beneath it was a waistcoat of white marcella, and with it cream or light sage cloth breeches, white silk stockings and black slippers. At the neck the lawn or muslin frill of the linen shirt flowed out over the waistcoat, and the cropped head was held high by the deep white neckcloth, folded round the neck and knotted in front.

This, the formal dress for evening, shows that the penetration of cloth into men's dress had already been completed; the fabric of informal, out-of-doors or country wear had become the fabric of formal wear also, and the varying richness of colour and texture of silks and velvets, of woven and embroidered pattern, had departed from men's dress.

[24] *Lady's Magazine*, July 1827.

[25] *La Belle Assemblée*, October 1826.

In morning dress the general form and fabric of the coat was the same, but the waistcoat might be buff kerseymere or striped silk, and the breeches leather instead of cloth. The breeches were the remaining link with the eighteenth-century style, but by 1810 this part of men's costume was changing. Breeches were worn long and well below the knee – 'the knee band extends almost to the calf'[26] – and gradually this form merged with the pantaloons which had been worn with high boots and the half-length hessians from the end of the eighteenth century (Pl. 81A). Pantaloons were now worn long and tight down the calf, with half-boots and slippers as well. They were often of knitted silk for the tightest effect, as well as of cloth or leather. 'Be so good as to buy for William [Wordsworth] 2 pairs of pantaloons of the knit kind, such as you got him before when he was in Town, one grey and the other drab.'[27] Pantaloons appeared in a variety of lengths and degrees of tightness by 1820 – 'my husband has bought ... a pair of loose pantaloons, puffed out like a hoop petticoat'[28] – and then they merged gradually into the full-length, straight-legged form of trousers, which for some years had been worn by young boys. By 1830 this new garment had become established in men's dress, long over the instep and strapped beneath the boot or shoe (Pl. 84). But the long, tight pantaloons were still worn for evening, and loose forms for day. Trousers had the centre front fastening, the return of an old fashion, in place of the flap front of breeches and pantaloons.

In 1810 there was still some richness of colour left in the cloth of the coat, and the contrast of the dark tone of the coat with the light-coloured breeches or pantaloons. But gradually blue and black, favoured by Beau Brummell, became the most general wear for the coat. Black silk breeches had been worn for evening in 1810, and black for this part of evening dress became more fashionable, so that by 1825 darkness, except for the waistcoat, the shirt-front and the cravat, had settled on for-

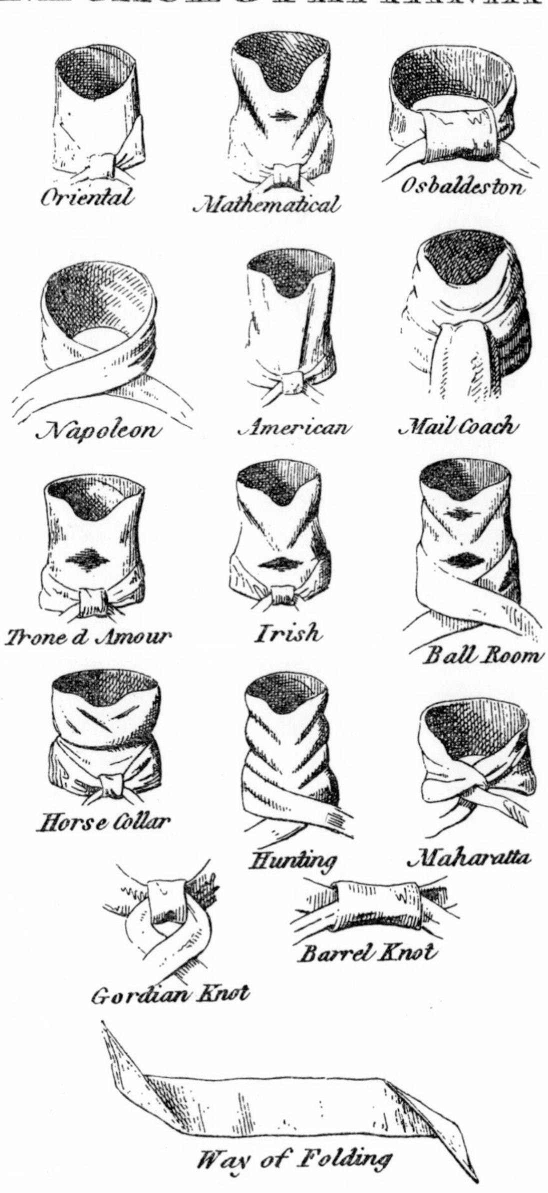


Fig. 3. The frontispiece of an essay on the neckcloth, showing some of the different ways of tying the cravat. Those with loose ends were held in place with tapes under the arms. 1818.

[26] Ackermann's *Repository*, January 1809.
[27] Hutchinson, S., *Letters*, 16 May 1813.
[28] *La Belle Assemblée*, July 1817.

mal evening wear. 'As black has been long the favourite dress of men of fashion, this together with the negligent kind of home costume of the ladies gave a look of gloom to the audience.'[29] For day wear light, neutral colour remained a little longer in the pantaloons and trousers.

The black or dark blue coat of evening wear kept the cut-away front and narrow skirts at the back; this was now the almost static style of a particular occasion. But there was change in the coat of daytime wear. The horizontal cut-away disappeared as the skirts curved over the thighs to meet in a point at the centre front, a style that was being worn, as well as the cut-away form, by 1820. The skirts then widened and closed in front, and by 1830 this new skirted form had replaced the cut-away style for daytime wear, although this remained in riding dress.

Men's dress was still sensitive to the movement of fashion, sharing with women's dress the changing line. The high cut-away line of the coat matched the high waist-line on women's dress, and in 1809, when this was lengthening, the fashion notes of men's dress make the same comment, that coats are long in the waist;[30] and it moved, slightly, towards the new higher level 1816–19. The skirted coat of 1830 had a marked and lower waistline, and swung out at the hips, 'the last button not buttoned, to make the coat sit more out at the hips'.[31]

During the 1820's the lapels of the coat curved open to display the waistcoat, shirt and cravat. The waistcoat it revealed had the same long curving lapels to the short waist, and by 1830 was showing the same flowering in its silk as the fabrics of women's dress.

For men the neck has always been the point, which, by expense of work, elegance or discomfort, has given the blazon of gentility, and for the whole of this period the cravat and its tying was an important part of dress (Fig. 3). The neckcloth was a large triangle of white muslin, which was folded into a band, placed round the neck or twisted in front. At the beginning of the period white could be worn on all occasions, and white only in the ballroom; for evening white was still the only wear in 1830, although black silk, a fashion previously military, and some coloured silks were being worn for less formal occasions.

Out of doors, single-breasted greatcoats were worn. Fur was fashionable for collars, cuffs and lapels in 1810. For travelling one, two, three or four capes were worn on the coat. Cloaks were worn for evening occasions.

Hats were of beaver or silk, black, grey or fawn; the crown grew higher after 1815, and by 1830 its sides, at first slightly concave, had straightened, and the brim had become flatter and narrower.

[29] *La Belle Assemblée*, July 1825.

[30] Ackermann's *Repository*, January, March, July 1809.

[31] *Whole Art of Dress*, 1830.

From Figgins' Type Specimen Book of 1821.

# *Jewellery*

(A) Necklace and pair of ear-rings, gold filigree set with emeralds, rubies, pearls and other stones. About 1820–30. *Victoria and Albert Museum.*

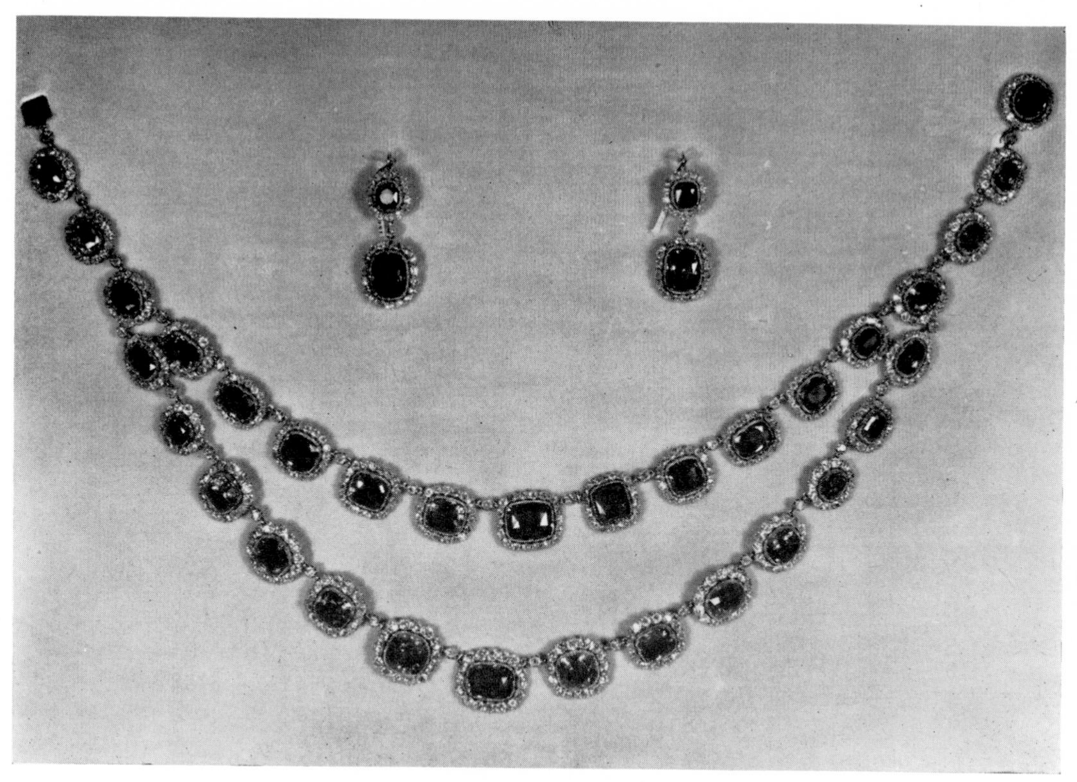

(B) Necklace and pair of ear-rings, composed of large sapphires set in gold and diamonds set in silver. Early 19th century. *Victoria and Albert Museum.*

PLATE 85

(A) Parure of necklace, ear-rings and clasp, filigree gold with tinted gold flowers, set with glass pastes imitating rubies. About 1820–30. *Victoria and Albert Museum.*

(B) Bracelet, gold filigree with tinted gold enrichments, set with amethysts and semi-precious gemstones. About 1830. *Victoria and Albert Museum.*

(C) Bracelet of interlaced gold wire, the clasp of gold filigree. About 1830. *Victoria and Albert Museum.*

(A) Tiara in two pieces, gilt metal set with imitation classical cameos of agate and onyx. About 1820. *Victoria and Albert Museum.*

(B) and (C) Bracelet of plaited human hair, the clasp set with a shell cameo, mounted in gold filigree. About 1820. Necklace of gilt metal set with roundels of cornelian, about 1810–20. *Victoria and Albert Museum.*

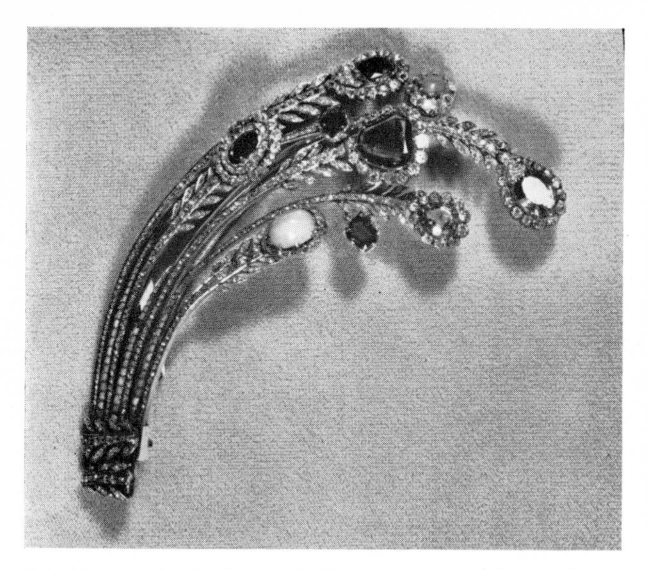

(A) Aigrette in the form of wheat-ears set with amethyst, emerald, turquoises, and diamonds. About 1820–30. *Victoria and Albert Museum.*

(B) Large floral spray brooch set with diamonds, early 19th century. *Victoria and Albert Museum.*

(C) Miniature portrait of a young woman, wearing a triple necklace of pearls, seed-pearl ear-rings, bracelets and belt-clasp *en suite* set with cameos. About 1820. *Victoria and Albert Museum.*

(D) Miniature portrait of Mrs de Wint, wearing ear-rings and necklace of coral. Probably painted about 1807. *Victoria and Albert Museum.*

PLATE 88

# Jewellery

J. F. HAYWARD

A complete transformation took place in jewellery fashions in Europe at the end of the eighteenth century; the early stages of this transformation were discussed in the jewellery section of the preceding volume of this series. Its causes were rooted in the social changes which had followed on the French Revolution and the ensuing period of European war. The new jewellery was devised to meet the needs and satisfy the tastes of the bourgeoisie, a class which had already emerged as an increasingly influential element in Western European society before the Regency period proper had begun. In discussing Regency jewellery we are therefore concerned not with the recognition of a new style, but with the development of a style that was already approaching maturity.

The process of democratization which is so marked a feature of early nineteenth-century society is strongly reflected in the jewellery of the time. Economic and political uncertainties and the changing balance of society led to the temporary suppression of the more valuable stones. The aristocracy followed the bourgeoisie in wearing jewels of modest intrinsic value. The fact that less expensive materials were acceptable for jewellery led, of course, to a great extension of demand. This change-over of demand from a small aristocratic clientèle to a far more extensive middle-class one was followed in a timely manner by technical improvements that made possible the production of expensive-looking jewellery at much lower cost.

It cannot be denied that in comparison with the better-quality eighteenth-century jewellery, Regency jewellery shows a certain tendency towards vulgarity. The settings which in the eighteenth century had been so finely and delicately made that they were almost imperceptible, broadened out and became heavier, more decorative in appearance. In spite of their apparent massiveness, nineteenth-century settings often contained a smaller amount of precious metal than those of the preceding century. The extravagant-looking settings of the 1820's, sometimes composed of gold alloyed with other metals to produce contrasting tints and, incidentally, to reduce cost, were in many cases stamped by machine instead of being constructed with painstaking craftsmanship by the goldsmith.

The delight in colourfulness, of which the use of vari-coloured golds is one manifestation, is a typical feature of Regency jewellery, but it cannot be claimed that the colour combinations were always harmonious. Whereas in the past the majority of jewels had been set with diamonds, rubies and emeralds only, or with cheaper substitutes, such as crystal, garnet and chrysolite, which gave similar colour combinations, now the use of semi-precious stones was greatly extended. Among the gems that were now added to the former range were amethyst, aquamarine, topaz, peridot and even the strident turquoise.

By restoring the importance of the setting, the new style brought more opportunity to the goldsmith, at any rate so far as the better-quality jewellery is concerned. Though the new mechanical techniques robbed him of one opportunity to show his skill, settings were now enriched with elaborate and often extremely delicate filigree work to which was soon added another decorative process, that of granulation.

Filigree was exploited at this time to a hitherto unprecedented degree. In addition to the usual technique of twisted wire soldered to the surface of the area to be decorated, we find the wire wound into whorls and built up in relief with minute leaves stamped from tinted gold sheets (Pls. 85A, 86A, B, C, 87B).

The process of granulation which was based upon that found on ancient Etruscan jewellery, was first introduced about 1815 in Paris and came over to England somewhat later. It consisted of depositing a large number of minute grains of gold on a prepared gold surface, and had the effect of giving a matt finish to the gold, thus providing a further alternative to the tinted gold already mentioned. Although Regency fashion as a whole took the lead from Paris, English manufacturing technique, particularly in the production of cheaper jewellery, was so renowned that no less an artist than Jean Baptiste Odiot, one of the creators of the French Empire style in jewellery and goldsmiths' work, sent his son to London in 1815 to study production methods.

During the eighteenth century jewellers had shown a most determined conservatism, and changes in fashion in costume had not necessarily been accompanied or followed by marked changes in jewellery design. In the nineteenth century the tempo of change was speeded up and fashions in dress began to exercise a greater influence on jewellery, which became more of a costume adjunct. The tendency to employ less expensive materials helped to make such changes possible, for the passing out of fashion of jewels made of shell or lava cameos, of amethyst or of seed-pearl, caused no financial embarrassment to a lady of fashion. As a special section of this work is devoted to costume, it will suffice here to refer quite briefly to the changes introduced in the first decade of the nineteenth century. The new Grecian fashion was fundamentally austere; in seeking to reveal as effectively as possible the form of the female body, it left little place, at any rate logically, for extraneous decoration in the form of jewellery. The Empire style in France, however, while adhering to the Grecian fashions of the Directoire, required a display of jewellery appropriate to the splendour of an Imperial Court. In fact, in spite of its apparent severity, early nineteenth-century costume provided a by no means unsatisfactory background for jewellery, though of a different kind from that worn in the preceding century. The high waists and simple bodices with square *décolletage* (Pl. 88D) provided an admirable setting for a rich necklace or a brooch in the middle of the corsage. The short sleeves called for a lavish display of bracelets. Contemporary portraits of fashionable women show them wearing ear-rings, a necklace, or a *sautoir* chain (of which more later) reaching down to the waist, one or more pairs of bracelets and, of course, the inevitable rings. Finally, the girdle which encircled the waist was often held by a large jewelled clasp. (Pl. 88C).

The parure, or set of jewellery designed *en suite*, though it had been known long before the Regency period, became very popular at this time, and quite a number still survive in the leather cases in which they were originally supplied. It usually comprised a necklace, brooch, ear-rings, and sometimes tiara and bracelets as well (Pl. 86A).

Most of the standard types of jewel were given a different form during the early nineteenth century. The necklace of the period usually consisted of a series of large coloured gemstones with wide settings (Pl. 85A) and, in the case of the more expensive pieces, diamond or half-pearl borders, with links set with smaller stones of similar type (Pl. 85B). Radiating outwards from the links between the larger stones were often pear-shaped pearls or pendants composed of stones of the same colour as those of the necklace. Such necklaces were worn low down on the neck and shoulders, and their width was sufficient to balance the wide expanse of the square *décolletage*. While the necklaces intended for daily wear were composed of inexpensive materials, some of those for evening wear were of great splendour (Pl. 85B). An imposing effect could also be achieved with semi-precious stones in die-stamped gold or gilt settings, but these cheaper and rather meretricious necklaces were often bulky and coarse in design (Pl. 86A).

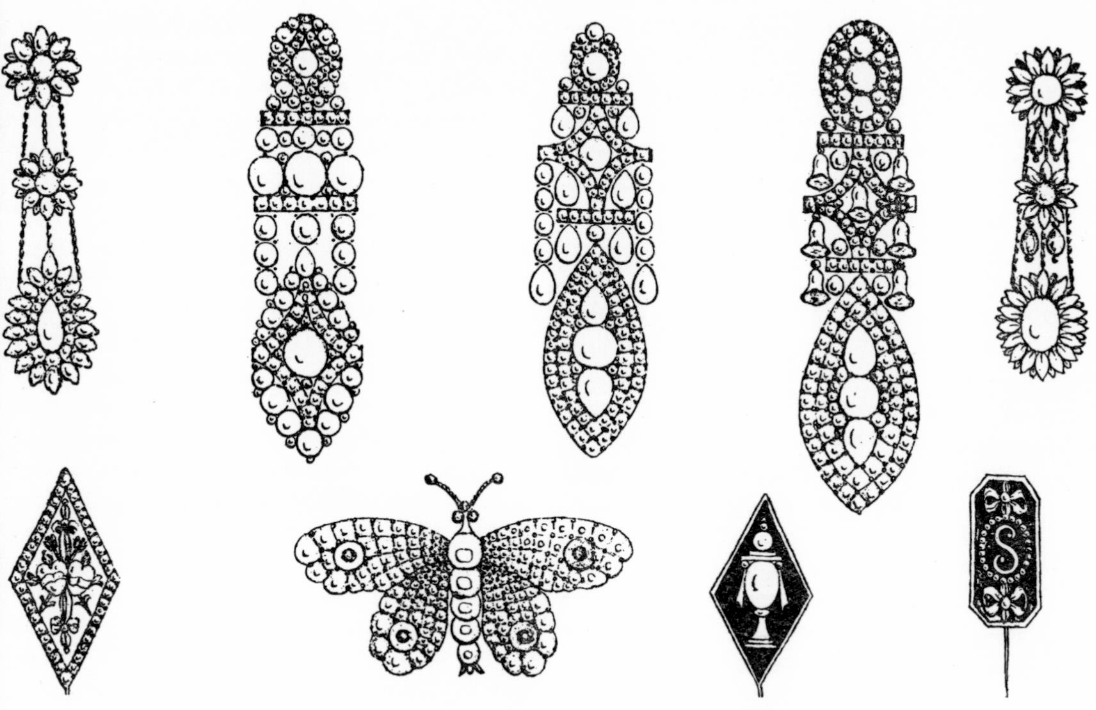


Fig. 1. Designs for ear-rings and a butterfly brooch set with pearls and pin-heads of enamelled gold. From an early nineteenth-century drawing. *Victoria and Albert Museum*.

Regency ear-rings also differed from those of the preceding century. Whereas the earlier ear-rings branched outwards and were almost as wide as they were long, the nineteenth-century type consisted of a single elongated pendant, shaped like a stalactite (Fig. 1). As the century advanced the length of ear-rings gradually increased; in 1817 a fashion journal already refers to 'Ear pendants of a prodigious length', and by 1830 they measured as much as two inches in length. Ear-rings formed an indispensible part of the parure and were worn *en suite* with necklace and pendant. For daily wear, however, the familiar pear-shaped pearl ear-ring, of the type that had been worn since the first half of the seventeenth century, was acceptable.

The bracelets of the late eighteenth and early nineteenth century had been lightly constructed of a series of plaques or cameos linked by slender gold chains, but towards the end of our period they also became much heavier in appearance, though the technique of stamping made it possible to produce them of quite light metal (Pl. 86B, C). During the Regency period bracelets enjoyed a popularity which they had never had before and never enjoyed again. The new fashion of wearing the arms bare gave hitherto unprecedented scope for their display. As many as three were worn on each arm – at the shoulder, elbow and wrist respectively. A cameo or some large semi-precious stone usually formed their central feature (Pls. 87B, 88C).

Along with bracelets, chains came into fashion, having been neglected since the seventeenth century. They were often of great length and passed several times around the neck, even so leaving a loop which reached down to the high waist. Like all other kinds of jewellery, they tended to become coarser, being composed of heavy links, interspersed with the inevitable cameos or plaques.

A peculiar fashion existed in France in the early nineteenth century for wearing a long chain over one shoulder reaching down to the waist, where it ended in a large locket or pendant. These baldriclike chains were known as *sautoirs*, and one finds references to them in English fashion journals of the Regency period, though it is probable that in England they were worn around the neck like the usual necklace. A fashion journal of 1828 records that 'Gold chains with small essence bottles suspended from them are much admired'.

The considerable demand for chains, for necklaces, bracelets and *sautoirs* resulted in the introduction of many new varieties; made of plaited gold wire (Pls. 86c, 87c), of inter-twined links (curb chain), of stamped and pierced links, and in a peculiar tubular form of up to half an inch in diameter which gave a heavy effect corresponding to the massive appearance of the jewels which were suspended from it (Pl. 86A). A Paris fashion journal of the late 1820's observes: 'The chains with which ladies now encircle their necks are becoming so large that their weight will soon become a serious problem. In one type each of the heavy and elaborately worked links is separated from the next by a star of matt gold. At the end of the chain a heavy cross, rings *à la chevalière* or other jewels of a Gothic character are suspended'.

The simpler hair style of the period no longer offered the same space for chains, pearls and pendants as had the monstrous coiffures of the late eighteenth century. It did, however, provide an admirable setting for the tiara which now became an indispensable item of court dress (Fig. 2). Few of the more splendid tiaras of the Regency period have survived, but even a lady of title did not consider it beneath her to wear one of gilt metal set with copies of Classical cameos, such as that illustrated in Plate 87A. This particular tiara is of unusually solid appearance even for a period which accepted massiveness as a fundamental principle of design in applied arts.

Another hair ornament which made its appearance towards the end of this period was, in fact, a revival of a fashion of the first half of the sixteenth century. This was the *ferronière*, so called because a similar jewel is shown in Leonardo da Vinci's portrait of a lady, known as 'La belle Ferronière' and formerly believed to represent the wife of a blacksmith who became the mistress of the king of France. The jewel took the form of a pendant suspended over the forehead from a chain which encircled the top of the head; in 1825 it was said that every woman of elegance wore one.

The catalogue of hair ornaments continues with diadems and combs in the Spanish style. The diadem was worn at the front of the head straight over the brow, and sometimes two or even three might be worn, one above the other, the ensemble being completed in the more extreme cases with a Spanish comb at the back of the head decorated *en suite* with the diadems. Some of these Regency diadems, of which only those composed of semi-precious stones have survived, are of most attractive design and delicate construction. Floral motives such as laurel leaves or ears of corn were among the most frequent designs for them. Though the Regency coiffures were simple, they were required nevertheless to support a profusion of jewellery with evening dress.

The design of all these various forms of jewellery was influenced more or less by the contemporary interest in the arts of Classical Greece and Rome. Cameos or intaglios, in some cases antique, but usually contemporary copies from Italy, were introduced wherever possible as prominent features of all kinds of jewellery from finger-rings to tiaras (Pls. 87A, B). So highly were such cameos regarded that they were mounted alongside gems of very great value without arousing any feeling of incongruity. In France the enthusiasm for cameos as jewellery reached such a pitch that in 1808 the Emperor Napoleon required the Director of the Bibliothèque Nationale to hand over 82 classical cameos and intaglios from the ancient Cabinet du Roi for mounting as jewellery.

It was partly in order to accommodate the cameos, which were of larger proportions than precious stones, that early nineteenth-century settings were broadened out till in some cases they became clumsy. Authentic antique cameos and intaglios had always been rare; reproductions in hardstone had been produced in Italy ever since the Renaissance, often for sale as antique, but now the great increase in demand made it unneccessary to pass off modern pieces as classical cameos. Many of these reproductions were of notable quality and of high

Fig. 2. Design for tiara and floral brooches set with brilliants. From a drawing, early nineteenth century. *Victoria and Albert Museum.*

cost, but the demand for less expensive cameos led to the development of a large industry in shell cameos in Naples and the surrounding country. As an even cheaper alternative cameos cut in lava from Vesuvius were made and mounted in bracelets or necklaces while cheaper still were those of moulded glass. The Staffordshire firm of Wedgwood had also been producing cameos of stoneware since the 1770's, and these continued in favour during the early nineteenth century, though they were not likely to satisfy the more archæologically minded ladies. The finest cameos were cut in cornelian, jasper or agate, and for those who could not afford to buy cameos in these materials necklaces and bracelets were produced set with plain medallions of hardstone, mounted in pinchbeck, a gilt base-metal, instead of gold (Pl. 87c). The most popular hardstones were, of course, those that had been used in classical times – namely, sardonyx, cornelian, onyx and agate.

The Empire style which dominated the early years of our period placed no exaggerated value on archæological exactness; it was sufficient that the jewels should be set with classical or pseudo-classical gems and that their design be appropriate to contemporary costume. Apart indeed from elements of obvious classical derivation such as the cameos, some of the main features of the Empire style had no particular relevance to antique jewellery. Among these may be numbered the emphasis placed upon harmony between brightly coloured stones and settings of variegated gold, and the preference for shining and contrasting unbroken surfaces.

The end of the Napoleonic epoch in 1815 did not lead in England to any drastic changes in jewellery style. But in France the sudden change of fortune found many persons of importance without the substance to support their position, and there was for a while a strengthening of the fashion for jewellery of small intrinsic value. In general, a revival of interest in styles less remote than that of Classical Greece and Rome manifested itself. By the 1820's we find the first results of the blossoming of the Romantic taste, the pseudo-medieval *style cathédrale*, the revived Renaissance beginning with the *ferronière*, and even a trend towards orientalism, this last encouraged by Byron's activities in Greece. The post-Empire interpretation of the classical style was far more serious in attitude and was much concerned with questions of archæological exactness. In the 1820's the Roman jeweller Fortunato Pio Castellani began manufacturing reproductions of Etruscan and Classical Roman jewels based on examples in his own collection, and continued to do so until his death in 1865. He was particularly famed for his skill in reproducing the extremely fine granulated surface characteristic of Etruscan jewellery.

Romantic Gothic jewellery followed much the same course as the revived classical jewellery, that is to say, in its earlier phases it was merely fashionable and popular in spirit with no pretence at accuracy, but later it became consciously and painfully academic in its effort to reproduce faithfully its medieval prototypes. Among the revivals of the post-Empire period were the diamond sprays and bouquet brooches that had been so popular during the latter half of the eighteenth century. So closely (Fig. 2 and Pl. 88B) do they follow the naturalistic designs of the preceding century that it is often difficult to distinguish with certainty between the Regency and the eighteenth-century examples – with the exception of those set in collets closed at the back, a type of setting which was abandoned in favour of open collets about the end of the eighteenth century.

The aigrette, which had been crowded out by tiara, diadem and Spanish comb, also returned to favour in the 1820's; a particularly attractive example set with the fashionable gemstones of the time, turquoise, topaz, amethyst, emerald and diamond, is illustrated in Plate 88A. The design is based upon an ear of barley, a form which is frequently encountered in jewellery of this period. A Paris fashion note of 1822 refers to the popularity of the wheat-ear in jewellery: 'Are you going to a new play at the theatre? Twenty, thirty, fifty, even a hundred coiffures will display ears of corn, some of gold, the majority imitating the real thing'.

As in previous periods, jewellery fashions continued to be international; jewellers still neglected to sign their work, and the problem of determining the nationality of a given jewel is no easier to solve. One can say that the popular 'Berlin' cast-iron jewellery was probably not of English manufacture but imported, as were the hard-stone and the shell cameos and the Florentine miniature mosaics with views of Italy or sentimental dogs that garnished so many brooches and bracelets. Jet, on the other hand, which was much used for mourning jewellery, was produced in England at Whitby and can usually be recognized as of English origin. Mourning rings remained in great demand during the whole period, though their designs were less imaginative than those of the preceding century. The charming little sentimental devices of the late eighteenth-century mourning ring gave way to massive gold hoops inscribed only with the name of the deceased in enamel, black for married persons and white for the unmarried. Another type of mourning wear was the hair jewellery which became more popular in the 1820's. In the late eighteenth century lockets and rings with the initials of the deceased worked in a lock of the hair had been worn, but now the scale became larger and we find whole bracelets formed of intertwined hair (Pl. 87B).

The various styles which have been referred to above, Roman, Etruscan, Egyptian and Gothic, eventually passed out of fashion in the course of the later nineteenth century, but the new materials which had been introduced in order to cheapen jewellery and make it accessible to a wider public, had come to stay. The jewellery of the second half of the century was dominated by semi-precious stones such as amethyst, topaz and turquoise, and settings continued to be constructed of stamped scrollwork, filigree and granulated gold work.

(A) Thomas Attwood, 1765–1838. *Royal College of Music.*

(B) Samuel Wesley, 1766–1837, by J. Jackson. *National Portrait Gallery.*

PLATE 89

(A) John Field, 1782–1837.

(B) Sir Henry Rowley Bishop, 1786–1855.
*National Portrait Gallery.*

(C) William Crotch as an infant prodigy, aged 3, by I. SANDERS, 1778. *British Museum.*

(D) Charles Dibdin, engraving from a miniature by R. W. SATCHWELL, 1819.

PLATE 90

## *Music and Musical Instruments*

# Music and Musical Instruments

ROBERT DONINGTON

### *Diluted Handel, Haydn and Mozart*

The glory of English music, so bright in the sixteenth and seventeenth centuries, yet so inexplicably diminished in the eighteenth, sank perhaps to its quietest state under the later Georges. No one really knows why; the period was by no means an uncreative one in England for the other arts. The fact remains that in musical composition we produced no men of undoubted genius at about this time, and very few of outstanding talent. As a natural consequence, such talent as did make its appearance was unduly influenced by models which were not indigenous. There were, it is true, a few exceptions; but their work, as we shall see, was either in too lightly popular a vein to carry much weight in the history of music, or too limited in scope.

This verdict is accepted by the general consent of historians. All the same, there is one sense in which it is too harsh. That the judgement of time has proved retrospectively unfavourable to most late Georgian music is not to be denied. But this judgement does not, perhaps, give an altogether fair impression of the state of that music as it affected its own contemporaries.

In the first place, whatever it may have lacked in quality it undoubtedly made up for in quantity. And as we read through its numerous contemporary editions and its still more numerous manuscripts, we are impressed by a certain impetus and vitality even in the least musically inspired regions of this imposing output. We are impressed by an unavoidable conviction that whatever monotony all these volumes of glees and ballad operas, anthems and oratorios, may hold for us today, they represent a tremendous amount of uninhibited enjoyment both in the writing and in the performance of them for the musicians and the general public of their own day.

That is one important consideration. A second of more lasting interest is that in spite of the amount of sheer paltry Handelian imitation that had been going on ever since his sojourn and death (1759) in England, in spite of the equally paltry imitation of Haydn and Mozart that later added itself to the medley, and in spite of the consequent insignificance of most of our late Georgian music in the main current of European musical development, there were nevertheless one or two features of English musical life at the time which were not foreign imitations but had a truly indigenous zest and reality. They were, in fact, not in the main current at all. They drew little from it and they contributed little to it. But they were alive in their own right, they were genuinely English, and they are genuine musical achievements.

### *The so-called 'Ballad Operas'*

One of these indigenous achievements was that form of entertainment which throughout its long history continued to go under the name of 'Ballad Opera', though in its later forms this name was no longer strictly appropriate. However, it was accurate enough when the species began. That was under the first George of England, in 1728, when the famous *Beggar's Opera* of Gay and Pepusch first took the stage. It is said on no lesser authority than that of Pope that Gay took his idea from a suggestion made by Swift to the effect that a 'Newgate pastoral', replete with jail-birds and their female appurtenances, might do very well for an operatic libretto. The suggestion was presumably meant satirically, and a fine satire Gay made of it: a satire at once of the Whig party with their leader Walpole, and of the ultra-fashionable Italian opera of the period with its leading exponents Bononcini and the great Handel himself. 'I hope I may be forgiven', says the prologue, 'that I have not made my Opera throughout unnatural, like those in vogue.' He had not indeed; it is all delightfully spontaneous, to (but not beyond) the point of enjoyable coarseness; and it is impossible not to see in this splendidly flippant and irresponsible affair the natural Englishman's answer to the excess of Mediterranean artificiality which, with all its undoubted musical excellencies, the Italian opera of the eighteenth century had come to represent.

Because it was natural and because it was English, the Ballad Opera took firm root. It has, indeed, the rare distinction of being one of the few English musical forms since the great harpsichordists of the early seventeenth century to have had any appreciable effect, though scarcely a weighty one, on continental music: it was one of the many starting-points of the German *Singspiel*. It had spoken dialogue (like the so-called '*opéra comique*'), not sung recitative (like 'grand opera'); and its airs were sung to tunes borrowed from the general stock of the ballad-mongers (itself often borrowed from folk sources), but as those were exhausted they were more and more commonly adapted from sophisticated sources which included Handel and the grand operatic composers themselves. Then, rather before the middle of the eighteenth century, the original craze for Ballad Operas petered out for a decade or two, and only a few were written.

Shortly before the period here under consideration, the Ballad Opera took on a second lease of life, at least as energetic and productive as its first. In this second phase, the borrowed ballad tunes were no longer a characteristic feature; yet the music composed for the airs in place of them kept a great deal of their easy-going popularity and directness. Among its most successful composers at this stage were Charles Dibdin (1745–1814), James Hook (1746–1827), William Shield (1748–1829), William Reeve (1757–1815), the short-lived Stephen Storace (1763–96), his exact contemporary John Davy (1763–1824), and the remarkable tenor John Braham (1774–1856), whose imperious habit it was to compose all the music of his own part (but not of the unimportant other parts!) of most of the operas in which he appeared. With these men should perhaps be named Henry Rowley Bishop (1786–1855), a most prominent and prolific composer of opera and theatre music in great variety, from grand to popular, but not a Ballad Opera composer in the same sense as was Dibdin, Hook, Shield or Storace.

The late Georgian output of Ballad Operas reached a remarkable total, and very largely maintained that forthright and robust vitality which is its chief recommendation. Perhaps of all this music the most enduring is that to which Dibdin set his justly celebrated songs of the sea. But many good tunes, genuinely rousing in their extraverted way, can be found; and the whole episode is one of which English musicians (incurable snobs excepted) can rightly be proud.

Towards the end of our period, it must be admitted that the Ballad Opera was beginning to wear a little thin. The robustness grew less convincing; the tunes more threadbare; the manliness a trifle forced. Yet the form itself was by no means finished with. It remained in being until the Victorians Gilbert and Sullivan fastened on it with something in no way short of genius; crossed it with Italian opera, not of the heavy Handelian, but of the sparkling Rossini strain; and produced a yet more enduring English operatic achievement, the Savoy Operas.

### *The Glees and the Glee Clubs*

A second late Georgian musical activity of an equally indigenous, and not far from equally popular, character was the fashion for what are generically known as 'glees'.

A glee is primarily an unaccompanied part-song. Some works known as glees for want of another name have instrumental accompaniments; the great majority do not. Many glees have a cer-

(A) Covent Garden Theatre, by Pugin and Rowlandson, from *The Microcosm of London*, 1808.

(B) Humming-birds, or a Dandy Trio. Drawn by 'J. S.' and etched by G. CRUIKSHANK, 1819.

PLATE 91

(A) Piano. William Stodart. Early nineteenth century. *Victoria and Albert Museum.*

(B) Portable Pianino. Chappell. Early nineteenth century. *Victoria and Albert Museum.*

PLATE 92

tain amount of contrapuntal workmanship in their construction; scarcely any have any elaborate artifices of this kind. Yet the workmanship is generally craftsmanlike; the parts are contrived neatly to give everybody a tuneful if not very independent melody to sing; the harmony flows skilfully if unsensationally; the rhythm is alive if not greatly varied.

In comparison with the finesse and subtlety of the best Elizabethan madrigals, a late Georgian glee is a somewhat obvious affair, and no doubt reflects a decline in the prevailing standards of amateur taste and musicianship. But not of musical enthusiasm; glee clubs founded specially for the enjoyment of such active music-making were numerous and well attended. As with the best Ballad Operas, the glees are attractive in proportion to their vitality. Unpretentious as they generally are, they make uncommonly good singing. Some of them, moreover, rise to genuinely poetic feeling, occasionally of extraordinary force.

Of the glee composers active within the years 1810–30, the following were among the more prominent; Samuel Webbe (1740–1816); William Shield (1748–1829); John Stafford Smith (1750–1836); John Samuel Stevens (1757–1837); Thomas Attwood (1765–1838); John Wall Callcott (1766–1821); Samuel Wesley (1766–1837); Reginald Spofforth (1770–1827); Mendelssohn's admired friend William Horsley (1774–1858); William Beale (1784–1854), some of whose glees are real madrigals; and the ubiquitous Henry Rowley Bishop (1786–1855). Quite an imposing list, and one that could readily be extended. Some of those mentioned in it were distinguished composers in other directions as well; some, such as Webbe and Stafford Smith, were not. It will be noticed that there is a certain overlapping with the list of Ballad Opera composers. Attwood, it may be mentioned, was a pupil of Mozart, and one of those who introduced a Mozartian style as a change from the perennial Handelian into the more serious forms of English music then prevailing. But unfortunately he was less successful as what was then an instrumental modernist than he was in the less ambitious indigenous form of the vocal glee.

In addition to its own musical value, the glee formed an indispensible link in that long tradition of unaccompanied vocal part-singing which has never been broken in England since the great madrigalians themselves, and indeed since far earlier. If our late Georgian forefathers had not been so fond of singing glees, our own generation might not so easily have taken to singing madrigals now that the Golden Age of English music has been brought out of the history books and into practical life again. The late Georgian composers were certainly unenterprising to a defect; but in so far as their lack of enterprise went with a healthy conservation, it had its corresponding virtues.

### *Interest in past music: Wesley and the Bach revival*

This conservatism, on its healthy side, is pleasantly evident in an institution which would not evoke any particular comment in our own generation, when interest in music of earlier periods has become a commonplace, but which was certainly unusual in the early nineteenth century. I have in mind the series of 'Ancient Concerts' founded in 1776 and continued until 1848, the rule at which was that no music was to be included of less than twenty years' standing at the time of the performance. In theory, therefore, the rule was a sliding rule, bringing in an interesting succession of music from perhaps a generation ago. In practice, the exaggerated reverence for Handel made itself felt here as elsewhere. The proportion of the programmes handed over to his music was not healthy at all.

It was typical of our English conservatism, once again on its healthy side, that a new edition of nearly two hundred older pieces, mainly English, appeared in 1812 under the decidedly slapdash editorship of Stafford Smith. Good editing of early music was hardly to be expected in an age so patronizing towards pre-Handelian music; but in view of that, it is striking enough to meet with so much practical enthusiasm. Stafford Smith had already published a quantity of early Tudor music in 1779; he had greatly assisted Hawkins in the preparation of the latter's famous *History of Music*; and he died possessed of an astonishing collection of early manuscripts, which were unfortunately dispersed at the sale of his effects.

Another example of creative conservatism which it is pleasant to record is the part played by distinguished English musicians in the revival of J. S. Bach. It is well known that Bach, though a greater and more profound composer than Handel in every way, and in the long run actually possessed of a wider popular appeal, yet passed through a period of substantial neglect while Handel's fashion came to its peak. It is perhaps less well known that Mendelssohn, whose championship secured the first performance of the *St Matthew Passion* since its composer's death, found an early and powerful ally in Samuel Wesley the elder (1766–1837).

In many ways Wesley is the most noteworthy of the late Georgian composers. His enthusiasm for Bach began very early in his career, and remained one of its guiding influences. He was evidently a most formidable exponent of the organ works both of Bach and Handel, and an indefatigable propagandist for the former's claims; he shared with C. F. Horn (1786–1849) the credit of first editing a portion of Bach's music for the English market.

Some of the excitement which Wesley found in rediscovering this supreme genius of the past made its way into his own composition. Remarkably enough for an Englishman of that generation, he avoided oratorio after two exceedingly precocious and by no means unsuccessful attempts, the second of them at the age of eleven years. Less surprisingly, perhaps, in view of his serious if somewhat erratic personality (the erratic side was plausibly, but not necessarily with truth, attributed to a serious fall at the age of twenty-one), he avoided the stage: he was not one of the fashionable Ballad Opera men. Neither, however, did he essay grand opera. He did write glees, but here he was capable, as only few of his contemporaries were, of truly madrigalian workmanship. His Church music ranges from brilliant passage-work in the Mozartian idiom, to soberly wrought and profoundly felt counterpoint almost in the old Tudor vein. As an instrumental composer he was prolific, and at times inspired. He had an excellent chamber vein, while as a symphonist of considerable structural abilities he was ahead of his English contemporaries. Altogether, he was both the solidest and the liveliest figure late Georgian musicianship could boast.

Two lesser church composers with some claim at least to solidity, if not to liveliness, were John Clarke-Whitfield (1770–1836) and William Crotch (1775–1847). The latter is the more substantial personage; he was a Handelian of Handelians, but in that line he was the best of his school, particularly in oratorio. What these two chiefly lack, however, is the quality of excitement which makes much of the elder Samuel Wesley so worthwhile.

### *A great Irish pianist-composer and others*

There was an exciting enough school of pianist-composers more or less in or of Late Georgian England, of whom the three best representatives were not any of them strictly Englishmen. One was an Irishman who worked much and eventually died abroad; the others were continentals who worked much and died in England. The Irishman was John Field (1782–1837); the continentals were Muzio Clementi (1752–1832) and John Baptist Cramer (1771–1858).

Of the two continentals, Clementi was the more talented as a composer, though it is only his masterly studies for the piano which still survive. The same is true of his pupil Cramer. But the Irishman holds a more important place in the history of music. He was not only, like the other two, a brilliant pianist; he was a composer of so poetic an imagination that only its extremely limited scope prevents our calling him a genius. Perhaps, indeed, we should admit that genius can show itself in miniature, and call him one outright.

Field's contribution to the history of music is that slight but deeply felt form of piano music known as the Nocturne. It is a form upon which a composer to whom nobody would deny the name of genius set his stamp: that is to say, Chopin. But it seems certain that Chopin based his conception of the Nocturne upon Field's, and that Field's conception of it was his own. It was the one late Georgian creative achievement in music which did pass into the main stream, and deservedly. Most of Field's music is strung to too slack a tension to be of enduring value; but his Nocturnes place him, however inconspicuously, among the immortals.

Apart from Field, we seem to have imported rather than exported our top performers at this period. Even in the seventeenth century, a foreign name was already a commercial asset for a performer, though at that time English virtuosi stood in the front rank. In the eighteenth century, the foreign fashion grew, particularly for Italian singers – and with some good reason in that respect. By the early nineteenth century, continentals had the preference in many fields, particularly that of violin playing, where the Italian school had been in the lead for many generations, though the German and Franco-Belgian schools were soon to dispute this lead with them. Later in the nineteenth century, it is the German names that are most conspicuous here; in the period now under discussion, it is Italian names.

Viotti, who was the last great Italian violinist of the classical school, though by no means the last great Italian violinist, aroused remarkable enthusiasm in England where he spent intermittent periods between 1792 and his death in London in 1824. He was among the active founders of the Royal Philharmonic Society in 1813; his pupil Nicolas Mori was made the first professor of the violin at the foundation of the Royal Academy of Music in 1822 – Mori being the son of an Italian, but born in London.

Both these foundations were of lasting musical importance. As usual in the nineteenth century, we find no lack of intense musical activity in this country; but we do find a lack of confidence in our own indigenous powers. Could it be that we exercised a baleful species of auto-suggestion upon ourselves, to the effect that only wild looks and a continental name seemed compatible with true musicianship? Is that how the Italian, and later the German, spell held our home products at such a tacitly admitted disadvantage?

### *A thriving trade in instruments*

Our makers of musical instruments, at any rate, as opposed to our performers, were at no such disadvantage. English keyboard instruments had a particularly high reputation not only in this country but abroad. English harpsichords were among the most favoured in the eighteenth century; and in the latter part of that century, the new art of piano-making received some of its most notable improvements at the hands of Englishmen. Indeed, at the time of which we now write only two piano actions were regarded as worth taking seriously, out of a multitude of less successful attempts. One was the 'Viennese action', with a supreme delicacy of touch and swiftness of repetition; the other was the 'English action', somewhat heavier and less volatile, but compensating for that drawback by an unrivalled sonority and depth of tone. Eventually the advantages of both were combined in the famous Erard 'repetition action' on which the double escapement actions of most grand pianos of the present time are based. It is not without interest that the great Sebastian Erard's son Pierre (his father being then too old to follow up his own invention) immediately patented it in England. The year was 1821.

Within the brief twenty years from 1810 to 1830 here under review, a number of English improvements to the piano were made, particularly with regard to the then novel principle of a metal-braced frame, the forerunner of the modern metal frames. The invention patented by Thorn and Allen in 1820 actually used metal tubes in an ingenious system by which their expansion and contraction at different temperatures compensated for similar changes in the strings, thus keeping the instrument in tune under varying conditions. This refinement was eventually abandoned; but the work done on it, together with other work carried out during this period by the firm of Broadwood, was of pioneering value in developing a frame capable of piano stringing.

The period was one during which a fairly rapid change was occurring in the nature and function of the piano, and the English contribution to this change was most important. The late eighteenth-century piano, the 'fortepiano' of Mozart's period, has thin strings and a light frame comparable to the harpsichord. It differs, of course, in having a percussive hammer action giving a continuous gradation of volume controlled by touch, in place of a plucked jack action giving little direct control of volume. But in the quality and colouring of its tone, the 'fortepiano' is very like a harpsichord indeed.

Not so the grand piano of 1810–30. By now the strings are thicker and tenser, yielding a more massive but less highly coloured tone. For as the thickness and tension of the strings increases, so does the proportion of energy sent into the lowest few harmonies of the natural harmonic series, while the proportion sent into the colourful high harmonies decreases. During the second half of the nineteenth century, this tendency was carried to extreme lengths, and the instruments of that time, though mechanically admirable, are tonally very different from those of the period here under discussion, and it is by no means certain that the difference is entirely for the better. The volume, however, is substantially greater. The English experiments in strengthening the frame were a necessary preliminary, especially since the period 1810–30 saw a disposition to enlarge the compass of the piano by adding further octaves, with a very considerable increase in total tension as a consequence.

In the year 1818, the firm of Broadwood sent a fine specimen of their newest grand pianos as a gift to Beethoven. This instrument made an extremely favourable impression both on the composer and on a number of distinguished continental pianists whom he caused to make a careful trial of it; on his death it came into the hands of Liszt. An instrument such as this, with its powerful and reliable English action and its strong yet resonant frame, represents one of the highest points in the history of the piano, being in its way quite the equal of any subsequent instrument, though dissimilar in the purposes for which it is most suitable. The modern piano is of a comparatively neutral, though big and beautiful, tone; but the Beethoven piano of this type, though already quite different from the harpsichord in tone, retains a stronger colouring and a more individual character, albeit less loud. There is no doubt that to hear a Beethoven concerto played on it, with the volume of the orchestra suitably adapted where necessary, can be a memorable and revealing experience.

In 1816 William Simmons took out a patent for a barrel mechanism to play piano, harpsichord, or organ automatically. In 1827, James Stewart patented an improved method of attaching the strings which effected a minor revolution in tuning technique and has not since been replaced. A more conspicuous innovation so far as appearances are concerned was Robert Wornum's introduction of the still popular cottage piano in 1811.

Wind and string makers, though not so markedly in the forefront, were very active. John Shaw's patent of 1824 for transverse Spring Slides on brass instruments may have inspired some important German improvements shortly afterwards. Boehm's famous systematization of the holes and keywork of the flute was influenced by the large holes of an instrument played to him by Nicholson in London, and it was the London makers Gerock and Wolf who in 1831 made an experimental prototype to his specification. The holes of the flute had previously been cut less large than is acoustically desirable, in order to be convenient for the normal size of finger-end; they had, moreover, been placed in positions other than those acoustically desirable, in order to be conveniently within the reach of normal fingers. Acoustically, in short, the entire system was a compromise. Boehm's plan was to reorganize the system on sounder acoustic principles, while overcoming the practical difficulty by using a set of padded stoppers worked through levers. These levers or keys were placed conveniently for the fingers; the holes could then be placed as widely apart and cut as large as the acoustic requirements suggest.

It is believed, though it is not at all certain, that this novel approach to the problem of the flute (which was later extended to some other woodwind instruments) had already been anticipated in England by Captain Gordon, an amateur maker. In most directions, however, the English makers of wind instruments were conservatives rather than innovators at this period. As such, they enjoyed an excellent reputation.

With the violin family, there was no longer a question of improvements at so late a date. The number of reputable English makers at work is surprisingly large: it included the younger Benjamin Banks and his brothers James and Henry; William Forster II and III; Henry Lockey Hill and his son Joseph III; and at least four of the Dodd family. These are all makers whose work is much in demand today, but there were plenty of others whose businesses were thriving at the time.

*A pedestrian but not contemptible musical activity*

So substantial a trade in musical instruments argues a plentiful supply of amateur buyers; even a flourishing profession could not have kept so many makers busy by itself. The piano trade in particular was clearly providing for great numbers of amateur performers, a majority of them content with the compact and economical 'square' (actually oblong) pianos so common under the misleading title of 'spinet' in the modern saleroom. Though pleasant enough when in good condition, they are not altogether satisfactory instruments, being neither incisive like a good harpsichord nor full-bodied like a good piano. Still, they served their purpose in very many music-loving households, both for solos and as instruments of accompaniment.

Glees must have been sung in household circles as well as in more formal glee clubs. On the other hand, nothing had arisen to replace the profound amateur chamber music of the viols, now forgotten for the best part of a century. The love of amateur string quartet playing which became so striking a feature of nineteenth-century Germany had scarcely yet reached England, nor did it ever strike root so deeply here. It was, indeed, an age of big orchestras and romantic virtuosos; the amateur came second where in Stuart England he had been very much to the front. All the same, countries do to some extent take turns in musical prominence. With the nineteenth century, Germany came to the top of the wheel, England to the bottom.

Yet even in this low trough of our musical fortunes, we made a better showing than the foreshortened view of history quite gives us credit for at this distance of time. We were not creative of any great benefits for posterity; but in addition to doing good trade, there is not the slightest doubt that we enjoyed ourselves. That may not be the only purpose of music; but it is one of them, and not the least.

[*By permission of the W. A. Harding Trustees and of the author*

Grand Piano with vertical stringing, by George Wilkinson, *c.* 1829.
From *The Pianoforte* by Dr Rosamund E. M. Harding, 1933.

(A) Binding by Charles Lewis, *c.* 1830. Longinus, *De sublimi genere dicendi*, Venice 1555. Brown morocco, gold-tooled. (Reduced.) *British Museum (Grenville Library).*

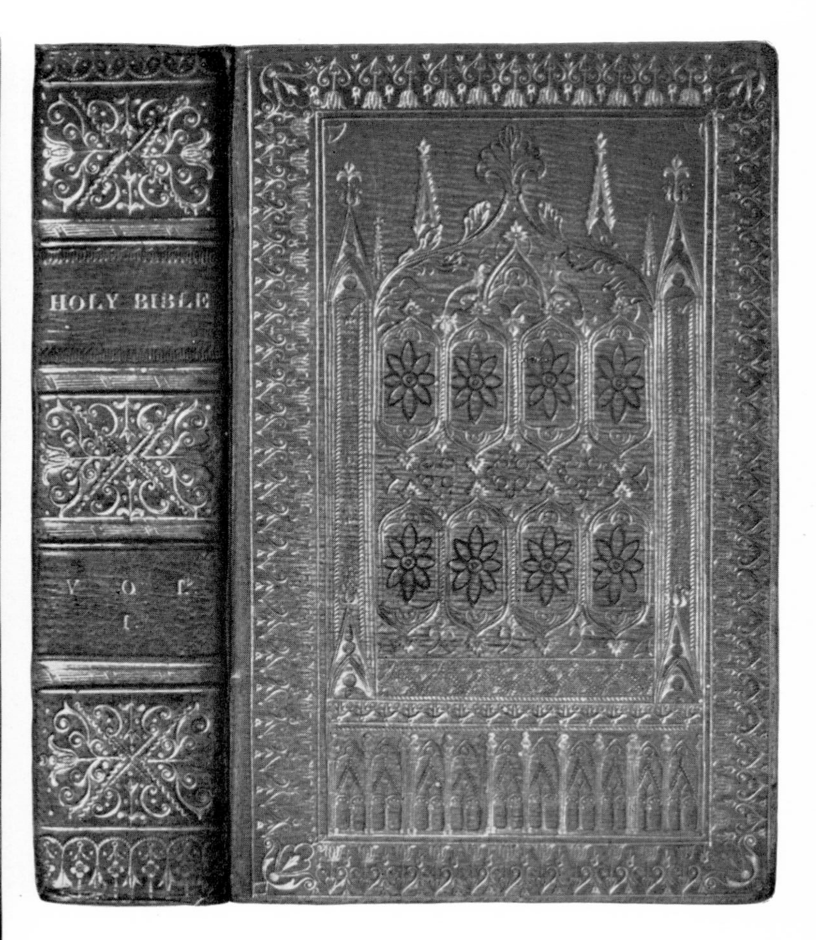


(B) 'Cathedral' Binding by William Lubbock of Newcastle-upon-Tyne, *c.* 1812. *Holy Bible*, Edinburgh, 1811. Red morocco, gold-tooled. (Reduced.) *Courtesy Mr and Mrs A. Ehrman.*

PLATE 93

Third Edition.
LECTURES
ON THE
Art
OF
WRITING,
Comprehending
*A Variety of Observations*
ON THE
IMPEDIMENTS WHICH RETARD THE PROGRESS OF THE
LEARNER;
*Including a brief History of the Art;*
And also of the
MATERIALS THAT HAVE BEEN IN USE FROM THE EARLIEST AGES TO THE
PRESENT TIME;
With Excellent Receipts
FOR
*MANUFACTURING INKS OF VARIOUS COLOURS;*
And likewise
Methods of Extracting Ink from Paper after it has been written upon.
*To which are added,*
SEVERAL METHODS OF ACQUIRING IMPROVEMENT IN
BUSINESS HAND WRITING,
*By a Peculiar Movement of the Pen,*
Containing
*A CURIOUS CLASSIFICATION of the LETTERS of the ALPHABET,*
And combining the excellence and uniform neatness of
English Manuscript.

*Interspersed with a great number of Plates and Examples*
WITH FULL AND COPIOUS INSTRUCTIONS HOW TO PERFORM THE SAME.

DEDICATED (BY PERMISSION) TO
HIS ROYAL HIGHNESS THE DUKE OF SUSSEX.

By J. CARSTAIRS,
*Author of Tachygraphy, or the Flying Pen—Abbreviated Arithmetic, &c. &c.*

*LONDON:*
PRINTED BY W. MOLINEUX, BREAM'S BUILDINGS, CHANCERY LANE;
*And Published for the Author, 77, Cheapside, Poultry; and may be had of all Booksellers.*
PRICE TWELVE SHILLINGS, BOARDS.

Dated 1816, this book (slightly reduced) shows the printed paper boards in which many books were issued before the introduction of cloth in about 1825. The 'shaded' type used for WRITING and the border are both Regency inventions. *Courtesy B. L. Wolpe.*

PLATE 94

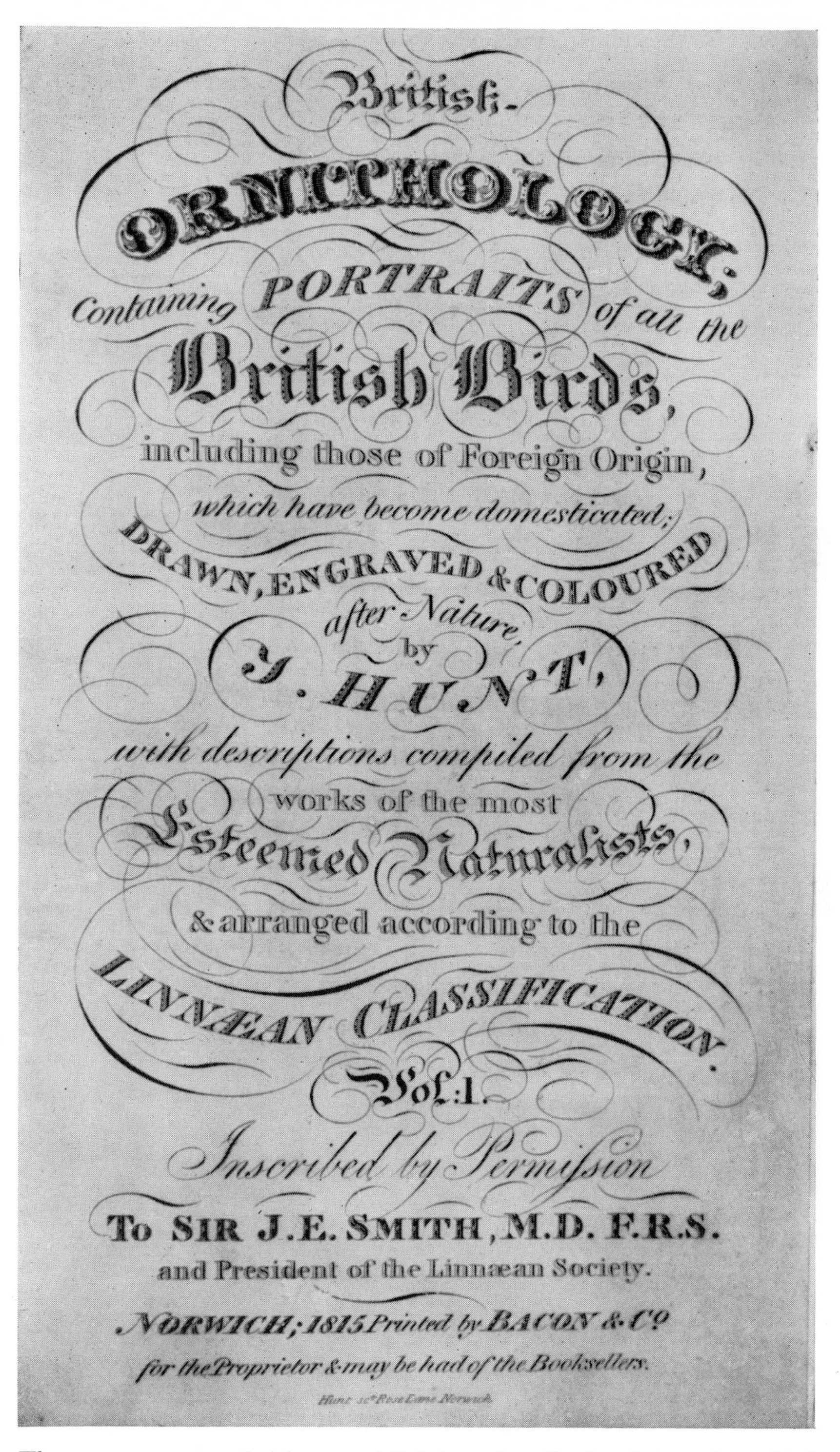

British
ORNITHOLOGY;
Containing PORTRAITS of all the
British Birds,
including those of Foreign Origin,
which have become domesticated;
DRAWN, ENGRAVED & COLOURED
after Nature
by
J. HUNT,
with descriptions compiled from the
works of the most
Esteemed Naturalists,
& arranged according to the
LINNÆAN CLASSIFICATION.
Vol: 1.
Inscribed by Permission
To SIR J. E. SMITH, M.D. F.R.S.
and President of the Linnæan Society.
NORWICH; 1815 Printed by BACON & Co
for the Proprietor & may be had of the Booksellers.

The copper-engraved title-page (slightly reduced) of a three-volume bird book published in Norwich 1815–22. The decoration of the engraved letters indicates a new trend also being followed by the typefounders. *Norwich Public Library.*

An example of Whittingham's Cabinet Library. The binding, contemporary, is in red morocco, gold-tooled. The title page is actual size. The illustrations were engraved on wood by S. Williams.

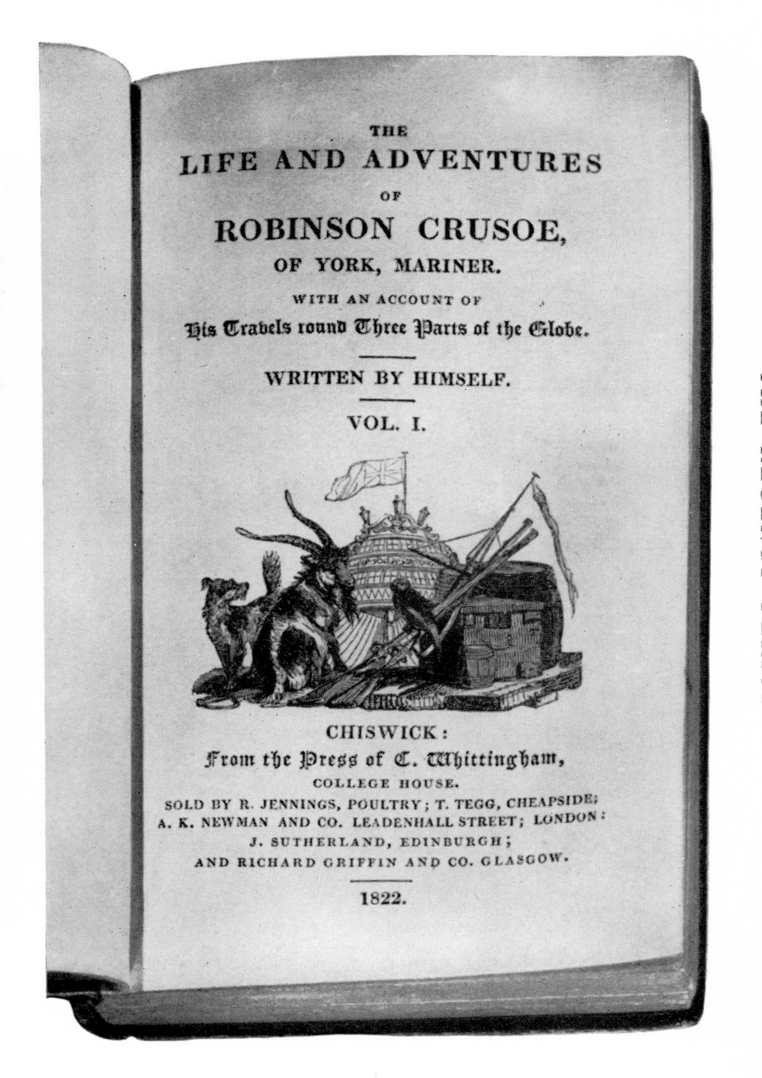

THE

LIFE AND ADVENTURES

OF

ROBINSON CRUSOE,

OF YORK, MARINER.

WITH AN ACCOUNT OF

His Travels round Three Parts of the Globe.

WRITTEN BY HIMSELF.

VOL. I.

CHISWICK:

From the Press of C. Whittingham,

COLLEGE HOUSE.

SOLD BY R. JENNINGS, POULTRY; T. TEGG, CHEAPSIDE;
A. K. NEWMAN AND CO. LEADENHALL STREET; LONDON:
J. SUTHERLAND, EDINBURGH;
AND RICHARD GRIFFIN AND CO. GLASGOW.

1822.

PLATE 96

*Bookbinding and Printing*

M

# Bookbinding

HOWARD M. NIXON

The years 1810–30 saw a revolution in the English binding trade, for it was during this period that the publisher's binding as we know it today was evolved. In 1810 the ordinary book was sold in stiffened paper wrappers or (sometimes printed) paper boards (Pl. 94), with the edges of the leaves untrimmed. A paper label on the spine, bearing the author's name and the title of the book, tacitly acknowledged that some buyers of the book might keep it on their shelves in this state, but this 'boards-and-label' style was essentially ephemeral: it had originally been conceived as a temporary covering for the sheets until they were more suitably bound in full or half-leather at the expense of the owner of the volume. By 1830 cloth, hitherto used only for chapbooks and school grammars, had achieved respectability, thanks to the efforts of the publisher William Pickering and the binder Archibald Leighton.[1] It was probably first introduced in 1822 or 1823 on one of Pickering's *Diamond Classics*, and the first examples have been claimed as the work of one Charles Sully. It is clear, however, that the development of bookcloth as a practical binding medium was the work of Archibald Leighton, who produced in 1825 a dyed glazed calico specially finished so as to be impervious to the adhesive. It was another seven years, however, before blocking in blind or gold was used on cloth-bound books, and up to 1830 decoration was limited to silk-bound annuals or to leather work.

[1] Cf. John Carter, *Binding Variants in English Publishing 1820–1900*, London 1932.

The leading figure in the 'West End' trade – the binders specializing in the best class of leather work – during the Regency period was undoubtedly Charles Lewis. His father, Johann Ludwig, had been one of the numerous German immigrants attracted to this country in the late eighteenth century by the passionate desire of the English collectors of the day to have all their books re-bound in full morocco. Once established in stylish premises on the ground floor in Duke Street, St James's, Charles Lewis secured the patronage of almost all the owners of great libraries of the day, including the Duke of Devonshire, Lord Spencer, Sir Richard Colt Hoare, Thomas Grenville, and Richard Heber. His style – doubtless in accordance with his patron's tastes – shows a steady deterioration from an early readiness to experiment, through a period of successful consolidation with linear designs and 'Aldine leaf' tools, to the skilful but insipid pastiches of 'Grolier' and other earlier styles which was to be the typical product of almost all European binderies from 1830 to 1880. Pl. 93A shows his characteristic linear style in the outer border and on the spine, combined with an interlacing lozenge and rectangle and a set of tools which are both copied directly from Grolier bindings of the 1540's.

Apart from Charles Lewis's ancestry and the continued existence of the firm of Hering, whose founder (another Charles) died right at the beginning of our period, the German influence of the previous thirty years faded completely. English binders were not entirely uninfluenced by events outside England, however, and the fashionable enthusiasm for all things Pompeian produced one or two interesting bindings by the firm of Dawson & Lewis, on which motifs based on decorations found at Pompeii were reproduced. The same firm was also among those who made use of Gothic decoration. The English 'Cathedral' bindings precede the French examples of the Romantic period and (except for late examples to be found on Prayer Books and Bibles of the 1830's) are normally built up of small tools, and not blocked from an engraved plaque. Sometimes the design depicts the west front of a church, as on Smith's *Antiquities of Westminster* in the Broxbourne Library bound by J. Mackenzie. More frequently the centre piece portrayed a rose window, while three or five lights from the window formed a type of fan decoration in the angles. Bindings in this style with heavily sunk panels were produced in George III's private bindery for the more important incunabula in his library, and are common on such books as Neale's *Westminster Abbey*, 1818–23.

Gothic binding was not the sole prerogative of London binders, however. Not only was it produced in Scotland and in Dublin, but also in English provincial centres, and Pl. 93B shows an adaptation of the style produced by William Lubbock of Newcastle-upon-Tyne. This was indeed the heyday of the provincial binder when, as Mr Charles Ramsden's collection shows, they often vied successfully with their London rivals. The proximity of Sir Mark Masterman Sykes's seat at Syston Park justified the existence in Grantham of two rival binders, S. Ridge and R. Storr, both of whom could produce gold-tooled work of competence, if not of taste. And the Earl of Leicester and Dawson Turner evidently provided enough work to keep John Shalders at work in various Norfolk towns.

One other London binder worthy of mention was Thomas Gosden, who combined the trade with that of bookseller and print-seller at the Sportsman's Repository in Bedford Street, Covent Garden. His sporting propensities confined his work largely (but not exclusively) to books concerned with angling and the chase, while his antiquarian interests are reflected in the heavy boards and bevelled edges, derived from the fifteenth century, which he deemed suitable for binding nineteenth-century editions of a seventeenth-century angling classic. He executed some excellent blocked work, however, using the design found on the title-page of the first edition of Walton's *Compleat Angler* in gold and portraits of Walton and Cotton in blind; his introduction of bronze medals of the same authors was original, if cumbersome; and many of his small sporting tools are charming.

# Printing

RUARI McLEAN

Thackeray (b. 1811) has described how, in his youth, children used to go on their holidays to look at the print-sellers' shops in Fleet Street, 'bright, enchanted palaces, which George Cruikshank [and Isaac Cruikshank, and Gillray, and Rowlandson, and Dighton, and Bunbury] used to people with grinning, fantastical imps. ... There used to be a crowd round the window in those days of grinning, good-natured mechanics, who spelt the songs, and spoke them out for the benefit of the company, and who received the points of humour with a general sympathizing roar. ... '[1]

[1] W. Thackeray, 'An Essay on the Genius of George Cruikshank', in the *Westminster Review*, 1840.

Fig. 1. Mrs Humphrey's print-shop in St James's Street, from a print by Gillray dated 1808.

We have a picture of such a print-seller's window, with a print in every pane, in Fig. 1 by Gillray (it is actually Mrs Humphrey's shop in St James's); and the publisher Tilt's window was drawn by Cruikshank. These windows supplied much of the public intelligence and news, for at that time many people still could not read, and the days of pictorial journalism did not start at least till the *Penny Magazine* of 1832. The prints were 'a penny plain, twopence coloured'. If coloured, it was by hand, by armies of girls and children, for colour-printing, by chromo-lithography, did not come in till about 1835. The prints were etched on copper, a process which the artist carried out himself, and could do almost with the speed of drawing on paper. Lithography, which had been invented by Senefelder in Bavaria in 1798, presented no advantages over etching until large editions (of, say, 1,000 copies or more) were required.

James Gillray (1757–1815), one of the greatest political cartoonists who ever lived, spent his life savaging politicians and the royal family, and died of drink; his successor George Cruikshank mirrored in his early prints the debauchery of the Regency, but lived on to throw his wildness into teetotalism and the illustration of fairy stories. The work of these two artists provides the most graphic pictures of the whole period, as future generations will recapture aspects of our own, not inaccurately, from the drawings of Giles.

### *Newspapers*

On the 28th November 1814 the London *Times*, first of any newspaper in the world, was printed on a steam-driven machine instead of on a hand-press. The machine was a German invention, but Koenig, its inventor, could not develop it in Germany and brought it to England, the leading country for industrial production, where he found a patron in Thomas Bensley, the great book-printer. The first machine to work was sold to *The Times*, as speed in printing was then of greater commercial interest to newspaper proprietors than to book publishers. Machine printing for books was not widely adopted till much later in the century.

Newspaper at that time was heavily taxed and every inch of paper had to be used, resulting in solid walls of type which appear formidable to modern eyes. Illustrations were few and cut on wood: the editor's difficulties are shown by the cut of Nelson's Funeral Car for *The Times* of 10th January 1806, which was made in advance and turned out to be inaccurate.

During the editorship of Thomas Barnes from 1817 to 1841 *The Times* rose to a position of great power and prestige and became known as 'The Thunderer'.

### *Books*

The most beautiful books published in Britain during the Regency were those illustrated by aquatint. Aquatinting was probably a French invention, but it was developed as a method of book-illustration in England by Paul Sandby and others from 1775 [2] and reached its greatest perfection during the 1820's and 1830's.

Aquatinting was a method of etching a copperplate to produce tints which looked like washes of water-colour, and came just at the time of the discovery of the Picturesque – of scenery, in fact – and the desire to paint and record it, exemplified particularly in the books of travel in Great Britain by the Reverend William Gilpin, illustrated with his own aquatints. If it is true that Gilpin 'discovered' the beauty of mountains (which, for example, were not at all appreciated by Johnson and Boswell in their tour of the Highlands), it is interesting to note that Gilpin took no pleasure in the flowering horse-chestnut tree, which in 1794 he described as 'a glaring object, totally unharmonious and unpicturesque'; it was Samuel Palmer who first painted and Tennyson who first described its beauties.[3]

The first aquatints were printed in one or two colours, but soon they were combined with hand-tinting in water-colour; and some of the hand-coloured aquatint books so issued were of great

[2] The first dated aquatints in England were produced by P. P. Burdett in Liverpool in 1771, but the full possibilities of the process were developed by Sandby. See J. R. Abbey's *Travel*, vol. 1, London, 1956, p. 142.

[3] G. Grigson, *Samuel Palmer*, London, 1947.

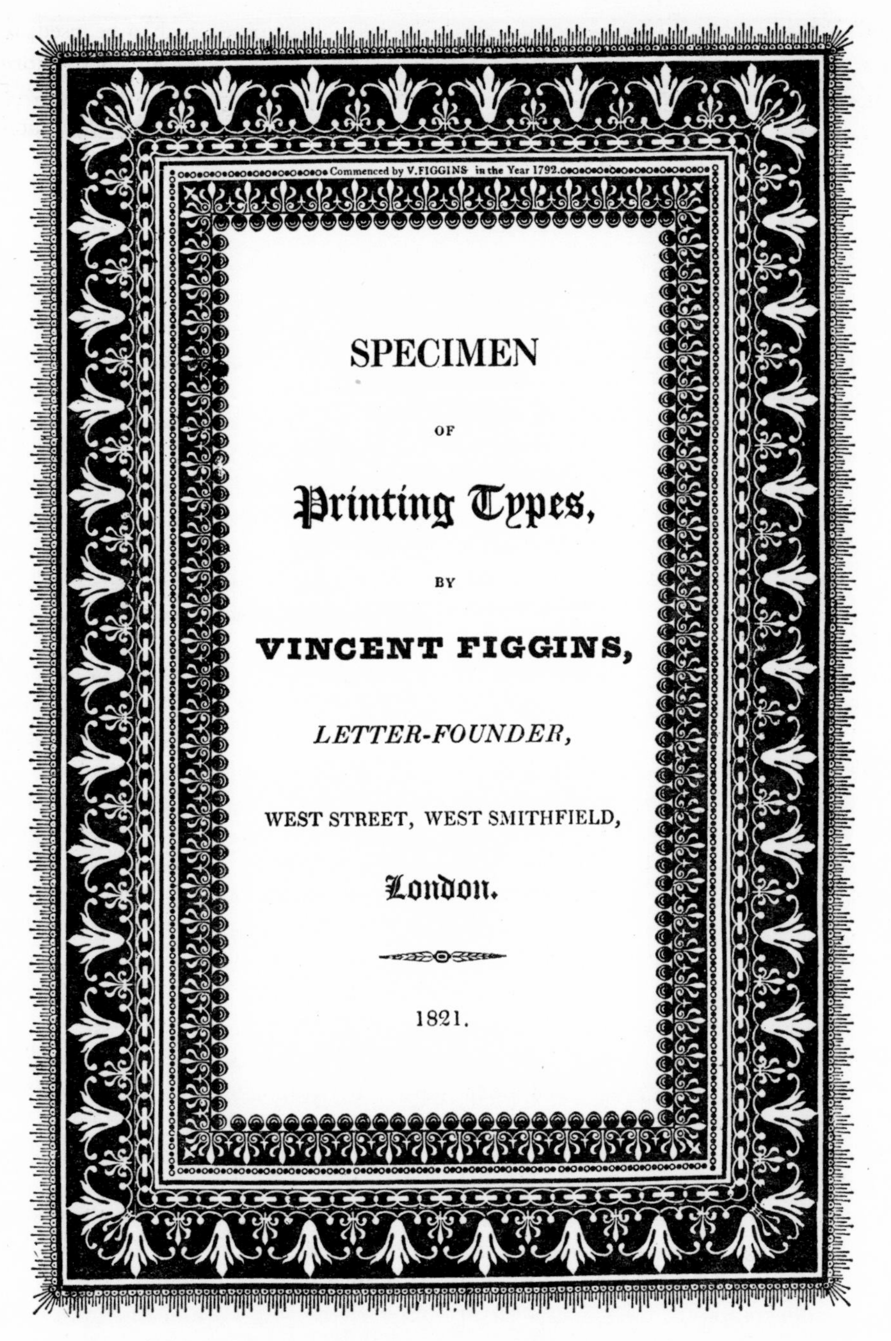

Commenced by V. FIGGINS in the Year 1792.

SPECIMEN

OF

Printing Types,

BY

VINCENT FIGGINS,

*LETTER-FOUNDER,*

WEST STREET, WEST SMITHFIELD,

London.

1821.

Fig. 2. The title-page of Figgins' specimen book of 1821, showing a border made up of type-ornaments which were then new. Actual size. *St Bride Printing Library, London.*

Fig. 3. The typographic borders here and on p. 174 are from Figgins' specimen book of 1821. Actual size. *St Bride Printing Library, London.*

delicacy and beauty and deserve, in fact, to be rated among the most beautiful artifacts of the whole period. One of the most famous of these books, and now one of the most valuable, was *A Voyage round Great Britain*, published in eight volumes between 1814 and 1825, containing over 300 coloured aquatints by William Daniell, R.A. Owing to the fact that aquatinting was a hand process and that the plates deteriorated in printing, the quality of individual prints varies considerably: but there is a softness and subtlety of colouring in the best that is entrancing.

Some of the colour-plate books, including Daniell's, were first issued in monthly parts in paper wrappers – a method of publication later adopted for the novels of Dickens and others. A book issued in this way which captured the spirit of its period more than any other printed work was Pierce Egan's *Life in London*, which began appearing in monthly parts in October 1820. Its heroes were Jerry Hawthorn (a gentleman), Corinthian Tom (a pugilist), and Bob Logic (an Oxford undergraduate), and each part (price one shilling) contained three coloured aquatint plates, usually by George Cruikshank's brother Robert. The book was instantly successful, was reproduced on the stage, and initiated a host of successors and imitators. The characters gave their names to the age, so that thirty years later Surtees wrote about 'The old Tom-and-Jerry days, when fisticuffs were the fashion', and added that 'Tom and Jerry had a great deal to answer for in the way of leading soft-headed young men astray'. The plates are still among the best illustrations of the London life of the period.

The publisher who specialized in large colour-plate books was Rudolph Ackermann (see *The Late Georgian Period*, p. 175): he had the brilliant idea of a series of topographical books with the architecture drawn by A. C. Pugin and the figures by Rowlandson, a collaboration successfully carried out in *The Microcosm of London*, 1808–10. Later volumes portrayed, in equal magnificence, the history of Westminster Abbey, the Universities of Oxford and Cambridge and the Public Schools.

Another category of colour-plate book of this period was the flower book. Perhaps the greatest of these appeared in France, where the great Redouté, patronized by Marie Antoinette and Napoleon, published his *Lilies* between 1802 and 1816, and his *Roses* between 1817 and 1824; but in England we had Samuel Curtis's *A Monograph on the Genus Camellia*, published in 1819 with magnificent hand-coloured aquatint plates by Clara Maria Pope, and the same author's even more magnificent *The Beauties of Flora* of 1820.

There were also the bird books. Audubon's *The Birds of America*, largest and most magnificent not only of these but almost of all books ever published, began publication in parts in London in 1827, with five hand-coloured aquatints in each part: the complete work contains 435 plates in four volumes, double elephant folio.

In the great colour-plate books, the typography of the letterpress did not usually achieve the same degree of magnificence as the colour-plates, unless it happened to be printed either by Bulmer, who died in 1830, or Bensley, who died in 1824; most of the best work of those printers was done earlier and is described in *The Late Georgian*

*Period.* They printed fine and expensive books worthy of the aristocracy and the wealthy merchants who were their principal patrons: the sort of books that were, perhaps, more often looked at than read.

### *The Chiswick Press*

Charles Whittingham (1767–1840) was a very different printer. He rarely printed anything larger than an octavo, but everything he produced was carefully and usually beautifully designed and printed. He foresaw the expansion of the reading-public and the coming increased demand for books that could be carried in pockets, and pioneered both in printing and publishing them. From the beginning of the century he was printing cheap and elegant duodecimos, which greatly annoyed other publishers, whose octavos and quartos were so much more expensive. In 1805 he was printing the British Poets in duodecimo, and in about 1814 came Whittingham's Cabinet Library, a series of tiny books measuring about 5″ × 3″ and selling at from 1*s.* to 7*s.* each, depending on extent and binding (Pl. 96).

Whittingham was one of the first printers to use iron hand-presses, machine-made paper, overlays for printing wood-engravings (in which he was a master), and steam-driven machinery (for pulping paper). He also pioneered in the use of gas for lighting his factory.

The 'Chiswick Press' imprint was first used by Whittingham when in 1811 he moved his press from London to Chiswick. Whittingham's nephew Charles, who became as great a printer as his uncle, was indentured to the Press in 1810, became a partner in 1824, set up on his own in 1828 and resumed control of the Chiswick Press in 1838, two years before his uncle died. The books produced by Whittingham the nephew and the publisher William Pickering will be described in *The Victorian Period*.

One of the most beautiful books printed by Charles Whittingham the uncle was Northcote's *Fables*, 1829, with wood-engravings after drawings by James Northcote, R.A. Of the same date was *The Tower Menagerie*, illustrated with wood-engravings by Branston and Wright. Both are octavos and show the art of printing from the wood at its best.

Thomas Bewick (1753–1828), who had published his *General History of Quadrupeds* in 1790, his *History of British Birds* in two volumes in 1797 and 1804, and his *Fables of Aesop* in 1818, was still working in his native Northumberland. In London, the most eminent engravers were Bewick's pupils, Luke Clennell and William Harvey, Robert Branston and his pupil John Thompson, W. J. Linton, and Samuel and Thomas Williams. Most of these men were artists in their own right, but most of their work was to interpret the drawings of others, which they did with a delicacy and fineness that make the best wood-engraving of the 'sixties look coarse. Many of George Cruikshank's drawings were engraved on wood by these men; for example, in *Points of Humour*, 1823; *Mornings at Bow Street*, 1824; *Three Courses and a Dessert*, 1830; and *Robinson Crusoe*, 1831. Cruikshank was the greatest illustrator of the Regency period; perhaps his best-known works of that time were his etchings for the first English translation

V. FIGGINS.

Fig. 4. The 'Egyptian' type-face, introduced by Figgins in 1815 in various sizes and in lower case as well as caps.

of Grimm's *Fairy Tales*, and *Peter Schlemihl*, both in 1823. His famous illustrations for Dickens, Ainsworth and other novelists were made in the reign of Queen Victoria.

### *The Type-founders*

The last aspect of printing during the Regency that can be mentioned in this short account is the output of the type-founders, an activity that merits a book to itself.[4] There was a great outburst of invention in the design of type-faces and type-ornaments, which resulted in a permanent enrichment of the printer's and decorative artist's equipment. The spate of invention did indeed continue far into the Victorian period, when it sadly degenerated: but the Regency saw the emergence of Sans Serif, Egyptian (which one critic has described as 'the most brilliant typographical invention of the century, and perhaps the most complete and concise expression of the dominant culture of its brief period; more inspired than contemporary paintings, combining the elegance of the furniture, and the weight of the architecture, and the colour and precise romance of Bulwer Lytton'),[5] Fat Face, shadowed letters, and the earliest and best of the long line of nineteenth-century ornamented types, magnificently rich, theatrical and English.

These rich borders and bold types (which included many new varieties of black-letter, with gothic ornaments) were a conspicuous part of the movement in search of the picturesque; and they were first used on the labels and printed paper covers of books issued in parts, many of which were themselves catering for that movement. They quickly came into use also for tradesmen's announcements, but such advertisements were still, during the Regency, small, discreet, and in good taste.

Names of individual designers cannot now be established: in many cases the designs were probably originated by the founders themselves, men such as Vincent Figgins, Edmund Fry, Robert Thorne, and William Thorowgood. Theirs was among the most notable artistic achievement of the whole century, and it is not a mere whim of fashion, but because their designs were sound and are now being justly appreciated, that so many of their types have been recently revived and used not only in Britain, but all over Europe and the United States.

[4] See Nicolette Gray, *Nineteenth Century Ornamented Types and Title Pages*, London, 1938.

[5] N. Gray, *op. cit.*

#### SHORT BIBLIOGRAPHY

G. Everitt, *English Caricaturists of the Nineteenth Century*, 1893. A. M. Cohn, *George Cruikshank, a Catalogue Raisonné*, 1924. J. Jackson, *A Treatise on Wood Engraving*, 1839. M. Weekley, *Thomas Bewick*, 1953. *The History of The Times*, 5 vols., 1935–52. S. T. Prideaux, *Aquatint Engravings*, 1909. A. Warren, *The Charles Whittinghams, Printers*, 1896. T. B. Reed and A. F. Johnson, *A History of the Old English Letter Foundries*, 1952. N. Gray, *XIXth Century Ornamented Types*, 1938. Sitwell, Buchanan & Fisher, *Fine Bird Boooks 1700–1900*, 1953. Sitwell, Blunt & Synge, *Great Flower Books 1700–1900*, 1956.

# *Index*

## A SELECT LIST OF CONTEMPORARY PUBLICATIONS MENTIONED